Sit Down Young Stranger

One man's quest for meaning

by **John Graham**

Published by
Packard Books
PO Box 759
Langley WA 98260

Manufactured in the United States of America
Cover and page designs: Susan Reed, Pixels (pixelsgraphics.com)

Sit Down Young Stranger
Title and lyrics taken from "Sit Down Young Stranger" by Gordon Lightfoot, © 1969, renewed 1998. Used by permission Early Morning Music

ISBN 978-1-45375-078-0

Graham, John, 1942 –
Sit Down Young Stranger
By John Graham
graham@giraffe.org
www.johngrahamspeaker.org

Sit Down Young Stranger

I'm standin' in the doorway, my head bowed in my hands
Not knowin' where to sit, not knowin' where to stand.
My father looms above me, for him there is no rest.
My mother's arms enfold me and hold me to her breast.

They say you've been out wandrin'; they say you traveled far.
Sit down young stranger, and tell us who you are.
The room has all gone misty; my thoughts are all in spin
Sit down, young stranger, and tell us where you been.

I've been up to the mountain; I've walked down by the sea.
I never questioned no one and no one questioned me.
My love was given freely and oft-times was returned.
I never came to borrow; I only came to learn.

Sometimes it would get lonely, but it taught me how to cry.
And laughter came too easy for life to pass me by.
I never had a dollar that I didn't earn with pride,
'Cause I had a million daydreams to keep me satisfied.

And will you gather daydreams or will you gather wealth?
How can you find your fortune when you cannot find yourself?
My mother's eyes grow misty; there's a tremblin' in her hand.
Sit down young stranger—I do not understand.

Now will you try and tell us you been too long at school,
That knowledge is not needed, that power does not rule,
That war is not the answer, that young men should not die?
Sit down young stranger; I'll wait for your reply.

The answer is not easy, for souls are not reborn.
To wear the crown of peace, you must wear the crown of thorns.
If Jesus had a reason, I'm sure he would not tell.
We treated him so badly, how could he wish us well?

The parlor now is empty; there's nothin' left to say.
My father has departed; my mother's gone to pray
There's rockets in the meadows and ships out on the sea.
The answer's in the forest, carved upon a tree:
John loves Mary—does anyone love me?

—Gordon Lightfoot

Contents

Part One

Making War

Chapter One

The *Golden Bear*, 1959

The drinking began that night in a thatched-roof, open-air bar, fifty yards into the jungle. The place had a dozen wooden tables on a dirt floor, each with a kerosene lantern and three or four bamboo chairs. A couple more lanterns hung from the rafters, swinging slightly. The bartender was a big Chinese guy with a shaved head, bare-chested except for a filthy leather vest. I think my friend Roy called him Han or maybe Hung. A half-dozen whores, barefoot in cocktail dresses, oozed among the crowd, about evenly divided between the ship's crew and local stevedores. One of the stevedores had a monkey that stole peanuts off the tables. Barely seventeen, I struggled to look like I'd been in places like this all my life. Meanwhile I forgot to breathe.

The whores headed for the American seamen and their dollars. Roy slipped a girl named Lucy a five-dollar bill and she sat on my lap, pulled down the top of her dress and pressed her left nipple against my face. I was paralyzed. Roy and the others roared with laughter.

"Gotta get your nerve up, man, then your dick," said Roy. With that, I downed a half-dozen rum and cokes in a very short amount of time. Lucy—and the bar—faded from view. I have no memory of what happened next. Roy told me later that I'd passed out and he'd all but carried me back to the ship. I missed not only the chance to end my virginity but also a pitched brawl with the stevedores that had trashed the bar and put two crewmen in the local hospital.

The crew was punished over that fight. I think Roy was docked some pay. I ended up with the mother of all hangovers. My head throbbed like the ship's turbines and I couldn't look at food for a day and a half. Getting blind drunk and then hauled from a dockside brawl was not the introduction to manhood I'd had in mind. Still, part of me was pumped, thinking of the stories I could tell at school.

But I'd say now that a bigger part of me was scared by the world I'd landed in that night and by my incompetence to deal with it.

It was the summer of 1959. Three weeks before, I'd sailed for the Orient aboard a freighter named the *Golden Bear*. I was the youngest member of a crew of 36, and this voyage was the first even remotely adventurous thing I'd ever done. Standing against the rail, watching the hawsers splash into San Francisco Bay, feeling the deck shudder with the first thrust of the engines, my throat had felt so dry it hurt. The trip was a deliverance, a stroke of fortune in a teen life I was sure was unmatched for misery.

I was skinny, had a face full of pimples, and was so uncoordinated I regularly stumbled going up the stairs. At St. Robert Bellarmine High School in Tacoma Washington, I put the chalk lines on the football field but never played on it. I won debate trophies, not girlfriends. The "in" crowd never invited me to their parties unless their mothers made them do it. I hung out with other social misfits and defended myself from real or imagined taunts by burying myself in books. Sitting, dateless, in the stands on Friday nights, watching classmates with padded shoulders and muddy uniforms do battle, listening to the cheers—I would have given anything to throw just one touchdown pass.

The revenge I swore for my humiliations was nonviolent. Someday all the bullies and jocks would be flipping burgers or selling washing machines when they'd see my face on the cover of *Time* magazine and be forced to contemplate their own miserable, unachieving lives. The anger I developed in high school pushed me for decades. It also left a dark residue that time and growth have never fully cleansed. I still avoid high school reunions.

The good thing about Bellarmine was the Jesuits who ran it. They made calculus and Homeric Greek exciting. They let me teach myself chemistry at home, taught me how to write and to speak in public, and steadily forced me to value all the things I could do well. It was a Jesuit who told me I could win a national essay contest—and demanded that I enter. The prize was a six-week trip to the Orient aboard a freighter. All I had to do was write 750 words about the Port of Tacoma.

I won—then almost didn't go when the sponsor told my parents I'd be going as a member of the crew. My Catholic mother feared that hanging out with seamen in exotic ports for six weeks would bring the "near occasions of sin" a little too near. I argued that her fears were groundless—and fervently hoped that they were not.

And why shouldn't she trust me? For seventeen years my whole life had been about doing everything right. I wasn't born in Tacoma—I stepped out of a Norman Rockwell painting there. I was an altar boy, an Eagle Scout, and turned in homework early. I never broke a law or missed a piano lesson. At a time when other kids were testing authority, I found purpose in obedience. I anticipated commands before they were given. I fed on the praise of parents, teachers and priests because it gave me a sense of accomplishment when little else in my nerd-world did.

I didn't see then the price I would pay for following the rules as closely as I did. Blind obedience may have been the only way I saw to make my life work as a child and teen—but the pattern it left slowed my capacity to think on my own, and to gain the courage to find and live a meaningful life. Had it not been for that summer on the *Golden Bear*, the delay would have been even longer.

This judgment is harsh. There are worse things than growing up in a safe, loving middle-class family in 'fifties America. But five decades later, I tell high school audiences what I wish I'd been told then—that thinking and acting for yourself are essential, and that rebellion is a necessary part of growing up.

I felt *some* unease at the straightjacket I wore, however, or I wouldn't have been so excited at the prospect of breaking out. The afternoon I heard I'd won the trip, I walked the two miles home from Bellarmine instead of taking the bus. The sidewalks and houses of Tacoma faded from view, replaced by scenes from every Jack London fantasy I'd ever had. Here I was looking tough and confident on spray-washed decks. That was me, striding down Asian streets dark with intrigue, and lying with exotic, willing women. I couldn't wait. None of the "in" crowd at Bellarmine could equal what I was about to do.

I drove down to San Francisco with my father to collect my prize.

My father, Albert, was a quiet, caring man who sold advertising for the *Tacoma News Tribune* for thirty-five years. He was tall, slender and balding, with the kind of quick humor that made him good with puns and quips. He was a private man; I have few memories of him ever hugging me as a child, except for awkward squeezes at bedtime. Mother had always hinted that there'd been a wild side to him, and I'm sorry I never saw it. Long before I was born, he'd had the stuffing kicked out of him by the effects of heavy drinking, including a series of stomach ulcers that had grounded him for good.

My father's early dream had been to be a writer, but the only job he could find during the Depression was in advertising, and he never made the moves to get out. By the time I reached my teens, he was living through my achievements, long having given up on his own. He'd take me up to the Elks Club for a swim, but we'd spend half the time interrupting bridge games in the clubroom so he could tell his friends about my latest report card. I hated the way my father was deaf to his friends' half-hidden groans when they saw him coming toward them with me in tow. I'd stand there, smiling and awkward, absorbing their dutiful compliments as if they were blows. My father was standing in my shadow when I was still in high school, and I was old enough to know there was something very wrong with that.

For most of that first day in San Francisco I signed papers to get a seaman's card, which officially made me a member of the crew. I was assigned a job—typing cargo manifests—although, under the terms of the essay contest award, I didn't do more than a few hours work the whole trip.

The next day my father and I went down to the ship—huge, black, sleek, half-again as long as a football field. We watched for hours from the bridge as cables whined and pallets of sacks and cartons swung through the air and settled softly into holds that filled the ship from her main deck to her keel. When the loading was finished in late afternoon, my father shook my hand and went ashore. I joined a line of seamen to sign on for the voyage in a large, frayed ledger. On line 29 was printed: "John Graham, Purser's Yeoman." When I signed above that printing and handed the pen to the man next in line, I felt ten feet tall.

An hour later, the *Golden Bear* glided out into San Francisco Bay. I looked up at the Golden Gate Bridge as we passed underneath, watching the movement of cars through the perforated decking and wondered if any of them might be carrying my father home. Then I walked as far back on the ship's main deck as I could, and leaned against the rail, watching the ship's wake boil out beneath me.

The distance that counted was not just from my father. Soon, I would also be seven thousand miles away from my mother and from the Catholic Church.

My mother, Madeline, was the third child of Croatian immigrants. She had a peasant's build, with dark hair framing a Slavic face with strong, angular bones. For generations, her family had scratched a living out of the thin limestone soil of Vis, a small, sunny island off the Dalmatian coast. Threatened by famine, they'd fled to America in 1898, carrying with them a commitment to their ancestry, to Catholicism, and to doing everything exactly as it had been done before. My mother was the most resolute person I ever knew. Until her final illness, I never saw anything stop her. In the mid-nineties, when Croatians, Serbs and Muslims were tearing each other apart in Yugoslavia, I was glad my mother wasn't over there. She could have singlehandedly kept the fighting going for years.

I could feel the vibrations in the rail as the ship's engines picked up tempo in the open sea, sending the bow rising and falling slightly, pointed toward the setting sun.

My mother's compass was as sure. She'd work long hours on any community or church effort to help the poor—and she'd publicly scold any teenage boy she thought needed a haircut. The sight of an interracial couple would have her fuming for days. Her political opinions pitted her against almost everything that happened after Eisenhower.

But at home, love poured from her. I remember her singing lullabies and, when I was sick, rubbing my cold-ridden chest with camphor. She gave up teaching for fifteen years to be at home when my older sister Wynne and I were young. The allegiance she invoked was so complete there were times I would have rather died than risk her frown.

Mother had a fearsome ally in the Catholic Church. If her rules weren't enough, the Baltimore Catechism had plenty more. My soul, said the Catechism, was like a bottle of milk, and through my weakness and disregard I allowed little black spots to pollute it every time I forgot to say my prayers or thought an unkind thought. "Mortal" sins turned the whole bottle black and poised my soul for eternal damnation until the sin could be confessed to a priest. Mortal sins were not just the really bad stuff, such as masturbation or missing Mass; eating meat on Friday would do it too. The Baltimore Catechism was a minefield that no healthy adolescent could ever cross unscathed. I wish I'd known that then. Instead I struggled to please both my mother and the Church. My failures were occasions of deep shame.

Now father, mother and Church were all receding with the California coastline into the dull evening light. I stayed on deck and followed the ship's wake until it flattened in the swells. For the first time in my life, I was on my own. No nuns, no priests, no teachers, no parents. No tests, no grades. No one's expectations but my own. When I shivered as the first stars appeared, it wasn't from the cold.

I bunked with a cadet from the Merchant Marine Academy. He was four years older than I. His name was Dave, and he was so annoyed at having to share his room, he said about a hundred words to me the entire trip.

My friend and guide aboard the *Golden Bear* was Roy. Roy was a thirty-five year-old, two hundred and fifty pound black man who worked in the engine room. He adopted me from the first day, introducing me to the rest of the crew and showing me every mast and bilge in the ship.

Roy was also my protector. The second day at sea, a gay crewman (something I was too innocent to spot) made a remark about me that Roy didn't like. In an instant, Roy slammed the man up against the wall, with his forearm hard against the man's throat until the guy's eyes bulged out. Roy then told the motherfuckin sonofabitch that if he so much as put his motherfuckin hand on me, he (Roy) would cut off the guy's motherfuckin dick and cram it up his motherfuckin ass.

I watched this in utter awe. I'd never until then even seen real violence, nor heard such magnificent cussing. I kept staring. The gay seaman blubbered his innocence, and Roy let him down; the man slunk down the hall, rubbing his throat.

At seventeen, I so much wanted to become a man. But my mother was the toughest person I knew, and that only further confused my search for models of manhood. Now, watching Roy, it occurred to me that *this* is what real men did, or at least must be prepared to do. I'd seen it in war movies and westerns, but that was nothing like seeing it for real.

My father couldn't physically have done what Roy did and, more to the point, he never would have tried. My father was an extraordinarily gentle man. Competing for promotions at work, he was constantly shoved aside by more aggressive men. When my mother would learn of another loss, she would, in her insensitive Croatian way, find ways to worsen the hurt. "Oh, Al!" she would say in front of the whole family that night, in a voice not of compassion but of disappointment, "Why didn't you fight back?" Father would look down at his plate and silently pick at his peas. And I would look away. Had my mother been in his shoes, and had it been another era, she would have been running the newspaper.

I was terrified that I'd inherited my father's gentleness and not my mother's spine. When I was a toddler, my mother had made me a wonderful doll with brown yarn hair and stuffed him with chips of foam rubber. I'd named him Sammy and loved him to death; when he began to fall apart after a few years, my mother made a second doll. But when the seams in Sammy II began to rip, some Croatian clock in my mother's head decided that, at age six or seven, I was too old to play with dolls and she refused to make another. So I "borrowed" her sewing basket and repaired Sammy's seams and re-sewed his yarn hair myself. When Sammy II then mysteriously disappeared, I sewed his name on the inside cover of the rubber pillow on my bed, and that pillow became my secret friend.

I not only never started a fight as a kid—I never fought back when bullies attacked. Once, two weeks into the fourth grade, a gap-toothed kid named Alex stole my hat—a large, dorky-looking one with big earflaps that splayed outwards—one no kid in his right mind would ever want to wear. My mother had bought it, however, and insisted that I wear it to school. Alex had lain in wait for me on the way home, grabbed the hat off my head, and taunted me to get it back. When I refused to fight, he'd dragged the hat through a mud puddle, then slapped me across the face with it. When he'd finally lost interest, I'd retrieved the hat, then sneaked into the basement at home to clean off the mud.

I worked as quietly as I could, worrying that my mother would discover me and ask what had happened. She would never have understood why I'd let myself be humiliated. Her barrel-chested brothers—my uncles—would have died first. What I dreaded most of all would be hearing: "Oh, John!" in a voice not of compassion but of disappointment, "Why didn't you fight back?"

Other bullies had followed Alex, and with each encounter I'd known I could not excuse my reluctance to fight as a principled avoidance of violence. I'd seen it instead as a lack of courage, an unmanliness passed down from my father—a weakness that I would have given anything to change.

I did the best I could. At twelve or thirteen, I simply stopped expressing, or even acknowledging, the gentle caring boy in me. I hammered boards over my heart, and hoped that that would make me tough. That Croatian culture clock in my mother speeded the process. At about the same time I started to shut down my emotions, my mother said I should stop hugging my father goodnight and simply shake his hand. I obeyed—then pushed her message to an extreme she never meant. I stopped hugging anyone, including her. For years she would complain about the disappearance of "that loving little boy I used to know," without ever understanding the role she'd played in chasing him underground.

It was a long exile. In seeing gentleness and caring as weaknesses, I condemned for decades a vital part of who I was.

Now, on board the *Golden Bear*, I finally had a model for how to be a man. If only I could be like Roy! The night of his encounter with the gay seaman, I practiced what he'd done in front of a mirror. Dave was on watch, so I didn't have him to laugh at me as I slammed my right elbow against the throat of an imaginary foe, then my left, then my right again. I looked as fierce as I could and I practiced saying "motherfuckin" with a snarl, just like Roy.

Across the Pacific, the Philippines were the first port of call. Threading her way south through the islands, the *Golden Bear* stopped to take on dried coconut in Iloilo, a jungle port in southern Mindanao so tiny its dock was barely a third as long as the ship. As we nosed slowly closer to the pier, I stared at the warehouses, shacks and muddy alleys. Tacoma was half a world away. Iloilo was where the rest of my life would begin.

I confided to Roy that I wanted to get drunk and get laid that night, if I could. He laughed and told me to stick with him because this would be the roughest port of the trip. The rougher the better, I told him smoothly, and was annoyed that he laughed some more.

Beyond booze and sex, however, there was something I wanted beyond what even Roy could show me. I wanted to rip open a curtain and see whole new possibilities for my life—ideas and visions and options that would free me from the cocoon in which I had been raised. I wanted something that would give me a sense of confidence and direction I'd never known. I had no idea what that something might be. But I knew it was out there, and that it would change everything.

The drunken brawl in Iloilo that night ripped open a curtain in my life all right, and I was lucky it hadn't ripped open my head as well. I never went out with the crew again. Like a prairie dog, I'd popped out of my hole for a brief look, then ducked down again, grateful for the safe, familiar cover of hard earth. Iloilo had been no grand rebellion against seventeen years of being good. It hadn't even been a successful sally into sin.

Back on the *Golden Bear*, I read guidebooks from the ship's library on the Philippines, Hong Kong, Okinawa and Japan and mapped out shore trips for each stop—sometimes going with a few of the ship's twelve passengers, and sometimes on my own.

In Japan I took off for three days on my own to look at temples and palaces, and to dodge busy people in cities like Kobe and Tokyo that mostly looked to me like America but with signs I couldn't read.

Hong Kong, however, was like watching Roy slam that crewman up against the wall. The harbor was a din of bellowing horns and shrill whistles. On the crowded streets, merchants called in sharp voices from stalls hung with plucked chickens and bright cloth. At night, from the top of Victoria Peak, ferries traced yellow lines in black water, and the near land glowed with neon signs and electric lights. Further back, where people lived, thousands of lights and lanterns and cooking fires pricked the darkness like fireflies.

I sent articles to the *Tacoma News Tribune* from the trips ashore that summer, and the paper published them. Reading them today I'd say they were technically well-written but dull. The people in them were furniture. Abroad for the first time in my life, bombarded with new sights and sounds, I was a detached and pinched observer. The Jesuits had taught me writing as a craft, but there was no heart in anything I wrote. I'd closed that part of me down years before, in my despairing struggle to become a man, as defined by what my mother wanted and my father wasn't. And in repressing the gentle and caring emotions that I thought were keeping me from manhood—I'd repressed everything. I'd become afraid to risk *any* kind of emotional response for fear that the wall I'd hammered around my heart would fly apart. I told myself that emoting was what women and children did, and steeled myself against it. At seventeen I couldn't put it in words, but from some deep place I feared that if I really tried to write about the excitement I felt in Asia that summer, I'd be waking a part of me safely stowed, and the consequences could be terrible.

After Iloilo, the voyage was all about covering ground, not about risking any of it opening up beneath my feet. I approached the rest of the journey as if it were a survey course, with an "A" given for the most sights seen, the most miles traveled—even though there was no one to grade my performance for seven thousand miles. Getting A's was what I knew to do, what I was praised for doing. It was my high card, and I wasn't brave enough to play others, even had I seen them in my hand.

Despite my caution, that summer changed my life. Roy and the other seamen had given me a new, brawny model of manhood and, in one night, introduced me to a raw, physical world totally different from anything I'd known before. And, wooden or not, simply being in those faraway ports had shown me much more than I could even imagine from Tacoma, and set off a thirst for foreign adventures that would push me for the rest of my life.

Both my parents were waiting for me on the wharf in San Francisco when the ship returned. I came clanking down the gangway with a seaman's duffel on my shoulder. The first thing I said to them was that I wanted to go back out to sea. I had seaman's papers and a union card; all I had to do was go down to the union hall and apply. My senior year at Bellarmine could wait.

Of course they said no, and part of me was glad they did. But with that one voyage, the circles of possibility for my life had rippled outwards. I'd seen the wider world. I'd tapped, however briefly, however softly, into a part of me I'd never touched before. I didn't know it then, but I'd also struck a spark that would eventually challenge all the conservatisms in which I had been raised.

Chapter Two

Harvard, 1960 – 1962

After the *Golden Bear*, my final year of high school was a speed bump on the road back out into a wider world. I got into Harvard, Yale, MIT, Georgetown and Stanford, all with scholarships. In the end, I decided on Harvard, more or less on the strength of pictures I'd seen in a magazine, waiting my turn at Travoni's barber shop in Tacoma. The pictures showed young men walking across Harvard Yard, looking cool and self-assured, obviously heading for lives of fame, money and power. The article said Harvard was the best university in America and that was good enough for me. I was tired of being bullied, of looking in from the outside. I wanted to be one of those cool, self-assured young men. Looking up through the fog of adolescence, I wanted to be powerful. I wanted to get to the top of the world, and Harvard, I thought, would take me there.

It didn't matter that my research was limited to a magazine in a barbershop or that I knew no one who'd ever gone to Harvard. It didn't matter that the Jesuits were pushing me towards Catholic universities. It didn't matter that my parents expected me to go to the University of Washington, where my father had gone and my sister was then enrolled; for my family, sailing beyond "the U" was sailing off the edge of the map. For me, after the *Golden Bear*, that was the point.

"Sailing" turned out to be more than a metaphor. I won the same essay contest that had sent me to the Far East the year before. This time the prize was a trip as a passenger on the *Flying Fish*, a freighter bound from California through the Panama Canal to Boston.

Other than a bad storm off the Mexican coast, and the day going through the locks, this sea trip was uneventful. The taxi from Boston Harbor to Cambridge, however, was a twenty-minute journey to Wonderland. Turning into Harvard Yard—seeing the trees and grass and buildings just like in the magazine at Travoni's—was like watching Iloilo come up on the port bow. Only this was no one-time sally into sin. This was about all the possibilities that Roy could not take me to. This is where the curtain to the rest of my life would open.

The cabbie waited while I fumbled for bills in my wallet, then reminded me, with more or less good humor, that I was supposed to leave a tip. I got out of the car, and joined other young men all trying to look cool and self-assured. The sound of pounding hearts must have been audible as we all followed signs for dorm assignments and bed linens and coupons for dinner.

My roommate freshman year was a sandy-haired doctor's son from Omaha named Michael Crofoot. Jesuit-trained like me, he'd arrived a few hours earlier and left a welcoming note on the door—in Homeric Greek. A high school swim champ, Michael was so soft-spoken I was never quite sure he was in this world. He had make-believe friends. He sometimes introduced himself to strangers as "Zanzibar Stupenzo." I could talk to him face-to-face and feel like I was on a long distance telephone.

For reasons I never understood, Michael's family was extraordinarily well-connected. When he introduced me to David Rockefeller's daughter that first weekend in Cambridge, I thought he was kidding. To my credit I recovered fast enough to avoid making a fool of myself.

My expectations for Harvard were huge. Harvard was where I would transform myself from outsider to insider, from boy to man, from misfit to master. Part of that transformation had to be physical; if I was to be as tough as Roy, I needed a body that worked better than the one I had. I was determined to become an athlete, and Harvard was where this would happen.

When I turned out for the Harvard freshman crew I was six feet four, weighed a hundred and fifty-five pounds and looked like the Before side of a Charles Atlas ad. Since Harvard was to crew what Notre Dame was to football, the odds of someone like me rowing for the Crimson were vanishingly small.

I didn't know that. It wouldn't have mattered if I had. I badly wanted the body that crew could build for me, and the risks of failure never entered my head. Besides, my father had rowed for the University of Washington and I knew from him that I had the height to be a rower. And very few secondary schools had rowing programs; crew was one of the few college sports where I wouldn't be competing with guys who'd had years of experience I lacked. When I walked over Eliot Bridge to Newell Boathouse for freshman tryouts the second week of school, it was with an optimism that belied the odds.

The boathouse was a squat castle of dark wood, hunkered down on the banks of the Charles River. The main hall was poorly lit, with heavy black floorboards worn smooth by many decades of young men's feet. Racks of rowing shells, four high, split the room from front to back. Pictures of the great Harvard crews of the past—national champions, Olympians—lined wood-paneled walls that smelled of resin and sweat.

The main room opened directly out onto a dock that sloped down to the river. There were forty of us there that afternoon, gathered to hear Harry Parker, the freshman coach. Coach Parker was young, passionate— and a world-class rower himself. Pacing up and down the dock, he told us that somewhere in our forty was another Olympic-gold-medal Crimson crew. Parker was charismatic; when he'd finished, there wasn't one of us who doubted him, or who didn't see himself Olympics bound. When Parker saw me in the line of nervous young men in shorts and T-shirts, however, I'm sure he judged that I would never be one of Harvard's stars. But he respected my being in the same line with guys thirty pounds heavier, and he went out of his way to encourage me.

I never missed a practice. I ran extra miles. I struggled to keep up with the cadences in the practice barge. I lifted weights until I could barely raise my fork at dinner. When the preliminary team list was posted in November, my name was on it. I called my father after practice to tell him the good news, and we talked so long about rowing that I missed dinner. Rowing had given us something to share.

When winter came and the Charles River froze, the team rowed on indoor machines or from a platform in the center of a huge tank with hydraulic pumps pushing the water past our oars. Coach Parker had us shovel the snow off a flight of steps in the football stadium and we'd run from the field up to the press box and back down to the field a dozen times—then run back to the boathouse where I'd lift more weights while the others showered. I put on fifteen pounds of muscle in three months. When the guys in my entry started calling me "the jock," it felt like Olympic gold.

I did very well in math and science my first semester at Harvard. A "C" in a freshman sociology course, however, was devastating. Sure, I hadn't expected to continue straight A's in college, but a C? As it turned out, the C on the transcript was the least of it. The hard part was the interview with the section leader, an earnest young assistant professor named Harvey Sprewell.

Sprewell was way down the Harvard pecking order and it took me a half-hour to find his tiny office, stuck far back in the warrens of a Civil War-era building north of Harvard Yard. He was in his late twenties, with curly brown hair and clothes that had never felt an iron. He moved a pile of papers off the only other chair in the office, motioned me to sit down and handed me my course papers. He told me I had a good mind that was running on one cylinder. I could memorize and I could analyze, he said, but I'd not shown the intellectual courage to turn my mind loose, to innovate, to risk mistakes and contradictions. My papers had been a brilliant job of regurgitating and a mediocre job of thinking for myself. Good enough for high school. Not good enough for Harvard. He hoped the C would prompt some intellectual audacity.

Nobody had ever talked to me like that before. I started to argue, but two other students were waiting in the hall, so I picked up my papers and left. I walked around in a pout for a day or so, remembering all the praise heaped on me by the Jesuits and sure that Sprewell's charges were unfair. After all, I was a National Merit Scholar and I'd won a national essay contest *twice*.

As the hurt receded, however, I slowly and privately began to acknowl-edge the truth of what Sprewell had said. My whole life had been about following orders. So why wouldn't I expect Harvard to give orders too—to feed me wisdoms I could accept and regurgitate? Instead, Harvard was insisting that I think for myself, and, for me, the concept was both revolu-tionary and threatening.

I was getting the same message in the freshman dining hall. When the dinner conversations weren't about women or sports, they focused on cur-rent events and the kind of philosophical puzzlers that freshmen love. When I trotted out the views I'd inherited from my parents or picked up from other adults, they were cut to pieces by peers who were at least as smart as I was. I soon learned to start separating what I knew through my own experience from what I had been told.

Harvey Sprewell and my quick-witted classmates raised huge ques-tions for me. What would it be like to think beyond authority, not just in writing term papers and debating with my peers—but in everything? And then—what would it be like to *live* beyond authority, outside the "shoulds" and "musts" in which I had been raised? I took these questions home for Christmas break. I spoke about them to no one, but they ran like television trailers under every holiday scene—turkey and mashed potatoes cooked as they had always been cooked, my parents' unchanging views on every-thing, and my friends already preparing to follow beaten paths. On the red-eye back to Cambridge, I pressed my face against the window and fol-lowed tiny farmhouse lights as they passed by in the blackness. Tacoma seemed less safe harbor now than anchor. The lines that tied me to my past were beginning to part. I was drifting away, heading for the horizon of what I knew now was not a flat earth, and the excitement I felt made it im-possible to sleep.

By spring I'd gained another ten pounds and learned pretty well how to pull the heavy oar through the water with the smooth cadence that row-ing crew demands. I rowed for Harvard that season as captain of the third-string heavyweight freshman crew.

I could deal with being third string—just being on the team was my victory. I loved the excitement of sending that needle of a boat through the water. I loved the echo of the oars when we rowed under the bridges. I loved the excitement of competition, seeing our boat gain a foot over a rival with every stroke. I loved the last fifty yards of a close race, when the cox-swain would up the stroke to twenty-eight, then thirty, then thirty-four beats a minute, banging out the timing against the sides of the boat, with the eight of us straining with every last bit of breath and will, streaking for the finish.

Rowing also let me, for the first time in my life, *belong* to something that mattered. I was part of a team in a sport where, if you're any good at all, teamwork is both exquisite and complete. When the eight of us in that boat were swinging back and forth in rhythm and balance, we could all feel the added power created not by any one of us, but by the whole. It wasn't as though we were like a fine watch, because a watch has many parts. It was more like we became one pulling machine—one team. I loved the synergy that rowing both created and demanded, because it meant that I was not alone.

We won all our intercollegiate races. I think Coach Parker was pleased although he seldom showed it. I remember one afternoon when he came alongside in his launch after an intrasquad practice. We'd just rowed our hearts out and still been crushed by the freshman first team. "At least they kept you in sight, Graham," he'd chuckled through his megaphone, "At least they kept you in sight."

The summer after my freshman year, I went back to Tacoma and worked in my Uncle Charlie's ice factory. With my new muscles, I shoved four hun-dred-pound blocks of ice around loading docks and lifted heavy bags of crushed ice into trucks. The best part of the job was icing railroad cars. A switch engine would push a refrigerator car under a narrow metal plat-form. Standing on a catwalk, I'd use an ice pick to turn a huge block of ice into bits in seconds, then maneuver the pieces down a moveable chute into lockers at each end of the car. The catwalk was slippery, the ice pick was sharp and I was twenty feet above the tracks. Not counting the hapless night in Iloilo, it was the first physically dangerous thing I'd ever done. I loved the way it made my heart rush and the hair on the back of my neck bristle against the collar of my mackinaw. I worked overtime icing cars and took other guys' turns.

At home that summer, tuna casserole on Friday nights was an old friend. The four of us ate, as we had forever, around the blue Formica table in our kitchen dining nook. My place was on the long side of the table, closest to the wall. My sister Wynne, home from her first year teaching school in California, sat to my left. My father was to my right and my mother across from me, closest to the stove. There was a half-inch chip in the tabletop near my place, caused by an ill-advised experiment with a hammer when I was six. I still felt guilty about it, and did my best to hide it with my plate.

Sophomores and upperclassmen at Harvard all lived in one of ten stately "Houses" near the banks of the Charles River, each in effect a small college of four hundred students in the middle of a huge university. Each House kept its own style and sense of intimacy; each had its own dining hall, library, sports teams and tutors. I was assigned to Lowell House, a classic ivy-covered building of Georgian brick with two large courtyards and a huge bell tower capped with a blue dome that could be seen for miles.

One of Lowell's distinctions was "High Table," a formal dinner series. The honored guest at High Table was usually a last-minute surprise, depending on who was moving through the campus. I remember that Jimmy Hoffa, Madame Nhu and Basil Rathbone all came by, as did a guy designing a tunnel under the English Channel. It was all part of Harvard's intellectual smorgasbord.

That smorgasbord did not extend to my social life. I had friends at Harvard, but none of them very close. I had particularly bad luck with roommates, who cycled in and out that second year. Michael Crofoot came with me to Lowell, but the tension between Harvard's focus on the real world and Michael's fantasy life eventually became too much and he dropped out. He would become a Navy SEAL, go to Vietnam, then spend years in a Navy psychiatric ward.

Another roommate was a brilliant, bearded recluse who finally left to live on an Indian reservation in Montana (no, it wasn't the Unabomber–*he* lived in the House next door at that time). A third was a prissy kid who'd been brought up with servants. What I remember most about him was that whenever the toilet would plug up—which happened a lot when he was around—he'd always insist that somebody else reach in to clear the mess.

I dated some, but nothing memorable. It wasn't for lack of women; while Harvard in those days was all male, Radcliffe students attended Harvard classes and Cambridge was surrounded by women's colleges. With more muscles and fewer pimples, I wasn't so shy anymore, but there was too much going on in too many other parts of my life for me to spend any serious effort with girls.

When I had to pick a major my sophomore fall, I decided on geology. It combined science—which was always the world to which I thought I was headed—with the outdoors, which I'd loved since my days in Scouting. As it turned out, geology at Harvard would introduce me to more than rocks.

My geology course advisor was a young South Indian professor named Rustam Kothavala. Rusty was brown-skinned with a huge black moustache, mischievous black eyes and a voice so soft no one in his classes sat in the back rows. He and I spent a lot of time together, especially during the two or three field trips his class took into the Adirondacks that fall. There were always others in the VW bus he drove, but he'd usually invite me to sit up front "because of your long legs" and I always accepted.

Rusty loved to talk religion and for a scientist like him, the rules of a tightly organized faith like Catholicism were an affront to reason. He never directly challenged me—he just asked one polite question after the other. It was like being hit with pillows. He'd start about the time we passed the Boston beltway and keep it up all the way to the mine or quarry or road cut we were headed for. And back.

Rusty picked apart every Catholic credo I 'd ever learned, from the Virgin Birth to the infallibility of the Pope. He turned the Baltimore Catechism inside out ("Why is it you'll go to hell if you eat meat on Friday in America, but not in Argentina? And if you go out for a hamburger next Friday in Cambridge with a Catholic student from Buenos Aires and the two of you are then hit by a truck, will you both be damned forever—or does he get off?") When I tried to answer from my years of indoctrination, he'd nod and there'd be a silence for a moment or two. Then, after the next curve in the road—"Oh I see, John, thank you. But what if… " and then would come more questions, subtler then the first. To my amazement, I found I couldn't explain or defend most of what I'd been taught about Catholicism. Getting caught with my arguments down in dining hall bull sessions was one thing. With Rusty, the stakes were far higher, or so I thought.

Surely there would be a price to pay for not chasing the doubts that Rusty raised. But no lightning bolts struck me down. What *did* startle me was the relief I began to feel as each unresolved doubt put more distance between me and the faith in which I had been raised. I shouldn't have been startled. With its emphasis on guilt and imperfection, Catholicism was a strong band that tied me to the conservative and self-doubting world of my childhood—a world of home and Tacoma that was already slipping away. Now, thanks to Rusty, that band was growing looser by the day. I started skipping Sunday Mass, and lying to my mother about it when she asked— which she regularly did during my calls home. When I did show up, I'd take the prayer book out of the wooden holder in front of me and think about what it said—especially the parts that told me I was unworthy and a sinner. I knew I was becoming more confident in my life—why would God want me to lose ground? I often left church angry.

I rowed my sophomore year, on the varsity but still third string. My Olympic dreams had faded, but rowing had given me what I wanted—a strong body and with it, new opportunities. That second fall at Harvard, I joined the Harvard Mountaineering Club because I wanted to test that body on something besides an oar. I was also curious—I'd backpacked a lot as a kid, but never climbed rock and ice with a rope.

What attracted me most about climbing in 1961, however, was its promise of physical risk. I remembered the rush I'd felt when Roy and I had tromped down the gangway on the way to the bar in Iloilo, and the way my heart had raced, edging out on the catwalk above Uncle Charley's railway cars. There'd been something seductive about those moments, and I wanted more.

The Mountaineering Club taught its beginners' class in an old granite quarry just south of Boston. When my turn came, the instructors tossed a rope down from the top of the quarry thirty feet above my head, and tied the other end around my waist. I started up, putting my tennis shoes on little knobs and bumps that I never thought would hold my weight. Reaching up, I jammed my hands into cracks in the granite, feeling the rough rock tear a layer of skin. I gained some purchase this way, put more weight on my feet, and pulled myself up. The rope pulled taut from above, pushing up against my rib cage. I gasped for breath, listening to my heart beat, and craning my head to look for higher holds. "Not with your hands," the instructor called from below. "Climb with your feet. Find places for your feet!"

I inched upwards. Just short of the top, both feet slipped off a tiny ledge and I fell, scraping hard against the rock. In the split second before the rope caught me, I was amazed at how fast my body had picked up speed. Fear choked any sound that might have come from my throat. The rope burned against my backside. I clawed back up to that tiny ledge, and found a firmer place on it. A minute later I was on top.

My right hand was bloody. My arms and ribs ached. Sweat ran down the small of my back. The guy holding the rope was a grad student who'd actually been to the Himalayas. He said "Good job," told me to find a Band-Aid for the scrape on my hand, and turned his attention to the next novice.

I hardly heard him. That little cliff was Everest and I wanted to shout my triumph at the top of my lungs.

Every other weekend, until the snow flew, the Mountaineering Club would pile into an old hearse one of our members owned and drive five hours south to the Shawangunks, a 300-foot cliff of hard gray rock in the Hudson highlands. Toward the end of my first fall of climbing, I'd mastered Shockley's Ceiling, an expert climb that included hanging by my hands from an overhang 200 feet above the ground, then doing a pull-up to a ledge above.

In the winter and early spring, we'd drive the hearse north to the White Mountains. The high point of the road trip was passing through little New Hampshire towns late at night. We'd dust somebody's bare leg or arm with flour and let it protrude from the back of the hearse. Then, at a stoplight, hidden inside, we'd all start to moan. More than one town drunk ran for his life.

The next morning we'd climb ice-filled gullies on the side of Mount Washington. The gullies were 700 feet high, and part of that was vertical waterfall ice. Ice-climbing equipment in the early 'sixties was primitive.

Crampons (foot spikes) then lacked front points, so we had to chop lines of steps up steep ice, which usually meant being exposed for hours, not just to the cold, but to avalanches and falling rocks. The ice screws we forced into the cliff as "anchors" were little more than oversized coat hangers. None of our safety gear was likely to stop a serious fall. When climbing in these icy gullies became more popular a few years later, every winter brought a fatality or two.

It's a stereotype that climbers have trouble explaining why they climb. That certainly wasn't a question I wasted sleep over at the time. It was enough that the sport was challenging and exciting—the pounding heart, the neck hair bristling, the sucking in of breath looking down into empty space that could kill you. But for most climbers—especially those who become very good at it—climbing is more than that.

That first year on rock and ice, climbing taught me an intensity of focus that I'd never until then mastered because I'd never had to. Focus in climbing meant slowly shifting my weight on a tiny foothold, sliding my hand up carefully to the tiny nubbin that I could push on with just enough force to sustain my balance. Focus meant seeing the hairline wrinkles and cracks on a face above that everybody but a climber would call plate-smooth. Focus meant every neuron assembled for a single task. Focus meant me and the rock, me and the ice, me and the mountain, in the moment, with nothing but nothing in between.

Gravity was unsubtle and unforgiving—either you stayed on the holds or you didn't. In a world of confusions and distractions, of shades of gray, climbing was black and white and immediate; it was enormously satisfying to achieve the level of focus needed to succeed.

Climbing was also a constant, intimate dance with fear. In climbing, I was learning to accept fear, to move with it, and to use it rather than be used. If the next smooth pitch, or expanse of empty air beneath my feet, scared me, then the dance was to use that fear to sharpen my focus and to make my moves more precise.

The irony was not lost on me that in a citadel of academics, the most important things in my life the first two years at Harvard were physical—rowing and climbing. Physicality was an entirely new element in my life, and building and using a body that worked was for me an epiphany. That it happened at a place like Harvard may have been strange. But that it *hap-pened* was one of the most important transformations of my life.

I soon found, however, that the physical challenges I'd begun to take were easy compared to what I faced in other parts of my life. Shockley's Ceiling was a snap compared to exploring my feelings and sharing them with other people; I was still the boy with the hidden heart, the one who'd written the wooden travelogues from the *Golden Bear*.

It was easier for me to pull an oar to the point of collapse than take on the intellectual challenges that Harvey Sprewell had seen me ducking. I was getting better at thinking for myself, but it was a hard pull against a current that had been rushing in the other direction since I was born.

Still—less than two years since I'd felt on the wrong side of that Charles Atlas ad—the confidence I now felt with my physical body was beginning to rub off on other parts of me.

One of those parts was my religious life. Toward the end of my sopho-more year I stopped going to Mass altogether. Pushed by Rusty Kothavala's questions, in the course of six months I'd dropped the religious structure that had ruled much of my life for almost twenty years. I saw no need of replacing it. The faith that I was building was faith in myself and that, I thought then, was the only faith I needed. That didn't mean I no longer believed in God. I just no longer believed in following someone else's inter-pretation of God, or rules to live by. God was a concept I was now free to explore on my own.

Harvard, crew, climbing, sharp-tongued young professors—all of it had ripped away that curtain I'd confronted on the *Golden Bear*. Now all the things behind that curtain—all the things that Roy couldn't teach me, all the visions and options and opportunities I wanted for my life—were sud-denly at my feet. I had a body that worked. I'd dropped the chains of the Catholic Church. Now, I thought, I could not only contemplate the possi-bilities that would carry me out of the cocoon in which I had been raised—I could seize them all, and do it on my own.

As my second year at Harvard ended, I believed this with the fervor of the converted. It was a huge step from where I'd been in high school. That it was also stupendously arrogant, I didn't figure out for years.

Chapter Three

Three Adventures, 1962

The summer after my sophomore year, I took a student charter flight to Europe, financed by washing more test tubes for the Harvard Chemistry Department than I thought even a great university could possess.

It had been three years since the summer of the *Golden Bear* and I hungered for the sequel. Making decisions for myself at Harvard, building a new body, doing well without the Church, thrilled with climbing steep ice and rock—the possibilities for my life now seemed endless. The Jack London fantasies that had fed my expectations in high school were still there, but my models now were all real-life adventurers like Sir Richard Burton and Lawrence of Arabia. I read their books and studied their lives. I wanted to create a lifetime of exploits like theirs. I wanted to dare as they had dared—not just for the excitement, but because I now saw physical adventure as my path to becoming a man. Taking risks would vault me past the bullies. It would prove that I wasn't my gentle father's son.

No longer the scrawny, uncertain kid, I was determined this summer to head for every adventure I could find. I didn't need Roy, I told myself, and this wasn't about screwing and drinking. This was about finding out what else was out there, and throwing myself into it with everything I had. There was more than a little swagger in me as I picked up my rucksack from baggage claim at the London airport and headed for the ferry to France.

Beyond the airfare, I had three dollars a day that summer to spend on food, lodging and travel. For over three months I lived on bread, cheese and sausages, splurging occasionally at workers' restaurants with plain wooden tables and flasks of oily red wine. I slept in youth hostels when I could find them, and haystacks or railway station benches when I couldn't.

A classmate gave me a ride north to Scandinavia, but a week there made washing test tubes seem exciting. It was 1962 and the height of the Cold War. In four months, the Cuban Missile Crisis would put the whole world on the edge of nuclear war. I was looking for adventure, and the prospects for finding it seemed a lot better behind the Iron Curtain than in spotless Swedish cities.

I took a ferry from Copenhagen to Warnemunde, a Baltic port in East Germany. That I could have been sailing into trouble I couldn't handle never occurred to me. Whatever happened—and I very much hoped something *would* happen—I was sure I was ready.

The East German police at the ferry terminal had no idea what to do with an American tourist. I had a transit visa, which they finally decided meant that I couldn't spend the night in their town. When they got tired of shouting at me, they marched me down to the railway station and pushed me onto the night train for East Berlin. Not only did that force me to burn up five days' travel budget in five hours, but I quickly learned how far East Germans would go to be nasty to an American. Every thirty minutes on that train, a huge woman in a blue uniform would shine a flashlight in my face and demand to see my visa. In East Berlin, at dawn, nobody would sell me food.

It took me half an hour to walk from the train station to the east side of the Berlin Wall. There were hints of pre-war grace in a few tree-lined boulevards, but for most of the way, massive gray tenements and government buildings blended with rubble left from the war. If I tried to ask a question in college German to a passer-by, the person would put his hand up in front of his face and quickly walk away.

I got as close to the Wall as I could, then walked up and down it for a mile in each direction. The apartment buildings nearest the Wall seemed empty, except for guard towers on the roofs, overlooking a strip of mined

sand bordered by rolls of concertina wire. Small groups of lounging soldiers came alert when they saw me coming. Each man followed me with
uncertain eyes, his machine gun dangling from a shoulder strap of black
leather. If I even touched the camera hanging round my neck, somebody
would instantly shout a warning. There were always footsteps behind me.

Walking the Berlin Wall that morning stiffened the hair on the back of
my neck just as climbing did, but I noticed that the nature of the fear was
different. In climbing, gravity is both impersonal and predictable—it works
the same way with everyone every time. The nervous young soldiers looking at me that morning were both sentient and unpredictable, and that
seemed to add a whole new level of risk and excitement. It was also not lost
on me that this adventure was not set in some nameless barroom in a
Philippine jungle, but in a place where World War III could start, right here,
by the four-story-high portrait of Lenin above my head and the scrawled
slogans that invited America to go to hell. Only that afternoon, when I
crossed into West Berlin at Checkpoint Charlie, did I notice how tired and
hungry I was.

Hitchhiking out of West Berlin was forbidden, so I took a bus to Vienna.
From there on, I thumbed rides everywhere. In 1962, before America's war
in Vietnam had begun in earnest, I quickly found that an American flag
pinned to my shirt would stop cars almost whenever I wanted.

The only destination I'd pre-planned that summer was the top of the
Matterhorn. Climbing with the Harvard Mountaineers had left me more
than ready for my first "real mountain" and, given the bravado that fueled
me, the most famous peak in the Alps seemed a good place to start. I hitchhiked to the youth hostel in Zermatt, begged and borrowed some gear, and
set out for the famous silhouette, spiking into a blue summer sky.

There's nothing technically severe about climbing the Matterhorn. Once
the route to the top had been worked out in the early part of the century,
summiting was like going up a very steep set of narrow stairs. The fact that
the stairs fell off 5,000 feet on either side, and that some of them were loose,
slanted or coated with ice, got the heart pumping, but by most measures of
mountaineering, the standard route on the Matterhorn is not a hard
climb.

I went up with a guide named Werner, a gruff fireplug of a man who looked old enough to be my grandfather—and who probably could have done the route in his sleep. We took a cable car to the shoulder of the mountain, then hiked up to a cabin at the base of the route, 5,000 feet from the top. At 3:00 A.M., roused by the hut keeper, we ate a bowl of hot soup and started up. Werner rarely spoke, in part because he kept a pipe in his mouth all the way up. I also kept expecting him to stop at the steeper parts and set up an anchor to steady the safety rope. He never did. The best he would do was gather in a few coils in one hand, steady his elbow on one knee, and growl at me to watch where I put my feet. By seven we were on top, a flattish area of snow and rock the size of a living room. There was only a soft wind, and not a cloud in the sky. The rest of the Alps spread out from us in every direction, a jumble of sharp rock and ice. Zermatt was a collection of house-dots at the end of a long green valley below.

I shook Werner's hand and we both sat down on a sun-warmed rock to eat a sausage and drink from a thermos of hot tea. I've been on many summits since, many of them harder and some of them higher, but none of them produced the heady feeling of this first. Looking down at the enormous spaces between me and the glaciers below, I knew without a shadow of a doubt that Alex—the bully who'd shoved me around as a kid—could never have done this; he would have looked at all that air between his legs and peed his pants.

By twos and threes, other climbers began joining us on the summit. Werner and I surrendered our warm rock and started down, carefully listening for the sound of any rocks kicked loose from above, and ready to duck.

Rockfall is a big reason people still die on the Matterhorn. Another reason is the Swiss attitude toward climbing safety. Coming down, Werner still never held the rope in any way that would have held a fall. If I'd learned anything from the Harvard Mountaineering Club, it was that smart climbers minimized the risks they had some control over and accepted those they didn't. Climbing was dangerous enough; there was no point in decreasing the odds by doing stupid or sloppy things. I started yelling at Werner to brace the rope over the parts where I could have slipped, but it was clear he wasn't going to change his ways for me. He'd grunt, and mutter something in Swiss-German he knew I couldn't understand.

The day after the Matterhorn climb, I picked up a copy of the *Paris Herald Tribune* in the youth hostel in Zermatt. The headline said that the war in Algeria was over—independence had just been declared. Below the headline were pictures of bombed-out buildings, clumps of bodies and settlers fleeing their homes. The country was in chaos. I looked again at the pictures, put down the paper, and headed south. I had no plan, except that something dangerous and exciting was going on only a few hundred miles away, and I was pulled toward it. East Berlin was the Cold War. This war was hot, or just had been. It was a new kind of adventure and I was not about to pass it up. The concept of something bad happening—like getting shot, or getting stuck in the chaos and missing my flight home—did not occur to me any more than it had in East Germany.

I hitchhiked to Gibraltar, took the ferry to Tangiers, then set out east along the Moroccan coast road to the border with Algeria. Ten miles past Oujda, a barbed wire fence cut across the empty desert. I had little trouble getting past. The French had left the border posts, and the Algerians had plenty to worry about in their two week-old country besides one curious American.

Hitchhiking in Algeria was easy because of the American flag on my shirt. People stopped from sheer surprise. Two Algerian soldiers picked me up toward the end of the first day, and before they turned off the main road, they stopped a truck going in my direction at gunpoint and ordered the driver to take me on. That was good fortune until the driver, a middle-aged Arab in a sweat-stained undershirt, put his right hand on my knee and began to edge it up under my shorts.

I shoved the man's hand away. He put it back, squeezing my thigh so hard it hurt. I hit his arm with my fist and he hit me back on the side of my head, swerving the truck into the oncoming lane. We were then moving slowly up a steep grade so I grabbed the door handle, kept my hand around a rucksack strap, climbed out on the running board, and jumped.

Thanks to the hill, and some soft sand on the shoulder, I survived the fall with minor scrapes and a sore shoulder. I sat for some time on the side of the road, rubbing my bruised parts and thinking that maybe, in Algeria,

I'd finally got in over my head. But then I realized—I'm unhurt because the truck, at that moment, had been going up the only hill we'd passed in twenty-five miles.

Had that been dumb luck? Or had I been protected in some way I didn't understand? By my mother's prayers, perhaps? I had no idea. At the time, the question wasn't that interesting and it faded, like the dot of that truck in the distance. The only thing that mattered was that I was still in one piece.

Ten minutes later, a German merchant in an old Citroen took me the last few miles to Orleansville, and left me with the detachment of French Foreign Legionnaires who ran the electrical generating plant for the city. The Legionnaires had been asked by the city to stay because, without them, the lights went out.

Beau Geste! Everybody knew about the Foreign Legion. My three hosts didn't disappoint. A thin-faced German named Dieter actually had a dueling scar on his face, or at least he said that's how he'd got the cut. Ahmad, a wiry Palestinian, looked and moved like a fox. Peter was a Brit, bald as a cue ball and built like a football lineman. All of them had skins burned deep brown by the desert sun.

Midway through dinner on their patio, a machine gun opened up fifty yards away. I dove out of my chair, scattering dishes and spilling wine. None of the Legionnaires so much as put down his glass. "We forget warn you," Dieter said. "They do this every night, just to scare us. They know they kill us, boom, no lights. So fuck them. We don't listen."

I sat down again and looked at Dieter, then at the other two, with awe. They were tough, brave, irreverent. They were, if anything, more impressive than Roy, my protector on the *Golden Bear*. They were outnumbered probably three thousand to three if it came to a fight, but they still looked and talked as if the few pistols and rifles they had would be enough to hold off the entire Algerian Army. How could they be this bold? Where did their brawny courage come from?

How could I tap into that same well and drink what would make me a man?

I'd never seen my own father as a model of manhood. I respected many of the Jesuits in my high school, and sharp, bold intellects like Harvey Sprewell and Rusty Kothavala. But my *heroes*—the male models I studied from every angle—were all swashbucklers of one kind or another. In the beginning, they'd been dead swashbucklers that I knew only from books. In Orleansville, I looked at those three live Legionnaires and wanted so much to be like them. Their personal lives may have been miserable—after all, most men joined the Foreign Legion fleeing either personal demons or the law—but I didn't think of that. Nor did I consider that they probably couldn't resist putting on a show for the wide-eyed American kid.

I stayed with the Legionnaires that night and the next day came at sunset to a small farming village just west of Oran. Like other villages that had once been French or Spanish, it was all but deserted, with most of the storefronts shuttered and barred. The inhabitants had fled to Europe rather than face the uncertainties of life under Arab rule.

But this village was not quite empty. Walking toward me down the dusty main street was a giant of a man, dressed in filthy overalls, unshaven, waving a bottle of wine in his right hand and yelling in French. When he spotted me and the American flag on my chest, he ran toward me. I started to retreat, then held my ground, more curious than scared. The man dropped to his knees in front of me and began to sob.

I stood there, not knowing what to do or say. The man finally struggled to his feet. I understood enough French to get that he wanted me to have dinner with him, and to spend the night at his house. Since I could hear firing around the village, I accepted his invitation rather than risk running into an Algerian patrol at night.

His name was John Grousillat. Six and a half feet tall and three hundred pounds at least, he was the only European who hadn't fled the village when the Foreign Legion garrison had pulled out two months before. He lived in a plain stone farmhouse not far outside the town. In the time since his wife and the other Europeans had left, he'd turned the house into a sty. Every dish was dirty and lay about on tables or on the floor. Dozens of empty wine bottles were piled with the trash. The whole house stank of garbage and sweat.

Grousillat closed the door, then drew six bolts across it. An old shotgun stood propped in the corner. He warmed some kind of lamb stew over a kerosene burner, wiped two plates with the end of a curtain, and we sat down to eat. The stew smelled of kerosene and tasted worse, but I was hungry and I ate enough of it to fill my stomach. Over dinner, John told me of pleasant evenings under the grape arbor outside the kitchen door. His wife had played the guitar and neighbors and Legionnaires would gather to dance and eat and drink red wine. Then the war had come, and he'd seen both friends and enemies in the village butchered. Now, he feared, the local warlords would turn on each other and a new war would start, even bloodier than the last. He was marked for death, he said, by Arabs who wanted his farm. But his family's roots on that land went back two hundred years, and he would not leave.

After dinner, he got up unsteadily from the table, went to a kitchen cupboard, and fumbled on a high shelf until he found a dusty bottle of cognac, which he said he'd been saving for a special occasion. He poured me a glass and him a tin cup. We clicked a toast and drank. He started to cry again. All I could think of was High Table at Lowell House. Black-tied dandies, we'd retire to a drawing room after dinner with the guest of honor and ask smart questions and make clever comments over little glasses of California brandy. Now that all seemed so sterile, so utterly unreal. John Grousillat was real, and there was nothing sterile about the chatter of machine guns in the distance.

He had one double bed. I went to sleep in my clothes, perched on one edge. Just before dawn, this giant, seized by a bad dream, raised himself up in the bed and began to scream at the top of his lungs and wave his huge fists. I rolled to the floor, grabbed my rucksack, slid the six bolts and ran out the door. I walked fast toward the first hint of light from the east. Roosters began to crow. I could still hear John Grousillat's screams. I guessed he would blow his own brains out before the Arabs got him.

Two miles down the road I passed a small orange grove. I picked some fruit, got out the last of a two-day-old crust of bread, and sat on a rare patch of grass, watching the sun break loose from the desert and rise into the sky.

I could hear what my Legionnaire hosts in Orleansville, would say about John Grousillat: "Fuck the bastard, he should have got out when he could."

But I couldn't dismiss him so easily. I imagined Harvey Sprewell's response from Harvard: "OK, John," he would have said, "now what did you learn from this experience about life and about death, about terror and loyalty and the fragile nature of men's minds?"

But Harvey's questions were too intellectual, and something in me understood that. The experience I'd just had with John Grousillat was in another realm, a realm of feelings and emotions that I'd closed off years before.

John Grousillat's course had the arc of a Greek tragedy. But this was no play. His stage was for real and I'd been on it. I'd felt his anguish, and I'd fled from it, too scared and uncertain to reach out to a frightened, lonely man.

In 1962 I had no models for doing that. My new heroes were all men of physical courage and strength, not compassion. And I still identified my father's gentle, caring nature with weakness—and feared I was my father's son. I was still trapped in the contradiction I felt between being gentle and compassionate—and being a man.

I didn't understand much—perhaps any—of this at the time. Sucking on an orange and looking back in the direction of John's farm, I had only a vague sense that, in running away from the pain in that farmhouse, I was ducking something important about *me*, but I couldn't identify what that was.

I could not and did not probe the confusion I felt. Instead, I pushed my arms through the straps of my rucksack, got to my feet, and moved out to the road. I wanted a ride that would take me to Algiers, and a boat back to France.

Chapter Four

Mt. McKinley, summer 1963

I came back from North Africa for my third year at Harvard, charged by the possibilities of an ever-wider world, and determined to explore as much of it as I could.

In the Mountaineering Club, seven of us that fall decided that the next summer—1963—we would climb the north wall of Mt. McKinley in Alaska, then one of the two biggest and most fearsome unclimbed mountain faces in the world. The other was the north face of Everest. No one told us that we were too young, too inexperienced and too poorly equipped. It wouldn't have mattered if they had.

McKinley, at 20,300 feet, is the highest mountain in North America. Its north wall had never been climbed because of avalanches—house-sized blocks of ice breaking off from cliffs high on the face and crashing nearly two vertical miles to the mountain's base, scouring out tons of snow along the way. Nothing in their path could survive. Since avalanches fell every day and a climb up the north wall would take weeks—the experts had pronounced any attempt suicidal.

But detailed photographs showed a shallow buttress, a wrinkle snaking up the center of the wall. It seemed to us that the buttress stuck out just far enough from the face to offer safe passage up through avalanches crashing down on either side. We were also betting that the tents, snowshoes and other gear we'd made ourselves or gotten from Army surplus would hold up on McKinley—home to some of the fiercest weather on earth.

It all seemed perfectly reasonable to us. Chris Goetze, twenty-three and already in grad school, was the old man of our team. Hank Abrons and Rick Millikan were seniors. All three had already been on other expeditions. For the rest of us, the McKinley expedition would be our first. Pete Carman and I were juniors and Dave Roberts and Don Jensen were a year behind us.

We spent weeks studying aerial photographs, plotting each twist and turn up the wall. We were sure the avalanches would miss. We were all good climbers—none of us would fall. And we had no doubt that, given enough good weather, we'd get to the top and down again.

Planning for McKinley took up so much time I dropped off the third-string varsity and rowed instead for the Lowell House crew. I continued to do well in geology but, after the last two years, a life in science seemed limiting and I talked that spring to recruiters from the Foreign Service. I came close to running a five-minute mile. I won a ten-dollar bet by swimming the Charles River in a tuxedo. My acting debut in April, 1963 drew what may have been the worst review ever printed in the *Harvard Crimson*.

I'd not been in Tacoma for well over a year. I'd called and written home often enough, but here was no way I was going to share with my parents the steadily expanding horizons of my life—including leaving the Church and the growing skepticism I was feeling toward a life in science. My parents saw a linear course for me, from Harvard to career to home and family of my own. I saw no benefit to sharing thoughts and feelings I knew would just worry them. They knew about the McKinley trip, of course, but not about the level of its risk.

Hank, Rick, Dave and I got to Alaska that June by driving a VW Microbus four days nonstop from Cambridge across Canada, then up the AlCan Highway. The bus was so overloaded with food and gear that we had to drive in reverse up some of the steepest grades, because reverse was the lowest gear. We linked up with Pete and Don at the train station in McKinley Park (Chris would arrive a week later), and finished sorting and packing our supplies. On June 18, we drove down a winding dirt road to within forty miles of the mountain, as close as we could get by car. None of us had seen our goal—McKinley had been hidden for days by heavy overcast. When we parked the car and looked south, all we could see was a wall of clouds.

Then, as if on cue, the top of the cloud veil slowly began to lift, and just the summit of the peak appeared, much farther up the sky than the spot at which we'd been staring. None of us said a word. I have a picture of Pete taken at that instant. Tough, steady and not easily impressed, Pete is pointing to the mountain, his mouth open in disbelief.

The clouds continued to part and the bulk of McKinley literally filled the horizon from east to west, with the north wall in our faces—huge, white and steep. We kept staring, at last understanding the size of the challenge we'd taken on. If we had any qualms, we kept them to ourselves. We strapped on seventy-pound packs and, whooping and hollering, stepped out onto the tundra, a treeless expanse of scrub grass and mosquitoes.

For the next three days we packed in over barren wilderness and across rushing streams to a Base Camp at 5,400 feet on the Peters Glacier. Our three homemade tents were dots at the bottom of a huge wall of ice and rock leading to vertical ice cliffs at 14,000 feet. If we could get up to the base of those cliffs, then find a way up through them, the remaining 5,500 feet to the north summit would be relatively easy going.

For the first two days, while we waited for an airdrop of supplies, we charted when the avalanches fell down the massive face and where. Three or four of them fell every day, but we found that most of them came down between 7:00 and 10:30, both A.M. and P.M.—triggered by the sun melting the ice on the upper face in the morning, and by the expansion caused by refreezing in the evening. The size of the avalanches was unnerving. Each one took twenty seconds to fall from 14,000 feet The large ones were so powerful that the blizzards of snow kicked up by their falling blotted out the sun and all but flattened our tents half a mile away. Still, as far as we could tell, none of the avalanches swept over the shallow buttress that was key to our route—and our survival.

It soon became clear from initial explorations, however, that the aerial photographs we'd studied had kept one vital secret: that crucial buttress didn't extend all the way down the wall to the glacier but ended in an unclimbable spur of rotten rock about 1,200 feet above Base Camp. The only way to get up to the bottom of the buttress was to climb up to the west of the rock spur—straight into the path of the avalanches and into the basin where they fell—then to traverse east onto the relative safety of the buttress. And we'd each have to make this dangerous trip not once, but many times, ferrying supplies. It was either that or give up the climb.

We never discussed quitting. We hadn't planned for a year and come all this way, just to back down before we'd even started. For a week, we played Russian Roulette with the avalanches, hauling supplies from Base Camp up to Camp One at the bottom of the buttress. To get there, we climbed a steep icefall of twisted blocks and towers of ice, then traversed the basin where the avalanches fell. We called this basin "the Cannon's Mouth," and each trip across it and back took forty minutes. We climbed only during the twilight that passed for night in the Alaskan summer, timing our trips across the Cannon's Mouth for the hours when the avalanches were least likely to fall. In all, we each made seven round trips through the Cannon's Mouth. Had an avalanche fallen during any one of them, there would have been no escape. "Thumbing our noses at the Almighty," my climbing diary notes. "Got to be one of the biggest thrills of my life."

There was never even a close call. Each night we picked our way across the basin through tons of new avalanche debris; when the avalanches fell, we were safely back in our tents on the glacier, listening to their roar. When our supplies were safely stowed at the base of our buttress, we were ready to move our tents up to Camp One, at the same altitude as the Cannon's Mouth, but at a safe distance from the avalanche path.

We'd escaped the Cannon's Mouth but hadn't counted on another danger—rocks falling from a 600-foot rock cliff now towering above our heads. Dave and I were the first to permanently move up to Camp One, where we pitched a tent and then spent the rest of the night exploring for a route up the cliff. Quietly intellectual and slight of build, Dave was probably the best technical climber on our team, and he led the first section. The rock was no harder to climb than the New England crags we knew, but it was cold, crumbly, and in places covered with ice. We were carrying packs loaded with gear. And above this cliff remained over 12,000 vertical feet of hard climbing in the middle of an Alaskan wilderness—not three hundred feet on a nice warm cliff in the Hudson Highlands, with cold beer waiting below. We had no radio. If we got into trouble in this remote place, we were on our own.

After a night of reconnoitering on the cliff, Dave and I rappelled back down to the tent to sleep. A few hours after we'd crawled into our sleeping bags, I woke to see daylight through two small holes in the ceiling, one on either side of my head, drilled by bullet-sized rocks falling from above. Suddenly I heard the sound of much bigger rocks crashing down the cliff face.

Dave had already left the tent to take a leak, and was protected by an overhang twenty yards away. I unzipped my sleeping bag and dove out of the tent into the snow. It was too late to run. A barrage of rocks, some of them the size of cannonballs, was heading straight for me. I stood there in my thermal underwear, frozen in place, and watched dozens of rocks whistle past my body on both sides. They smashed some supplies and equipment, but not one touched me.

Dave Roberts would become one of America's best-known mountaineering authors and in several of his books describes this incident as one of the damnedest things he'd ever seen. I remember staring up at that cannonade as if in a trance and watching the event in slow motion; I could even make out patterns of color and texture in individual rocks as they flew by, some of them all but parting my hair.

When it was all over, and the last pebbles had clicked down the face, I stood there silently. We'd all assumed that none of us would die on the mountain, but the odds on my surviving this rockfall had probably been one in a thousand. For a moment, I felt the same questions rising in me I'd asked after leaping unhurt from the truck in Algeria the summer before. This time the questions seemed more urgent. Was my survival dumb luck? Was some higher power protecting me—maybe not my mother's Catholic God but *something*? I still hadn't a clue. I took a deep breath, pulled on my pants, and helped Dave search for buried gear.

We sent out a new two-man team every night to push the route farther up. The rest of us hauled supplies, following fixed ropes anchored in place by the lead teams. It took us three days to find a way up the rock wall in front of us to Camp Two, at 7,100 feet. But even when we'd climbed the rock and anchored fixed ropes over the hardest parts, the route was too difficult to climb with heavy packs. Splicing thin fixed ropes together, we rigged an enormous pulley system from the top of the cliff and, in a single night, hauled all our supplies up to Camp Two. We'd crossed the Cannon's Mouth and now had overcome the first real climbing obstacle on our route. As we looked up through the sharp ridges and towers of rock and ice ahead, our spirits soared.

We continued to climb during the night and to sleep when the sun was highest and the snow least stable. The strategy of climbing the buttress was right. Once on the route, we watched one avalanche after another crash down to our right or left, so close that we were often caught in blizzards of wind and snow created by the force of their falling.

Halfway up the wall, just below Camp Five, Hank and I were packing loads up a steep snow ridge. We'd been up and down the ridge twice before during the night; the snow had been hard, and the steps we'd kicked into it had stayed firm. But the ridge was topped by an overhanging cornice of snow and ice, made by winds steadily blowing from the west. Cornices are shaped like the frozen crests of breaking ocean waves. Unsupported from underneath, they are always dangerous, even in the hard freeze of night.

Hank and I knew that if we started down for a third trip, the sun would hit the snow and begin to melt out our steps and weaken the cornice before we got back up. A deliberate man, with a sense of gravity about him that none of the rest of us possessed, Hank came closest to being the *de facto* leader of our team. I suspect on this night, however, it was me that talked both of us into foolishly daring one more run. We got down to Camp Four quickly, loaded our packs with boxes of food, and started back up. It was Hank's turn to lead when we reached the steepest part, and he kept as far from the cornice overhang as he could. When he reached the end of the rope that connected us, he anchored himself to the ridge with a long aluminum picket driven into the snow, then yelled for me to follow. I started up, carefully following his steps.

Suddenly the entire cornice gave way with a soft sound like the blowing out of a candle. Tons of snow and ice beneath my feet suddenly dropped away and I was left standing on air, looking down past my boots at four thousand feet of nothing. I hung there for a millisecond, like the Roadrunner in a Saturday morning cartoon. That millisecond was time for one swing of my ice ax. It bit into what remained of the ridge top and I hung on it until Hank pulled the rope taut from above. I crawled back onto the ridge and caught my breath, thankful that our homemade picket had held just as we'd thought it would. I climbed up to join Hank and the two of us struggled up to Camp Five before the snow got even softer.

There, the dice continued to roll. We'd pitched our tents on a rare flat expanse of hard snow, protected on the uphill side by a fifteen-foot ice cliff. Late that afternoon, we awoke to start the next night's climb. Rick crawled out of his tent first, then ambled a few feet ahead and began to pee a hole in the snow. Suddenly that hole got bigger and bigger, as the yellow snow began to fall away into a crevasse so big that he could not see the bottom. We'd pitched our camp next to—or perhaps directly over—a fragile snow bridge over a monster void.

Rick stared, then carefully backtracked to the tents and quietly told us that we could at that moment be pulling on our socks on top of two hundred feet of air. One at a time we slowly and carefully got out of the tents, pulled the stakes, then gently dragged or carried everything out of harm's way, choreographing our moves to put the least possible strain on whatever supported us. All this took five minutes, but it seemed forever.

Steadily and carefully we inched upward. We used homemade rope ladders with aluminum steps to force a route over rock towers too vertical to climb with packs, unaided. We kept our balance climbing steep ice walls by hanging onto ropes anchored with ice screws or pitons. At this stage of the climb, after the routes were established by the lead teams, the rest of us were climbing each section three or four times, ferrying heavy loads through thinner and thinner air. "I frankly don't know what keeps us going," my journal notes after one particularly grueling night. "It is murder. Physically exhausting and extremely dangerous. When we reach the tents after this last haul, we fall like dead men. But boy we feel like kingpins for pulling it off."

On July 8, we reached the ice cliffs at 14,000 feet where the avalanches start. Exploring that night, Rick and Pete found a wide vertical crack in the cliffs and cut foot and handholds up through it. The next night we moved ourselves and our supplies up these steps. Now we were on top of the wall, and only a smooth, 40-degree snow slope lay between us and the north summit. With easy climbing ahead, and the colder air at this altitude keeping the snow firm, we reversed our pattern and began to climb during the days.

We also no longer needed to send out lead teams to find the route and fix ropes. It was obvious where we had to go—up. The slope was now so clear we could slide down on the seat of our pants on our supply runs. Of course we overdid it. "On one slide I miss the snow bridge and catapult myself thirty feet down into a crevasse," I wrote in my journal. "On another trip I just miss getting badly cramponed…it still was damn fun!"

My journal stumbles trying to describe the views as we get higher and higher. The McKinley River was a silver ribbon snaking across the tundra in the distance. The stupendous towers and cliffs on the wall were just the foreground for a panoply of ridges, peaks and glaciers. On clear days, the sunrises—following hard on the sunsets—were spectacular shows of light and shadow.

On July 12 the weather, which had been amazingly good for McKinley, shut us down. For four days a blizzard pinned us in our homemade tents on a shelf we'd hacked out of the slope at 17,400 feet. We had one book, *Northwest Passage*. We ripped it into seven pieces and read and reread them in any order we could, with the wind screaming against the fragile sheets of nylon above our heads.

The greatest danger during the storm, other than the tents shredding, was from the inevitable calls of nature. When they could no longer be ignored, we had to crawl out of the tents into the storm, drop our pants, jam our ice axes deep into the uphill slope and lean backwards, literally hanging onto the axes for our lives. Back in the tents, we spent hours amusing ourselves composing the letters we'd have to write to each others' mothers, in the event one of those axes failed: "Dear Mrs. Roberts, your son Dave crapped out at 17,000 feet…"

July 16 dawned clear and almost windless. By 7:00 A.M. we'd struck our tents and headed for the north summit. Halfway there, the weather began to worsen again, but we had little choice but to keep going—our safety now lay in getting off the windswept face and making it to shelter on the lee side of the summit. Deep snow and the thin air at 19,000 feet made each step an enormous effort. By 1 P.M. we were only 500 feet from the top, but battling

55 mile-an-hour winds and temperatures below zero. We could see only a few feet through the blizzard, but this close to the top, as long as we kept going up, we couldn't get off the route. Often we were forced by the winds to our hands and knees to keep from being blown off the mountain.

At 3:30 P.M. there was no more "up." We'd reached McKinley's 19,470 foot north summit. Cold and exhausted, we stopped only to take a picture of our club flag, blown taut by the gale, then started down to a flat area we knew from photographs lay only a short distance past the summit. Pete and I were roped together, and he started inching his way down first, soon disappearing into the storm. Suddenly the coils of rope at my feet began to spin out rapidly—Pete had fallen, and was sliding out of control. Starved for oxygen, my brain did not react; I just stared at the rapidly disappearing coils. Hank was in better shape and screamed in my ear. My neurons finally fired, and I anchored the rope just in time to stop Pete's slide, and to keep myself from being pulled after him. I waited for Pete to climb back up, pulling in the rope and panting hard to force more oxygen into my brain.

We still weren't done. McKinley is so big that its two summits are almost four miles apart. After three days of easy going, we reached the south summit, at 20,300 feet.

It had taken us over a month to go up the mountain from the north; it would take us only three days to come down, taking the easy route on the other side. Back on the glaciers at the mountain's base, we circled around to our original Base Camp where we stopped to devour a case of canned fruit cocktail we'd left behind the month before.

It had taken us three days to pack in to Base Camp; now, our heads filled with thoughts of steaks and hot showers, we crossed the mosquito-infested wilderness in two. When we reached the McKinley River in late afternoon, we could see our van on the far bank, a half-mile away.

The water level in rivers like the McKinley varies dramatically, depending on the time of day. Sunlight had hit the north side of the mountain in the morning, melting the snow and ice. Now the meltwater was roaring past us in full flood.

There's a prime directive in crossing dangerous, glacier-fed rivers—wait until low water. For us, that would have meant at least a six or seven hour delay. The snow and ice on the mountain would start to refreeze once the sun had disappeared, and the river where we needed to cross would be at its lowest point in the early hours of the morning. The smart move would have been to catch some sleep on the riverbank, then cross.

But we remembered that the manager of the McKinley Park Hotel, a man of little charm, had made a public bet that the Harvard team would never climb the north wall and live to tell about it. If our "sheer folly" succeeded, he'd said, he would treat us to all the steak dinners we could eat. His hotel was an hour away, once we got to the van. We'd been living on rice and freeze-dried food for weeks. We could smell those steaks.

We looked at the river rushing past us. The floodwaters were almost waist high and moving very fast. The roar was so loud we had to yell in each other's ears to be heard. What to do?

It was unanimous. We'd just made the first direct ascent of one of the highest and most dangerous mountain walls in the world. We were unstoppable. And we wanted our steaks. Waiting for low water might have been prudent, but it also would have required patience we did not have.

We roped up in one team of three and two teams of two and started across the eleven braided streams that formed the river. The weight of our packs helped us keep our footing as we crossed the first ten streams. Pete fell on one of the crossings but was hauled to safety with the rope.

Hank and I were the last team to reach the final braid. Hank plunged in and was just reaching the far bank when I started. At once I stepped into a hole the others had somehow missed, lost my balance and was dragged under. I struggled to get my face above water, gasping for air, but my pack had now become a deadly anchor. Tons of fast-moving water pummeled me against rocks on the stream bottom. Swimming was impossible. Hank had made it to the far bank but had been pulled off his feet by the rope that joined us, and was being dragged backward across the gravel toward the flood. The others were too far away to help in time. In the next thirty seconds, either the pull of the rope would pendulum me onto the far bank, or the force of the river propelling me downstream would pull Hank in too and we both would drown.

Hank spread-eagled himself on the bank, desperately trying to resist the pull of the rope, but there was nothing to hold on to and he was pulled foot by foot closer to the edge. I was helpless, one moment smashed against the rocks on the river bottom, then up, gasping for air.

I smashed into the far bank seconds before Hank was dragged the final few feet into the river. Moments later, the others pulled us both to safety. Lying on the cold gravel, battered and gasping, I could hear Dave saying something about my "luck."

I couldn't explain it, but from some deep place I knew then that Dave was wrong. In Algeria, I hadn't known whether jumping unhurt from that truck was "luck' or something else. Surviving the rockfall at Camp One had raised the same questions but still with no answers. But now—adding the collapsing cornice and now the river—the odds were too long for it to be luck. *These survivals formed a pattern*, and as I lay gasping on the river-bank, I saw that as clearly as I saw the cracks in a small piece of driftwood that lay beside my nose.

Of course, we'd all cheated the avalanches and we'd all survived falls on the climb, pulled to safety with ropes. But none of the others had faced the multiple brushes with death on this trip that I'd faced. We were all full of youthful bravado but, as far as I know, only in me, after that trip, would invulnerability become an act of faith. From that moment on the gravel bar, I simply *knew* that the pattern of deliverances would continue, that no physical adventure would ever do me in. Other people would call me lucky or foolhardy or even brave, but for me it was none of these. For me the odds were simply different, and I came to believe in that as I believed in gravity.

But pattern to me implied purpose—if I was being spared, didn't it have to be for a reason? What was that reason and who or what was behind it? These questions flickered across my mind that evening like distant light-ning. There were no answers, and the questions themselves were quickly overwhelmed by the simple pleasure of being alive—and the stings of a hundred minor cuts and bruises. No bones were broken, and with hot tea and dry clothes, the warmth slowly returned to my body.

When we got to the Microbus, we found that someone had changed the "Harvard" taped on its side to "Yale."

We drove eighteen miles to the McKinley Park Hotel to collect on our bet—an event that turned out to be more dramatic than we'd expected. Unknown to us, three weeks before, a bush pilot had reported seeing our tracks disappear into avalanche debris, and "Harvard Climbers Missing" had turned up on front pages all over the country. Hopes for us had "dimmed" when the four-day storm had hidden our tents from view, just beneath the north summit. At about the time we were having so much fun composing outhouse letters to our mothers, my own was saying rosaries and talking quietly with her friends.

When the storm had cleared, our tents had been sighted, but good news travels slower than bad. When the seven of us tramped into the dining room of the hotel—gaunt, unshaven, red-eyed, sunburned—a few astonished patrons looked at us as if we'd returned from the dead. After we'd eaten two steak dinners apiece, the manager, a poor loser, expressed his disappointment that the mountain had not finished us off.

Back in Tacoma, in the weeks following the McKinley climb, I was happy to let my mother's cooking put back lost pounds. But I didn't dare talk to her about the questions that had pursued me south. Who was protecting me in the face of these risks—and why? My mother would have immediately said that God was protecting me, but I no longer believed in her God (although I wasn't about to tell her that). Still, if it wasn't luck, and if it wasn't my mother's God, then what? There were plenty of dead young daredevils. Why was *I* still alive?

The shallowest part of me said that I was being protected because I was just plain special—like my parents believed and the Jesuits had said. But another niggling part of me suspected a *quid pro quo*. What if I was being saved to serve some purposes other than my own? If so, then what were those purposes? And whose?

The questions were too difficult and, as my senior year at Harvard started, they faded from focus, if not from view.

But my life had changed. Certain of survival, I took more risks. By the time I was forty I would have survived close calls with violent death many more times. The near misses never got me to back off—often just the opposite. With age and rank, my risk-taking began to affect the lives of many other people, and it was only then that I started to seriously reflect on it.

As to the risks on McKinley—no one has ever duplicated our climb; at least one person has died trying. Forty-four years later, a popular climbing guide to McKinley describes "the Harvard Route" as too dangerous to attempt.

I will always be proud that we did it.

Chapter Five

The High Road I, 1964

Harvard is not much impressed by anything, but headlines about the "missing Harvard climbers" had appeared in hometown papers across the country that summer of 1963. Many friends returning to Cambridge, thinking the seven of us dead, did the same double-take as the patrons at the McKinley Park Hotel.

I took graduate-level courses in geology my senior year, passed the exams for the Foreign Service and did well enough in a creative writing course to suggest that writing could be a life's work too. Senior year was supposed to be about leaning into the future, but I was leaning in so many directions I was losing my balance.

"Are the glories of spring lost on you entirely, Mr. Graham?" boomed a familiar voice coming from the walkway to my left. "The birds are singing, the sky is blue, you're graduating in two months—and you look miserable as a dog."

Elliot Perkins was the Master of Lowell House. Dressed in English tweeds, walking straight as a pole, swinging his ivory-handled cane with the precision of a drum major, Professor Perkins was famous at Harvard, as much for his total commitment to the men of Lowell as for the fierce stare he used to unnerve anyone who crossed him.

It was always best to prepare for an encounter with Perkins, but now I was caught completely by surprise. "Yes, sir… I mean, no sir," I said, trying to cope with the ambush. "I mean I've got a decision to make and I don't know what to do."

"And what might that decision be?" Perkins asked, as if, with his total attention to the young men in his charge, he didn't know.

I exhaled. "Two weeks ago," I told him, "I won a National Science Foundation Fellowship—four years at Berkeley to get a Ph.D. in geology. Yesterday Dean Porter called to say I'd won something I hadn't even applied for, something called a "Knox Fellowship;" it'll pay all expenses for a whole year at any university in the British Commonwealth, no strings attached. I've got to turn one of them down. The NSF is the best science fellowship in the country. But the other one sounds incredible—what I could do, where I could go…"

Perkins fixed me in his steely gaze while he methodically tapped the bricks in the sidewalk with his cane. "Aren't you the one," he said finally, "who got a story published in the *Boston Globe* about hitchhiking in Algeria?"

"Yes, sir, that was me."

"And weren't you one of those damn fools who almost got themselves killed on some mountain in Alaska last summer?"

"Yes, sir."

"And didn't you tell me last month that you'd taken the exams for the Foreign Service because you thought that would be more exciting than drudging about in some laboratory—and that you'd passed?"

"Yes, sir. If I get through the rest of their screenings, the Foreign Service could offer me a job within a year."

Perkins tapped his cane louder and faster. "Then dammit, Graham, think!" he barked. "If someone said they'd give you a silver spade if you would dig your grave with it—would you take it? Would you? Think, man, think!"

With that, Perkins gave the sidewalk a final blow, nodded curtly, and strode off toward the Yard. He knew, as I knew, that this decision was not about a fellowship, but about the whole direction of my life.

The choice couldn't have been starker. The NSF grant was the most prestigious way possible to launch a career in science; it was a well-traveled fast track to the best professorships and top awards. Accepting it would make the next four years, and probably the rest of my life, both comfortable and predictable.

I'd never even heard of a Knox Fellowship. Taking it would be a huge step into the unknown. Maybe it would link up with a job in the Foreign Service and maybe it wouldn't.

I turned down the NSF grant that afternoon. The decision did far more than effectively end a career in science; it forced me to think as deeply as I could about what I wanted my life to be.

At 21, that wasn't very deep. Harvard had kicked away the rote answers of my childhood, and what was filling the void was a belief in myself and what I could do, and a fascination with taking risks that was overwhelming everything else. Choosing the Knox was opting for adventure over security. In 1964, what I wanted for my life was to step off as many cliffs as I could, trusting that I'd fly. The thought from Mt. McKinley that maybe my miraculous survivals would demand a *quid pro quo*—that they might point to a life purpose higher than my own adventuring—was no more than an annoying whisper, lost now in the roar of the wind fast filling my sails.

I knew my parents would be unhappy with my choice. Having a son with a Ph.D. and in a safe, respectable profession fit their hopes for me. They'd see any turn from that path—especially one with no clear career goals in sight—as a foolish mistake. I wrote them a letter and took it to the mailbox on Boylston Street. Perkins was right—it was a lovely spring day; the birds were singing, and the sky was a brilliant shade of blue.

That evening I poured over the atlas in the Lowell House library, looking for the Commonwealth country farthest from Massachusetts, and the most exotic possible route for getting there. I thought about South Africa until I realized that if my destination were Australia, I could head east along the Silk Route, over the Khyber Pass, through India and Southeast Asia—then come home across the South Seas. And if I hitchhiked most of the way, and kept my living costs low, I could stretch the Knox budget to cover months on the road.

My geology professors thought I was nuts to turn down an NSF grant, but they were kind enough to arrange a desk for me in the Geology Department at the University of Adelaide in South Australia. No coursework, no papers, no teaching—and I could take four months to get there.

I flew to Paris the day after graduation, then took the Orient Express to Istanbul- which was, in 1964, the end of the beaten track. Two months after my encounter with Perkins, the last rays of sun washed over Europe at my back and lit the way east. Outside the window of the youth hostel, an imam stood silhouetted in his minaret and chanted the day's last call to prayer. When the prayers ended, shutters clattered shut on the shops below. Distant hills echoed with the horns of ships on the Bosphorus and ferries on the Golden Horn.

The next day at dawn I headed for the road south to Lebanon, walking out through the Grand Bazaar past pushcarts of fried fish and water sellers bowed under the weight of casks slung at the ends of long poles. The morning sun filtered through canvas awnings, splashing light on piles of vegetables and spices piled high on brass trays. I was on my way.

From 1962, I knew the moves. I knew where to look for the cheapest places to eat and sleep and how to deal with merchants and thieves. I carried a wash-and-wear suit in my rucksack, rolled in heavy paper to prevent wrinkles. That suit, a clean shirt and a pair of loafers got me into swank hotel lobbies from Beirut to Singapore, where I could clean up in the restrooms and sit unhassled, reading English-language newspapers. As before, I hitchhiked with an American flag pinned to my shirt. That flag would bring cars and trucks to a stop sometimes even before I could raise my thumb. A few years later, as the war in Vietnam escalated, American flags would be burned in village squares along the same route.

The Middle East that summer was wavering through an uneasy peace, and I traveled in it through checkpoints and police patrols. Not all the challenges were people with guns. Two days south of Istanbul I'd stopped at a street cafe in a small village on the Turkish coast to clean my contact lenses. The villagers, thinking I was some kind of sorcerer removing his eyeballs, started grumbling and pointing. Soon a dozen had collected, and the grumbling turned to angry shouts. My fifteen words of Turkish weren't enough to explain what I was doing. I left that village at a fast trot just as a few stones sailed past my head. Ten minutes later, I stopped a truck carrying burlap sacks of flour, and rode all the way to the Lebanese border on top of the load. When I jumped down from the truck to show my passport to the border guards, I didn't notice I was ghostly white from head to toe. The startled guards trained their rifles on me until one of them broke into a laugh.

Beirut, a few hours south of the border, was in 1964 a fresh, cosmopolitan city, with a string of plush seafront hotels that made it look and feel more like Monte Carlo than the Middle East. Its Christian and Moslem populations still lived in relative peace, and the city itself was still untouched by the fighting that would soon turn much of it into rubble. I stayed only a day, then rode with a Syrian businessman to Damascus, a short journey east over a range of low hills.

Damascus was neither cosmopolitan nor peaceful. The morning after I arrived a man was hung outside my hotel window, accused of being an Israeli spy. His broken neck was bent forward over a paper smock that listed his crimes. I stayed indoors until a mob chanting around the gallows had gone home.

Drifting south from Damascus, I spent four days in the West Bank, which in 1964 belonged to Jordan. In Jericho one evening, a dozen young men collected around my table at an outdoor cafe, eager to practice their English and unload their politics. Their English was better than I'd expected. Their political views were stark and unanimous: kill Jews; push Israel into the sea. I had little knowledge of the Middle East then, and no strong views, so mostly that night I listened.

What moved me most was the contrast between the anger and hatred of these young men and the peaceful look of the land around them·—the gentle hills, the holy places, the hard, simple life shared by both Moslems and Jews who worked the land. The curled lips and angry eyes I saw that evening belied this peace. None of the carnage in the West Bank since 1964 surprises me. You could see it coming. The young Palestinians I talked to were ready to die to kill Israelis, and some of them probably did die in the wars and intifadas that followed. I'm guessing that some watched with pride as their own children, or their friends' children, strapped bombs around their waists and head for crowded Israeli malls and busses.

It would be three more years before the West Bank—and the Middle East—would erupt in a shooting war. But there was one place near my route that summer where bullets were already flying. In late July, I backtracked to Beirut and bought a plane ticket to Cyprus.

The *Boston Globe* had given me press credentials for this year on the road, on the strength of a story I'd sold them from Algeria two years before. The foreign news editor had suggested I do my first piece on the long struggle between Greek and Turkish Cypriots for control of their island. The conflict had again turned violent, and that spring the fighting had become so vicious that a UN force had been sent to stand between the warring sides. The *Globe* would pay a fee for my story that would more than cover the airfare from Beirut.

With the *Globe*'s credentials I obtained a press pass from UN headquarters in Nicosia and used it to move back and forth between the battle lines, talking to Greeks, to Turks, and to the UN forces in the middle. This was best done during the day when UN peacekeeping was working. I saw villages leveled by artillery fire and torn bodies lying in the dirt. I talked to people with no forgiveness in their eyes.

By night in Nicosia, the capital city, there was sporadic firing as small patrols from both sides slipped back and forth through the UN net across a ceasefire boundary called the Green Line. Unwilling to miss any of the action, I put on the lightest-colored clothing I had and returned to the Green Line every night, shouting "Press" whenever I got close to Greek or Turkish guns poking from behind sandbag walls or overturned cars.

That this was dangerous to the point of lunacy never occurred to me. That piece of paper from the *Globe* made me a "war correspondent," and taking risks was my picture of what war correspondents did. Never mind that the *real* correspondents on Cyprus spent their evenings getting drunk in hotel bars. But it wasn't just ignorance that led me out to the Green Line at night. Ever since the McKinley River, I knew I wouldn't be hurt. Each time I returned in one piece only deepened the conviction.

Over dinner my last night in Cyprus I interviewed the UN commander, a spit-and-polish French-Canadian colonel in his mid-forties. He invited me to his villa in Bellapaix, a Greek village in the hills overlooking the harbor of Kyrenia. The sun went down that evening behind the crumbling tower of a 700-year-old abbey. Below us the tiny farms, the whitewashed houses and then the coastline slowly faded into night.

The meal was roast lamb, rubbed with garlic. A phonograph played soft guitar music, and patterns of candlelight darted off leaves in the arbor above our heads. Just to the south, muzzle flashes lit the sky around the Turkish fortress of St. Hilarion. Below us, flames leapt up from the harbor; commandos from one side or the other had torched the British marina.

Cyprus, like Algeria two years before, was a place where real people suffered and real people died. The colonel, however, talked only about the politics and battle news, and I did not push him further. I never asked him for any personal reactions to the human suffering around him. That would have meant asking myself what I felt, and that was still ground I was unwilling to explore.

If anything, my press credentials helped me bury my reactions to the human tragedies on Cyprus even deeper than I'd buried my response to the plight of John Grousillat in Algeria, two years before. I used those credentials not just as entrée, but as armor. Reporting with the objectivity I thought the *Globe* demanded gave me an excuse not to even look for my feelings, let alone express any I might have found.

The morning after the interview, I found a ride to the port of Famagusta and boarded a Russian steamer bound for Egypt. My plan was to go up the Nile all the way to East Africa, then double back north to Saudi Arabia and Iraq, before heading east again.

I'd become a savvy traveler, but there were lapses. In Giza, I was scammed by a bunch of kids who bet me I couldn't beat their leader to the top of the Great Pyramid. We bet two dollars, which was a small fortune to them and not insignificant to me. Looking at the spindly-legged kid challenging me, I felt confident. What I'd neglected was the importance of route-finding. The run to the top meant going up several hundred blocks each three feet high. Time had eroded many of the blocks, however, creating foot and handholds that made the climbing much easier—it you knew where those holds were, which, of course, this kid did. He had time for a nap on top before I got there.

Deck-class passage up the Nile from Cairo on a river steamer cost practically nothing, if you didn't mind sitting on stinking piles of untanned skins and being sprayed with DDT by health officials at every stop. The ride ended in Aswan where, in 1964, the Egyptians were building an earthen dam on the Nile more than two miles long and a half-mile thick. They were doing it the same way their ancestors had built the Pyramids—using humans as beasts of burden. Thousands of half-naked men carrying straw bags of dirt on their heads snaked in endless lines across the desert. The scene was straight from a Hollywood Bible epic. It was not just pre-Industrial Revolution, it was pre-wheel.

I would spend years of my professional life studying the politics and economics of the Third World. In that time, I never forgot how they built the Aswan Dam. *Our* part of the world could put a man on the moon and create the Internet, but ignore how another, larger part of the world still lived. We would raise the expectations of people like the serfs of Aswan through television—while doing little to help them raise their standards of living. They could collect in a headman's house to watch *Dallas* reruns and deodorant ads on sets powered by foot-pedal generators while their kids died from bad water and preventable diseases. That would feed an envy and sense of injustice that extremists would easily fan into anti-American passions. There's no mystery, at least to me, why so many people in the Third World cheered on 9/11.

From Aswan, an old steam train headed south into the Sudan, across the Nubian Desert to Khartoum. The Nubian Desert was as far as this train got.

A sandstorm in the Nubian Desert starts as a thin dark line on the horizon. If you're a dumb foreigner, you watch that line grow thicker as all the locals scramble back on the train, yelling stuff at you in Arabic you can't understand. You realize what's happening about thirty seconds before the storm hits, which is time enough only to throw yourself on the ground, hopefully behind something that will keep you from being sandblasted raw. Then you choke on sand for ten minutes until the storm passes.

With the train now stuck in the sand, I gave up on Khartoum and found a ride on a truck into Kassala, a town in eastern Sudan that for three thousand years had been a crossroads for camel caravans moving north to Egypt, east to the Red Sea, and south to the headwaters of the Nile. Low brown buildings, built with clay bricks, fronted narrow streets and alleyways that must have looked the same when the Pyramids were a construction site. There were a few Land Rovers in the town, but camels outnumbered them a hundred to one.

Kassala was as far as I, or anybody else, traveled for the next three days. An hour after I arrived in town, more dark clouds blew in from the west, carrying water instead of sand. Heavy rains, the kind that fall once in a decade, quickly turned the town and the surrounding desert into a sea of mud. Flash floods washed out the roads and created muck so thick that not even the camels could move through it.

This made the camels very angry, and Kassala was suddenly overrun with wet, bellowing beasts, chased through the streets by gaunt nomads with enormous bushy hairdos, flashing black eyes and curved swords tucked into cords that cinched their flowing robes. The drovers hated being stuck even more than their camels did, and they fought with anyone who crossed their paths, shaking long spears and screaming at the top of their lungs.

The drovers weren't the only problem. No sooner had I got to town than a man wearing a long white robe and an enormous turban began following me everywhere on a bicycle. He said he was the local chief of police and that it was his job to keep infidels like me from making trouble. Taking pictures was definitely against the rules, and the man threatened to throw me in jail if I even took my camera out of my pack. I don't think he ever slept, and I couldn't shake him for the whole three days I was stuck in his town.

Finally the rains eased, the camel trains departed, and a southbound truck with oversized tires took me across thirty miles of drying mud to the steep escarpment that guards the entrance to Eritrea and the Ethiopian Plateau.

Eritrea was in 1964 either the northernmost province of Ethiopia or a separate country, depending on the views of the various bands of armed men who stopped the vehicles traveling through it. At the first roadblock, just outside Tessenei, all the males on my bus were lined up against the side of the vehicle with our hands in the air, facing a half dozen guerrillas with automatic weapons pointed at our stomachs. Suddenly I thought of the American flag pinned to my shirt. Were we the good guys to this bunch— or not? Would that flag get me a hearty clap on the shoulder, or get me cut in two?

I sweated for five minutes, until the gunmen let us all back on the bus. Apparently, the U.S. had stayed neutral in this quarrel, or at least neutral enough to keep me from becoming a statistic. When we got back on the bus, I decided not to push my luck and stuffed the flag in my pocket.

Chapter Six
The High Road II, 1964

The dirt road from Eritrea to Addis Ababa runs south along the Ethiopian Plateau, winding as high as 12,500 feet through bulky green hills slashed by deep gorges and swift torrents. The danger in traveling this route during the rainy season was not from soldiers and guerillas. The danger was from bus and truck drivers who, glassy-eyed on the local hashish, forded rushing rivers at high water—often in sight of the wrecks of other vehicles flung downstream by the swirling brown floods. If the crossing was particularly fearsome, the driver would throw a rope across the flood to an ally on the far bank, who'd then drag across a cable and tie it to a tree. The driver would then use the winch on the front bumper to pull his vehicle across, rocking and skidding a foot downstream for every three it moved forward. Every crossing was an adventure.

The terrain we passed belonged on another planet. Sugar cane, bananas, and a strange bushy cactus grew at an altitude only a few thousand feet lower than the summits of the Alps. Cattle with huge, curving horns often blocked the road. Hyenas hunted in narrow meadows, baboons played in eucalyptus trees, and brightly colored birds the size of condors wheeled on rising currents of air.

Hidden from the world in this barely accessible place, peasants wrapped in rags or even old newspapers huddled in the bone-numbing rain and cold. At every stop, crowds of them would surround the bus to beg. Many of them were lepers or blind. Many were children with distended bellies and death stares. Worst of all were the "Spider People," victims of a disease that so deformed their legs that they could move only by scuttling sideways on their haunches, their useless legs bent at grotesque angles underneath them.

The misery here was far worse than anything I'd seen in Algeria or Cyprus. Amazed that anyone could live like this, I looked at these wretches as if they were animals in a zoo. I was there, but I wasn't.

More than four decades later, I can still see the vacant eyes of those starving people, and still remember the confusion I felt in staring at them. In 1964 I was defining my life by my adventures, each more dramatic and daring than the last. And as the stakes rose, so, in my mind, did the need to keep my heart as hard as the rest of my body. I was now the tough guy, as tough as Roy, my hero on the *Golden Bear,* or the three Legionnaires in Orleansville. There was no way I was going to risk this hard-won success by letting my emotions undercut the self-control I thought I needed to stay tough. A few years later, the whole world would learn about what was the worst famine of the twentieth century but, coming face-to-face with it, I was soul-dead. As in Algeria, as in Cyprus, I refused to let myself react to human pain. I felt uneasy about that at the time, but not uneasy enough to risk the introspection that might have opened my heart.

Rains blocked land travel south of Addis, so I flew south to Nairobi, then for two weeks roamed through Kenya, Tanganyika and Zanzibar.

In the town of Morongu, on the slopes of Mt. Kilimanjaro, I met a Chagga tribesman named Francis, who invited me to spend the night at his village, four miles from town up a trail winding through tea plantations and jungle. Francis' home was a mud and straw hut. Inside, a single oil lamp flickered over walls bare except for a large Coca Cola poster and, since Francis was a Christian, a crude tinfoil altar on a shelf hung from the opposite wall. A single table and chair stood in the center of the hut. In the corner nearest the altar was a bed made out of orange crates. The room smelled of oil and untanned skins. The smoke from a small iron stove was thick enough to burn my eyes.

The floor was dirt, stamped into a hard surface and swept clean by Francis' wife, a bent young woman with only a cotton dress to keep off the mountain chill. A naked baby was strapped to her back. A palsied grandmother huddled in another corner, muttering in Chagga, her hands pressed against her face.

Dinner was a kind of tomato stew, with coarse bread. The night got colder and colder, and I found it hard to sleep. I had just drifted off for the tenth time when Francis shook me awake, saying only that we had to leave the village right away. The urgency in his voice and the pre-dawn chill brought me fully awake and I followed him out the door and down the trail. Francis knew the way even in the dark. Only when we were almost back to Morongu did he slow his pace. "I'm sorry," he said. "But when my wife went out to make water, she overheard three men in our village, three bad men, planning to rob you just at dawn."

Francis, the Christian, said that he believed my guardian angel had sent his wife out to pee at just the right moment.

Maybe so, but my Catholic youth with its angels and devils was way back in my rear view mirror. Still, it had been clear to me ever since the McKinley River that my escapes were not luck. There was a pattern, and here was yet another proof of it. Francis' earnest explanation only revived the questions that had niggled me since Alaska. *Who* was protecting me— and why? Was this some kind of Faustian bargain that would ask something in return? The question didn't press for long. I was still willing to accept a free lunch without worrying too much about who'd bought it.

I rode from Morongu nearly to Dar es Salaam with a Swiss missionary who insisted I pass out her gospel tracts to the groups of Masai warriors we met along the road. From Dar, I worked my way north with a telephone repair crew, then curved inland through a string of game parks. By the time I'd seen enough elephants and lions, it was early September. Feeling some pressure to at least point myself toward Australia and the Knox Fellowship, I flew from Nairobi to Jeddah, a Saudi Arabian port on the Red Sea. From there I intended to go north to Baghdad, then turn east toward India.

The Saudi police grabbed me at the Jeddah airport and took me to a small, windowless room. A thuggish inspector with a small clipped mustache accused me of intending to sneak into the holy city of Mecca, thirty miles distant—and off-limits to all non-Muslims. While that idea had crossed my mind, I denied such intentions. The more I remembered that the Saudis cut off peoples' hands for stealing chickens, the more emphatic my denials became. The inspector finally shrugged and ordered his heavies to push me onto a plane for Dhahran, in the eastern part of the country, well away from Mecca. I was also given twenty-four hours to get out of the country—or else. The closest I got to Mecca was twenty thousand feet up. Arriving in Dhahran that night, only one flight left in time to get me out of Saudi Arabia before my twenty-four hours were up. It was heading for Teheran and I took it.

Without a visa for Iran, I expected trouble, but it was scarcely dawn when I arrived at the Teheran airport and a sleepy guard waved me through. Assuming that I was legally in the country, I wandered around Teheran for a day, then headed west by road to Baghdad, which is where I'd planned to go from Jeddah before the Saudis threw me off course. When I reached the border with Iraq, at the village of Qasri Shirin, the Iranian border police noticed that I had no visa for their country. They concluded I must have snuck into Iran. I was, therefore, a spy.

The policemen were overjoyed. After dreary months of looking for low-level smugglers and camel thieves, they'd nabbed a real American spy! I was paraded through the village to the local jail, a mud hut with bars. I shared not one word of any common language with my captors and I was forbidden from sending any message to the American Embassy in Teheran, five hundred miles east. At dinnertime, I was paraded again through the town to a local restaurant, a hut with an open fire under an iron grill and an earthen oven for baking bread. Villagers collected in groups of four or five to look at me, and to hear my guards tell and retell the story of my capture.

I had, of course, not the foggiest idea what the Iranians intended to do with me, but took it as a good sign the next morning when I wasn't blindfolded and taken to a wall. Instead I was marched back to the restaurant for breakfast, then taken under armed guard east to Khoramshar, where an English-speaking Army colonel told me my crime was "serious" and that my fate could only be decided back in Teheran.

Six hours later I was back in the capital, this time facing a civilian magistrate, a young, Western-educated guy who just laughed at my predicament. He dropped the spying charges but ordered me deported anyway. My biggest worry was that the Iranians would bounce me back to Saudi Arabia, where jail, or worse, awaited. Instead, they put me on a plane to Baghdad, where I'd been headed before my arrest. Considering the alternatives, this was a good result, although the unplanned series of plane flights I'd been forced to take since Jeddah had devastated my travel budget.

From Baghdad, I had to turn east again. I didn't want to re-enter Iran, but the road to India went through Iran and I had no choice. I got an Iranian visa in Baghdad, then headed back to Teheran by road. A different crew of border guards manned the checkpoint at Qasri Shirin and I crossed into Iran without being recognized as last week's spy. The next day I arrived in Teheran for the third time in two weeks. After a few days in the city, I took a local bus to the road east. My luck continued to change for the better. The first ride I thumbed—with two Mormon girls in a Microbus—took me three thousand miles, all the way to the Indian border.

Ella, an American, and Anna, a Swiss, had just finished a missionary assignment to convert the heathen of Switzerland. Both were a few years older than I was. Anna was small, dark-haired and quiet. Ella was a tall brunette, with the kind of lively blue eyes and lilting laugh I wouldn't have expected in someone who'd just spent two years passing out religious tracts in the suburbs of Zurich. Now the two of them were taking the long way to Salt Lake City. They'd made it this far, but the road ahead went across some of the loneliest terrain in the world, and through countries where the status of women was just above that of camels. They were as happy to see me as I was to see them and their bus.

In 1964, the paved road to India ended just ten miles east of Teheran. From there, a thousand miles of washboard track stretched to the border with Afghanistan across a flat desert whose only feature was a line of telegraph poles disappearing into the horizon. Blowing sand stalled the VW from time to time, but we used Ella's nail file to clean the engine points. The monotony of the land was broken by a few mud and straw villages. Most of them were walled, and after sundown the gates were locked. Venturing too close provoked a barrage of stones; we quickly learned to sleep in the desert.

There was, in all this emptiness, plenty of time for the three of us to talk. This was not, from my point of view, a good thing, since neither woman's missionary zeal had ebbed since leaving Europe. To them, the Book of Mormon had all the answers, and when I started to question what they told me about their faith—just as Rusty Kothavala had riddled my Catholicism at Harvard—their brows would furrow and their lips would tighten in frustration. Since I really didn't want to be left in the middle of the desert, I starting keeping my questions to myself, which unfortunately convinced both of them they were making progress.

A few hundred miles short of the Afghan border, the Muslim holy city of Mashad springs out of the desert. Remembering Muslim sensitivities in Jeddah, I would have avoided Mashad if we could, but the road not only went through the town, it went right past the sacred mosque. Anna was driving, and before I could stop her, braked the bus and leaned out the window to take a picture. Big mistake. In thirty seconds a howling mob formed, and we left Mashad weaving and bouncing through a hail of rocks and curses.

Anna had a few unkind words to say about the "fanatics" that were still waving their fists in her rear view mirror. When I commented that Muslims didn't seem any more fanatic about their faith than she did about hers, she gripped the wheel until her knuckles were white and neither woman spoke to me for the rest of the afternoon.

A day after fleeing Mashad we reached the Desert of Death, an utter emptiness where wind-whipped sand howls across the barren flatness twenty-four hours a day. In the middle of this desert is the frontier with Afghanistan, and what must have been the most God-forsaken border crossing in the world. On the Iranian side, there wasn't even a barricade, just a weather-beaten shack, and two guards with sheets of cloth wrapped around their faces so all you could see was their eyes.

Within hours of crossing into Afghanistan, however, the wind stopped and the land softened to low brown hills and broad valleys, some of them cultivated and green. The people softened too. Afghanis were as pleasant as Iranians had been hostile. When we had a flat tire near a village outside

Kandahar, within minutes we were surrounded by people offering tire patches and watermelon. I pinned the American flag back on my shirt. There is no permanence in politics. In this part of Afghanistan, the dark-eyed little boys waving at us would grow up to be Taliban, and the dirt tracks south of Kandahar would lead to the training camps of Al Queda.

We continued northeast to Kabul, nestled in grey-brown hills growing northward into the remote summits of the Hindu Kush. To our delight, we found a hot shower in Kabul. More than that, we found hamburgers and hot fudge sundaes, served up in an improbable oasis called the Khyber Restaurant by a Californian named Roger who was, he said, determined to get as far from L.A. as he could.

From Kabul we headed up into the Khyber Pass, a long slash in the mountains that for millennia had been the only passage between Afghanistan and the fertile lands of the Indus Valley to the east. That morning was my turn to drive, and I gently coaxed the little bus up one hairpin bend after the other, more than once forced to the edge of a precipice by a kamikaze truck careening down the mountain in the middle of the road. At the top of the pass we entered Pakistan where, to my horror, traffic now drove on the left. I'd never done that before. We got down the cliffs in one piece, but I remember having to pry my fingers off the wheel at the bottom.

Once over the pass, we continued southeast to Islamabad and then, a day later, headed for the Indian border. It was again my turn to drive, and by mid-morning I was carefully piloting the van through a small village. It was market day, and the narrow road was lined with women selling yams and peppers. Naked children chased each other, laughing. Merchants called to us from open storefronts.

Maybe I was driving a little too fast. When a chicken ran in front of the bus, I couldn't stop in time and dared not swerve for fear of hitting people on the sides of the road. I clobbered the chicken with the right front wheel. I stopped, intending to pay for the dead bird—until I heard the first rock crash against the side of the bus. I jumped back in the bus and we sped off, with angry villagers in hot pursuit.

Ella said nothing for ten minutes. Then: "You killed that chicken."

"Yes, I know," I answered. "If I'd swerved, I might have killed a human being."

Ten minutes more silence, then: "But you deliberately killed that chicken. What if it had been a child—would you have killed it too?"

I'd stepped on a landmine, either one the Mormons had given Ella or one she'd invented herself. She believed that the taking of any life, for any reason, was a sin, and I had just committed it. For the rest of the afternoon she described the hell-fire I would now be facing. I stared at the road.

At the Indian border, as luck would have it, the insurance papers for Ella's bus were not in order, and she was told she couldn't take the vehicle into India until the mess was straightened out. Chivalry be damned, it was time for my exit. I got my pack out of the bus, said goodbye to both of them and walked around the candy-striped barricade into India. I never saw either one of them again.

I hitchhiked north to Kashmir, then traveled east across northern India heading for Nepal. My goal was to get to Kathmandu in time for the Durga Puja, a religious festival that, over the years, had also become a kind of annual vagabonds' convention. From Istanbul to Zanzibar, the word on the high road was: "Meet at the Globe Restaurant in Kathmandu at Puja-time."

There were perhaps thirty of us at the Globe that year, from a dozen countries, eating yak steaks and drinking Nepali beer, spinning stories of adventures from Maracaibo to Mandalay. Outside the restaurant, Kathmandu shook with the sound of drums and gongs. Processions of worshippers wound through the narrow streets, blowing high-pitched horns, chanting and scattering flowers. Red-tongued Hindu gods glared from the corners of hundreds of little temples and lesser figures pranced in X-rated poses along the rooflines.

Looking back, the innocence of life on the high road in 1964 seems incredible. America's role in Vietnam was about to make it very foolish to wear an American flag anywhere in the Third World. The Middle East and Afghanistan would erupt in war. Khomeinis and Husseins and Talibans would come to power. Terrorism would become a global weapon of the discontented. Governments would collapse or turn inward. Borders would close.

In 1964, you might find a little hashish in the backpacks of vagabonds. But very soon that whole scene would be awash in drugs, bringing down brutal treatment from local police, who up until then had mostly been content to let the crazy young foreigners alone. Those of us who collected in Kathmandu that year thought the good times would roll forever. But an age of innocence was ending, not just for us but for the world, and the high road would never be the same.

Other things, personal things, were changing too.

I'd gone to Kathmandu in part because my life on the high road was becoming uncomfortably lonely. I'd found no youth hostels after Istanbul and, except for the long ride with Ella and Anna, had headed out on the road each day by myself. I was proud of the autonomy and self-reliance I'd forged for my life, but I also was beginning to realize how much I missed experiences like the Harvard crew or the McKinley climbing team. I thought I might feel some of that camaraderie with the other vagabonds that would collect in Kathmandu.

My adventures were as exciting and my stories as good as anyone's and I should have felt at home with this crowd. But as the celebrating and tale-spinning went on, I began to feel more and more out of place and, for a few days, didn't understand why.

Then I did. Most of my peers at the Globe Restaurant were dropouts; they would probably always live on the edge of whatever societies they might end up in, and they seemed comfortable with that. What I finally realized was that dropping out wasn't the life for me. Sitting at my table, listening to the clanging and singing outside the restaurant, there was no way I wanted to spend the rest of my life on the outside looking in. I'd done that all through high school and I wanted no more of it. Part of me was already thinking of what I'd be doing "back in the world" after my time in Australia.

Some of that push to stay engaged, in retrospect, came from my mother and the Jesuits, and their assumption that a life, in order to have meaning, had to be connected to organizations and systems. But some of it came from *me*, from something very deep inside that was beginning to sense the emptiness of a life not engaged with other people and with the world. This sense was weak and undefined in 1964. It was like walking in a dense fog and seeing then not-seeing the shapes of trees. Still, it was strong enough for me to realize that, after this year on the road, I needed to find a source of adventures that *didn't* include dropping out—some path or profession that would give my adventures context and significance in the wider world. I left Kathmandu finally understanding that I wasn't a member of the foot-loose fraternity that collected there and never would be—no matter how adventurous my life became.

But if I didn't want to be a lifelong outsider and I didn't want to be a scientist—where was my place in the world? The Foreign Service might offer me a job, but it had been eight months since I'd passed their exams and there'd been no offer yet.

Another option was staring me in the face—I could be a journalist, a foreign correspondent. I'd already sold major stories to the *Boston Globe*. The paper was pleased enough with my dispatches to ask for a series from Southeast Asia, beginning with the war in Laos—and at double my previous rate of pay. Enclosed with my last check was a letter from my editor urging me to think of a career in writing.

From Bombay I wrote the profs in Adelaide that I would be delayed even longer. They wouldn't like it, but it seemed to me that this trip had turned into a major means for finding out what I wanted to do with my life, and it made no sense not to play out the search as far as it would go.

Chapter Seven

Southeast Asia, November 1964

The Burmese Government wouldn't let me travel overland through their country, so I used the *Globe*'s money to fly from Bombay to Laos, a country that was in 1964 part Wild West and part Land of the Lotus Eaters. The capital, Ventiane, was a small moldering town on the banks of the upper Mekong, its French colonial buildings in need of whitewash and repair. A sign in my hotel asked patrons to check their guns at the door. Opium and plucked chickens were for sale from the same pushcart. The streets were dirt, the toilets didn't work—but the town was organized for the instant satisfaction of any vice. What little legal commerce and government there were in Ventiane shut down for a festival every two weeks when people got drunker and more stoned than usual and fired their guns at the moon.

The war in Laos didn't disturb any of this, since what little fighting there was took place in a large valley called the Plain of Jars, sixty miles to the north. Three armies—roughly representing the political right, left and center—huffed and puffed at each other, but no side ever gained more than a temporary advantage. The strings for this war were pulled in Washington, Moscow, Peking and Paris, and those powers, for the moment, were content with a standoff.

Generals from all three sides used Ventiane as their headquarters, not just for the war, but for managing a lucrative trade in opium, grown by peasants and controlled by warlords who played all sides against each oth-er. Most of this plotting took place, not just in the one town but in one seedy bar and whorehouse in that town. Its name was the Vieng Ratray, other-wise known to correspondents and freebooters all over Asia as "The Green Latrine."

The Green Latrine barroom took up the bottom floor, and the whore-house the top, of an old French hotel that knew its best days were past and had stopped caring. The barroom was barely lit, except for candles on tables and a string of pale lights over an elegant wooden bar against the far wall. Clouds of smoke from cigarettes and small hand-rolled cigars drifted in the gloom. Booths lined a second wall, each closed off by a curtain of beads. The rest of the room was tables, except for a small dance floor near the bar where two Laotian girls swayed slowly against each other to an old Edith Piaf record. Sitting at the bar and around the tables were warlords, drug runners, whores, mercenaries, spies and soldiers from the three armies.

The Green Latrine was definitely a step up from the jungle bar in Iloilo where I'd passed out on my night of inaugural sin five years before. Standing just inside the door, letting my eyes get used to the semi-darkness, I'm sure I saw no connection between the stupid kid on the *Golden Bear* and the tough, confident man coolly assessing what was no doubt one of the most impressive collections of thugs in Southeast Asia under one roof.

I was, of course, much too sanguine about the improvements those five years had brought. Muscles and experience had changed me all right, and I certainly *looked* more like a man. In other ways, however, I'd progressed very little. My heart was as closed as it had ever been. I'd traded a blind faith in my mother's God for a faith in myself that, in retrospect, was equal-ly blind. I thought I'd shaken off the chains of Tacoma but—as I began to make big decisions on my life over the next few months—would soon find out that I had not.

"You reporter? I tell you who CIA man is," purred a bargirl in a black silk sheath when I arrived. "He the one with the short hair."

A press card in a place like the Green Latrine is golden. Everyone has a story, and wants to see it in print. Even the "CIA man," a miserable alco-holic who said his name was Bob, spilled his guts over tumblers of gin and tonic. I didn't get out of the place until three in the morning.

I never bothered to go to the Plain of Jars to see this non-war. Instead, I flew to Bangkok, filed a story on Ventiane, then took an old coal-burning train through the jungle to within ten miles of the Cambodian border. A crowded local bus went from the end of the rail line another eight miles east. I sat on a pile of sugar cane, wedged between a couple of toothless old men, while somebody's jars of preserved garlic dripped steadily on my pants from a rack above. The bus stopped at the last village in Thailand, a collection of huts standing on stilts as protection against the rains, with goats and pigs penned underneath. From there, I walked two miles down a narrow dirt road to the Cambodian frontier.

Thais and Cambodians have hated each other for a thousand years, so there wasn't much traffic across the border. The crossing itself was a gate of scrap lumber and chicken wire hanging by one hinge. I woke up the Cambodian guard, showed him my visa, and signed myself into the country. A place this deserted was no spot to be choosy about a ride, and I ended up bouncing sixty miles in a motorcycle trailer down a rutted dirt road to Angkor Wat.

The ruins of Angkor are home for ghosts. A whole civilization simply picked up and moved south in the twelfth century, building a new capital at what is now Phnom Penh. The jungle quickly covered the old city, and it stayed buried until French archaeologists uncovered the place in the late 1800s.

Angkor is huge. I rented a bicycle, but it still took most of three days to see it all, pedaling miles down narrow paths hacked through the jungle. By day, monkeys chattered in the jungle around gray stone temples and palaces, many of them still partially shrouded in the vines and trees that claimed them 800 years before. By night, moonlight played on the promenades and parapets, and there was no sound except for the occasional cries of animals and birds.

This peace was not to last, not for Angkor and not for Cambodia. I got to Phnom Penh just in time to see the nation's leader, Prince Sihanouk, launch a huge anti-American rally, ending years of careful neutrality. From the press stand, I listened to Sihanouk and a crowd of Communist ambassadors rail at America's growing role in Vietnam. When the rally finally ended, with a parade of tanks and a MIG fly-by, I walked quickly back to my hotel, my American flag stuffed deep into a pocket. I spent the evening at a little floating cabaret on the Tonle Sap River. Kerosene lanterns on sampans bobbed with the current. A soft, steady rain fell with a hush into the water. The swollen river rushed seaward about as fast, it turned out, as Cambodia was rushing to her doom. It would take more than a decade, but the country's destruction would be total, much of it at the hands of its own people. The rally in Phnom Penh that day was just the beginning.

Next door, America's war in Vietnam had also begun.

In November 1964, bicycles in Saigon still outnumbered motorbikes, the black market was modest, and the graceful trees along Rue Catinat had not yet been cut down to make room for Army trucks. There were only 22,000 U.S. troops in South Vietnam, all of them in advisory roles. The first waves of American combat troops would not wade ashore in Danang for another five months, and the names that would be carved onto black stone slabs on the Mall would not yet fill half a panel.

After two days of press briefings in Saigon, the U.S. Army helicoptered me south to Phu My, a village in the Mekong Delta captured by South Vietnamese troops (ARVN—or Army of the Republic of Vietnam) from the Viet Cong ten months before. A battalion from the ARVN 7th Division was garrisoned in the village, advised by a small U.S. Army team, led by an amiable lieutenant from Kentucky named "Duke" Snyder.

The story of the war the ARVN and the Viet Cong were fighting in 1964 was a story of mud and fear and a lot of ugly ways to die. It was a war of night ambushes, booby-traps and hidden mines—and a war for people's minds. Both sides depended on recruits and informers in the hamlets. The peasants wouldn't sign on with either side without promises of protection, so each side struggled to build an image of strength—and ruthlessness—in the countryside.

Snyder let me go on a dawn patrol with an ARVN squad the day after I arrived in Phu My. The morning market was already crowded with farmers setting out wicker baskets of rice and vegetables. Here, where ARVN protection was reliable, people waved and called out to us as we passed. Ten minutes later, passing through contested hamlets less than a mile away, the mood was completely different. People either looked at the ground as we approached or stared at us with eyes flattened by fear. Nobody waved, not even the small children. There were no young men anywhere. Any found would have been interrogated as Viet Cong suspects, or sent to the ARVN induction center at Can Tho.

Beyond the hamlets, we moved through the jungle along a narrow trail, the soldiers with rifles at the ready. After half an hour we came to a shot-up pagoda, surrounded by coconut trees stripped clean by artillery blasts. Laid out in front of the pagoda were the bloated bodies of four Viet Cong, three young men and a girl. They'd been surprised in an ambush two nights before, then left to rot in the sun. Secondary ambushes had been set up near the bodies the next night, but no one had come to take them. Anyone coming in daylight to bury the corpses would be arrested, and probably tortured, in an effort to track down more of the enemy.

The patrol stopped for a mid-morning snack of small cakes of sticky rice. One of the younger ARVNs turned the girl's body over with his foot, sending a cloud of black flies swarming into the heavy, still air. The other soldiers swatted at the flies and yelled angrily at the man to stop. It was the first time I'd smelled rotting flesh. The girl's now-upturned face was twisted into what seemed a smile. What could she have been happy about as the life ebbed out of her? What must it be like to believe in something so much you were willing to die for it? I had no idea. Snyder offered me an energy bar, and I said no.

Back at battalion headquarters in Phu My that evening, ARVN artillery and mortars thumped and barked. Parachute flares drifted across the moon; from under dark trees, tracer bullets flicked into the night sky. A friendly outpost not far away had fallen under attack. There would be bodies draped on the barbed wire in the morning. I was in on the end of the beginning of America's war in Vietnam. Seven years and fifty thousand American lives later, I would be back for the beginning of the end.

I sent my story from Saigon and picked up a check from the *Globe* at the same time. Just as my life as a correspondent was gathering speed, however, my commitment to the Knox Fellowship got in the way. I headed resolutely south. Two months overdue, I finally arrived in Adelaide, Australia, greeted by Santa Claus and plum pudding and midsummer temperatures of 100 degrees in the shade.

Chapter Eight

Two Decisions, 1965 – 66

By the time I arrived in Australia, in December 1964, I'd been stoned, deported and jailed, caught in sandstorms and mired in mud. I'd forded torrents on the Ethiopian Plateau and tracked across the Desert of Death. I'd slept in jungles and deserts and fourth-class trains. I'd felt the ghosts of Angkor, danced at the Durga Puja and stalked the Viet Cong. Now I was supposed to settle down to an academic's life at the University of Adelaide, in a city known for churches, cricket and the fact that its pubs closed promptly at six.

Not bloody likely.

I told the profs at the Geology Department in Adelaide that my interest was in field work and they arranged a series of trips to mining districts all over the country. In January I began criss-crossing the Outback, the vast emptiness that is Australia beyond its coastal cities. I'd visit one or two mines on each trip, staying a week or so at each. Part of each day I'd be underground, learning how to follow a vein of ore. The rest of the day I'd be on the surface, surveying, prospecting and chasing kangaroos in a Land Rover. Most evenings, I'd be drinking beer in tough little saloons in tough little towns a thousand miles from the nearest city lights.

I returned to Adelaide after each trip, where I had a desk at the University but very little work to do. I was asked to give a couple of lectures on the research I'd observed at Harvard and I struggled through them without too much embarrassment. I lived at St. Mark's College, a hyper-formal institution in the Oxford mold where I had to wear an academic gown to dinner and the character-building showers deliberately ran cold.

St. Mark's College and the Outback saloons were the two poles of Australia's identity crisis n the 1960's. The wide-open spaces encouraged an informality and even rowdiness. But the isolation from the rest of the English-speaking world bred a sense of inferiority that drove many Australians to adopt every stuffy practice from Mother England they could remember, whether it made sense or not.

I spent as little time in Adelaide as possible. The University rowing team let me train with them whenever I wished. I learned to play cricket pretty well, although I never could stop calling a hard whack over the cen-ter fielder's head a "home run." Some weekends I went body-surfing with friends from the University at Chiton Beach, just south of town. But mostly, those first few months, when I was in Adelaide I spent most of my time planning for the next trip out.

In March I was prospecting for gold near Tennant Creek, a one-street cow town in the very center of Australia. The only hint of the Down-under autumn was a slight dip in the afternoon heat reflecting off the red earth. I'd found no gold but hardly cared. I was fast picking up an Australian ac-cent and my bush hat was beginning to look like it hadn't just walked out of the company store.

The one street in Tennant Creek was dirt, and the town looked and felt in 1965 like I imagined Dodge City did in 1880. As far as I could tell, there was no creek anywhere near Tennant Creek, unless the pioneers who started the town counted the bare gullies that cloudbursts filled once in a decade.

The other thing lacking was a local sense of humor. Soon after I arrived in the area, I'd been sent out by a mining company to put up large metal flags—surveying targets—on seven-foot poles on several of the low hills surrounding the town. Before I'd painted the flags, I'd seen a headline in the local weekly that Sukarno, the volatile Indonesian leader, had just threatened to invade Australia. Nothing stood between Tennant Creek and Sukarno's army but lots of very flat ground. So I'd painted my surveying targets red and white—just like the Indonesian flag. When the good citizens of the Tennant Creek woke the next morning they'd found themselves surrounded! When I'd showed up in the saloon that night, I was almost run out of town.

That stunt captured my state of mind at the time, that is to say, empty. The grand adventure of getting to Australia was over. My career as a correspondent, if that's what it had been, was temporarily on hold. So I'd quickly fallen into the "I'm all right, Jack" frame of mind shared by most Australian males in the 60's: don't work too hard but play as if your life depended on it. There weren't many temptations to engage in serious thought. I'd become pretty good at knocking down anthills with a Land Rover and knocking back beers in the local pubs. For the time being, anyway, not a lot else seemed to matter.

Tennant Creek was where The Letter caught up with me, in an envelope with a blue eagle and the words "Department of State" in the upper left-hand corner. The security background check for the Foreign Service must now be complete, and this could be, finally, the hard offer of a job.

It was. A training class for new diplomats would start that July in Washington D.C. Given how long it had taken the letter to get to me, I had less than a week to respond.

I put the letter back in the envelope, folded it in two and stuffed it in the back pocket of my shorts. I'd already started a career. After my stories from Southeast Asia, a senior editor at the *Boston Globe* had written me that I had a bright future as a correspondent, and asked me to stay in touch. Now this letter from the State Department was forcing a choice that, as far as I could see then, would determine the course of the rest of my life.

That night, alone at a campfire in the middle of nowhere, I fried a steak, drank some warm beer and leaned back against a gum tree to read the letter again. Sparks danced into a clear and moonless sky, lit by a billion stars. Dingoes howled. A rustling in the spinifex grass meant kangaroos, foraging in the cool of the night.

I'd written off a career in geology. Professor Perkins had been right: my life was not about rocks and laboratories, and it never would be. Skylarking around the Outback for a few months was one thing, but a whole life spent looking for ores or analyzing them in a laboratory would be quite another. My time at the mines only confirmed what I already knew.

Any image of myself as a permanently footloose vagabond had disappeared in the Globe Restaurant in Kathmandu. I knew now I could never stay dropped-out for long.

But a diplomat? Images came of men in striped pants drinking champagne at formal parties. My parents would be overjoyed at the choice. Harvard and the Foreign Service! Add a loving wife and kids and I would have succeeded beyond their dreams.

Then I rubbed my chin and remembered I hadn't shaved in three days. Wouldn't the Foreign Service cramp my style? Besides, my career as a correspondent was launched. All I had to do was pick it up again once the time in Australia was over. I closed my eyes and savored images of what my life as a journalist could be. Lean and suntanned, I'd return from dangerous field assignments to file my stories and be pursued by beautiful women in places with unpronounceable names. I'd go back to the U.S. to accept Pulitzer prizes and go on book tours and talk shows…

But if I played my cards right, why couldn't a diplomat's life be just as exciting as a correspondent's? Wasn't the hero in Michener's *Caravans* a Foreign Service Officer (FSO)? More images of romantic adventures in exotic places danced like the flames before my eyes.

Besides, I thought, diplomats had the social confidence and skills I'd envied as a high school nerd and still felt I lacked. Heroes like Roy on the *Golden Bear* and the Legionnaires in Orleansville were hardly models of cool. Harvard didn't teach social skills; events like High Table were more about intellectual jousting than being suave. Crew and climbing had been intense, physical, all-male pursuits. My life on the high road hadn't given me much practice as a social being either; I was far more comfortable dealing with thugs in bars than I would have been making conversation in some boardroom in a coat and tie.

Many of the correspondents I'd met on the road had been alcoholic louts. But if I became an FSO—wouldn't some suaveness rub off on me? I'd seen the first James Bond movie in Adelaide, and 007 was the very picture of dashing smoothness I wanted for myself.

I took another swig of warm beer, then got up to forage for more wood. I could make it as a correspondent—but the State Department had just offered me a job, and that was no mean thing.

It had now been a year since I'd taken the oral exams for the Foreign Service, sitting at a bare wooden table in a dull concrete building just across the river from the Lincoln Memorial. Three senior male ambassadors in dark suits had faced me from behind another table, on a raised platform. For an hour they'd rapid-fired questions on economics and current events, then for a second hour had asked me how I'd respond to a series of hypothetical crises. They'd deliberately kept interrupting me in mid-sentence, trying their best to rattle me.

When they'd called me back in to say I'd been chosen, one of them said that my interview had been a Hail Mary pass. With a major in geology and a relatively poor score on the written test, they hadn't given me much of a chance.

Now I was in.

I tossed the sticks I 'd found into the fire, and watched the sparks shoot up into the Milky Way, a broad smudge of light arcing over my head.

The more I thought about it, the Foreign Service offered me much more than teaching me to be cool.

I'd realized at the vagabonds' bash in Kathmandu how important it was that my adventuring have a context and significance beyond myself. My mother and the Jesuits had contributed to that understanding, but so had my own vague but growing discomfort with a completely self-focused life. Now the Foreign Service, I thought, offered the broader canvas that I sought, a place in the wider world.

But what finally swung my decision that night was something that until then I hadn't thought about much at all.

The Foreign Service could make me powerful.

In college, I'd been so caught up with re-inventing myself that I hadn't focused on what I'd *do* with the re-invention, beyond the next level of taking risks. I'd never thought of a career in business or politics. I'd never run for any student office. My decision to turn down the science fellowship in favor of the high road had been motivated by adventure, not ambition. But now, forced to make a decision about a career, I stared into the campfire and all I could see were the magazine pictures from Travoni's barbershop of the young men of Harvard heading for powerful lives. I was surprised that night at how much it meant for me to head there too.

I shouldn't have been surprised. Being powerful was part of my image of being a man, and my search for manhood then was the most important thing in my life. I wanted to be powerful because my father wasn't. I wanted to be powerful to get back at the bullies of my childhood. What choice would be the biggest come-uppance to those creeps? What career path would lift me farthest past their unanswered taunts?

Correspondents, I reflected, didn't make things happen; they only told people what had *already* happened. As a diplomat, however, I'd be solving important problems and making decisions that would change peoples' lives. What could be more powerful than that? And if I got to the top of whatever profession I entered, which summit would be the highest? At the end of my career, would I be more powerful as Secretary of State or editor of *The New York Times*?

Secretary of State won hands down.

I drove into Alice Springs the next day and wired my acceptance to the State Department.

Four decades later, that's as close as I can come to reconstructing one of the most fateful decisions I ever made. What strikes me most about that night is how much, despite my fervent belief to the contrary, I was still being jerked around by Tacoma. I chose the Foreign Service based on doubts about my manhood, angry memories of schoolyard bullies, and my own romantic imaginings and untested notions. While part of the push came from my wish for a broader context and significance for my life, my becoming a diplomat was about power, not public service. Any niggling feelings from the McKinley River that my life had been spared to serve a higher purpose were overwhelmed by reactive, self-centered reflections.

That night a path was set. Too many wonderful things have happened on it since for me to say that my decision—so breathtakingly shallow—was wrong.

I met Jean in April, over the beer cooler at a surfing party at Chiton Beach. She was twenty-four. She was a reporter for the *Adelaide Advertiser*. She was tall, blonde and beautiful. We fell in love instantly, profoundly, completely.

I'd see her when she got off work and we'd pour out our hearts to each other in little Greek coffeehouses in South Adelaide. I canceled trips to the mines, and Jean and I went camping in the Flinders Range, wine-tasting in the Barossa Valley, and sneaking off for lost weekends in Sydney. I played cricket with her brothers. I met her parents. I told her that I'd send her a ticket from Washington D.C., where I was about to train for the Foreign Service, and we'd be married there. When Jean said she didn't believe I'd ever send that ticket, I was hurt.

Instead, I should have seen what was coming.

At twenty-three, I'd built a whole life around controlling my emotional reactions to anyone and anything. By the time I'd met Jean, I'd created a wall around my heart so thick I had every reason to fear what would happen if it were ever breached.

With Jean, that collapse was explosive. It took all of ten minutes. The extraordinary thing was that I saw what was happening and didn't care. Falling in love was a total change from everything I'd ever been and done, and I was as consumed by the magic as a blind man by sudden sight. I knew the magic would disappear if I tried to control what was in my heart so—for the first time in my life—I didn't. I lost myself in Jean. I thought of nothing but Jean. The three months we were together in Australia were by far the happiest time of my young life, and I savored the passion with every part of my being.

So long as I was in Australia, so long as I could talk to Jean, touch her, love her, I was so caught up I didn't care that I was on a high wire without a net, leaping and spinning. Charged by the last leap and eager for the next, I never looked down. It seemed that my life and everything about it had changed forever.

It hadn't. Jean was a mortal threat to the emotional discipline that had closed my heart since childhood, and that part of me wasn't about to give up without a fight.

It was an unequal battle.

When I left Australia that June to join the Foreign Service, I looked down from the high wire, and I panicked. The passion that had taken out my defenses, that had obliterated my self-control, scared me more than flying bullets or raging floods. Within twenty-four hours, I knew I didn't dare go back to that high wire. I would not send that ticket, and I would not spend my life with Jean. And I wondered how Jean, from the start, had known that too.

What I did know was that I'd just given up something that had made me very happy. I told myself that it was an infatuation and would have ended quickly anyway. I reminded myself that the Foreign Service wanted spouses to be American, and that marrying Jean would have postponed my career until she filed for U.S. citizenship. I found other rationalizations—but the truth was I fled Jean because I was too scared by the passions we lit in each other, and by the loss of control they caused.

I had no models then for an emotional life as a man; certainly none of my heroes from the high seas or the high road qualified, and I was unwilling to see my gentle, caring father as a model for anything. My search for manhood was anchored in a tightly controlled toughness I'd created in response to my bullied childhood. It was a toughness that had kept my heart closed to the sufferings I'd seen in Algeria, Cyprus, Ethiopia and Vietnam. Now threatened by what Jean had tapped in me, it was a toughness that forced me to give up a happiness I'd never known possible.

I crawled around New Zealand for a few weeks, depressed and lonely. I stopped in Fiji, Tahiti, and Hawaii on the way home, but the romantic sunsets and white sand beaches only increased the sadness and frustration I felt.

I sent Jean lies that she must have seen through. Four decades later, I don't regret not marrying Jean; but I regret my cowardice and dishonesty toward her more than any other mistake I've ever made.

Jean joined the Red Cross and served with the Australian forces in Vietnam. I headed for the Foreign Service Institute in Washington, D.C.

I stopped in Tacoma on the way. Starting a career about which I knew little, confused and brooding over Jean, I was happy to spend a few days with my parents. Tacoma was temporary shelter from a world I suddenly felt much less confident in than the one I'd faced setting off on the high road the year before. I savored my mother's meatloaf with the ketchup baked onto the top, and I laughed at my father's puns. Both my parents were pleased that I'd hauled myself out of jungles and deserts and signed up for a profession as respectable as the Foreign Service. My mother told the local newspaper how glad she was to see me "all dressed up and out of those dirty clothes."

There was no way, of course, I could talk to either of them about Jean. I missed Jean. I missed us together, and the thought she was gone forever made me lonelier than I'd ever felt. Now the Foreign Service would soon send me to some distant part of the globe where I would spend more years by myself.

I suddenly realized I didn't want to be alone anymore.

Mimi Petrich was the girl next door. She was pretty, vivacious, well-connected, and the only child of wealthy parents. We'd both grown up in the same Catholic parish in the north end of the city but had hardly known each other then. She'd gone to a girls' academy in Tacoma run by Dominican nuns, then to Manhattanville, a top-drawer Catholic women's college in Purchase, New York. In those years, Manhattanville's mission was to groom the wives of the country's Catholic elite. Mimi arrived for freshman year with a white Mercedes and a mink coat. She once told me that she learned there how to eat a banana with a knife and fork. We'd dated three or four times in college, with only the slightest hint of interest that neither of us pursued.

I dialed her parents' number in Tacoma, and her mother told me Mimi was then in summer school at the University of Wisconsin, in Madison. Still in lingering love with Jean and totally unsure of how to deal with the loneliness I felt, I decided I would put any connection with Mimi in the lap of the gods. I would call her in Madison and tell her that I was coming to Chicago on my way to Washington to join the Foreign Service. If she drove down to meet me in Chicago, then I would pursue whatever might start there. If she didn't offer to come to Chicago—or if she invited me to detour to Madison—then that would be the end of it and I'd fly straight to DC.

Today, it's still hard for me to believe that someone with as much physical courage as I 'd shown by then could be so utterly spineless when it came to affairs of the heart. Still cringing from the mess I'd made with Jean, I was now failing to take responsibility for a relationship with somebody else. This time the price would be enormous.

When I called, Mimi interrupted me in mid-sentence to say she'd love to meet me at O'Hare, and suggested fun things we could do in Chicago. When I met her and her white Mercedes outside baggage claim, she was as pretty and lively as I'd remembered, and the sunny Sunday we spent together in the Loop was the most fun I'd had since Australia. When she left me at the airport, we hugged awkwardly and promised to write.

The Foreign Service held its Basic Course in an ugly blue office building in Arlington, Virginia, just across the Potomac from Washington DC. There were twenty-four of us in the course that summer of 1965, mostly men. I was the second-youngest, the only science major and one of only six without a graduate degree. The Service expected recruits to learn on the job, so its basic course was short. In six weeks we learned how the State Department was organized, how embassies worked and how to handle classified documents, write reports, interview visa applicants and help Americans in trouble overseas.

My classmates, half of whom were married, were likeable enough, and we played softball after class and shared dinners. One afternoon, all the guys took a bus to a men's store in Baltimore that offered big discounts to the Foreign Service and we ordered two suits apiece. I roomed with a short, dark-haired recruit named Bill Creech, with a Missouri accent you could walk across. When it was our turn to host a class dinner, Bill and I got recipes from our mothers and served up Yugoslav spaghetti and some strange dessert from the Ozarks that was better in the telling.

Like everyone else in the basic course, I was impatient to get to work. Unlike most of them, I got stuck for another four months in a total immersion course to improve my French.

Meanwhile, friendly but cautious letters flowed back and forth between Washington and Madison, words skittering on the surface like dragonflies above a pond. I felt none of the passion for Mimi that I had for Jean. I didn't come anywhere near to pouring my heart out to Mimi the way I had to Jean in those coffee houses in South Adelaide. Mimi was as safe as Jean had been dangerous. No out-of-control emotions. No chance of panic and humiliating retreat.

I already felt lonely and knew I was facing at least two years by myself in some far-off part of the world. So with each exchange of letters, the idea grew of asking Mimi to marry me before I left. With her upbringing, education and social skills, Mimi would be the perfect Foreign Service wife. I knew she'd already spent a year in India during college, and was eager to live abroad again. Then there was the job. The State Department had made it plain, even before I got to Washington, that it preferred new FSOs to be married. 75 percent of entering classes were male, and considering the social responsibilities of Foreign Service work, hiring a married male meant getting two employees for the price of one.

I approached the idea of marriage in a letter to Mimi in the most timid and hypothetical way I could. When she called two nights later and said "I accept," I had no idea what she was talking about. By then, of course, it was too late. I flew out to Madison with a ring.

I told Mimi in Madison that I loved her, and I believed then that I did. Responsible love. Mature love. In-control love. Non-Jean love. What I'd felt for Jean, I told myself again, was not love but an infatuation, a bittersweet memory to be shared soberly, and with feigned reluctance, when the time came to advise my sons on affairs of the heart.

No Professor Perkins stepped up to denounce the outright lies, slick rationalizations and thunderous stupidities behind this sterile marriage of convenience. No Professor Perkins told me that I'd not only closed off my heart, I'd begun letting my mind pretend it *was* my heart. That way I could remain safely loveless, yet still use the language of love. I could avoid passion. I could stay in control.

As it turned out, a marriage without passion would suit Mimi, for her own reasons, as much as it did me. She was as self-centered as I was. She was no more eager to get lost in me than I in her, no more willing to lose control. More honest than me, she used the word "respect" to describe what she felt for me. In the first of many fantasies I built around that marriage, I assumed the problem was in her syntax; I assumed she meant "love."

When I returned to Washington, I finally sent a truthful letter to Jean. There was no reply.

When I finished the French course, I asked to be sent to Vietnam, where the action was. Instead, the Foreign Service assigned me to the American Embassy in Liberia, a placid English-speaking country in West Africa. It was my first experience that, in the Foreign Service, what made sense to me didn't always make sense to my masters. As it turned out, being sent to Liberia was another deliverance: the FSO who *did* go to the post I eventually would fill in Vietnam was taken prisoner in the Tet Offensive.

In early January of 1966 I went back to Tacoma and married Mimi in the same church where we'd both been baptized. We left the church in a snow-storm. My Yugoslav relatives said that snow on the wedding day was a sign of great good luck.

Both our families thought Mimi and I a perfect match, and on paper we were. My parents were happy to see me marry into one of the city's most prominent families, and the fact that the Petrichs were Catholic thrilled my mother. The prestige of the Foreign Service met the expectations of Mimi's family and her class. It was a natural extension from Manhattanville and the Junior League.

Beyond the practical advantages, I really thought the marriage would work. After all, we liked each other. She was smart and fun to be around. But the best thing about Mimi was that she was no Jean. No sparks flew when we were together and I sensed, correctly, that they never would.

Had we both been more autonomous than we thought we were, this desiccated arrangement might have worked. But the truth was—a truth I would have strongly rejected at the time—we were both emotionally very needy people, entering into a relationship that guaranteed those needs could never be met. We both wanted to be loved, but consented to a mar-riage that was loveless. Worse, neither of us had much capacity or willing-ness to listen, to give, or to forge the compromises that any marriage re-quires. That much was clear in the first forty-eight hours after our wedding. Mimi insisted on cutting short our honeymoon so she could complete a navigation course for her private pilot's license—leaving me to mumble embarrassed explanations to our parents and friends. Things went down-hill from there.

With the sprite Jean had loosed back in his bottle, however, I ignored the reality of Mimi and me and fell back into the *Saturday Evening Post* cov-ers that described the Tacoma of my childhood. This time the picture was Perfect Marriage: responsible husband, pretty wife, nice job and (soon) two beautiful children. Mimi and I presented this picture to the world for the next fifteen years. Outsiders may have thought we were happy because our marriage was rarely stormy. What they didn't understand was that there was not enough energy in it for fighting.

Chapter Nine

Africa, 1966 – 1970

In late January 1966, the Foreign Service sent Mimi and me to the American Embassy in Monrovia, the capital of Liberia, a small English-speaking country on the bulge of West Africa.

The Embassy put us up temporarily in a small, cramped apartment at the edge of a tribal village on the outskirts of town. On our second night in country, we'd just fallen asleep when the night erupted with the wild thumping of drums. We jerked ourselves awake to see the reflections of small flames darting off the mirror in the bedroom. Running to the balcony we watched as a nine-foot apparition on stilts, clothed in animal skins and a long raffia skirt, whirled and chanted in the flickering light of hundreds of torches. The apparition wore a fierce wooden mask and a headdress of monkey fur. It shouted and waved a heavy staff at the tribespeople, who seemed numb with fright, moaning and offering gifts. After an hour, the specter suddenly vanished, as if absorbed by the night.

"So you saw a 'devil dance' on only your second day," Ben Hall, the Embassy's Admin Officer, said the next morning. "Lucky you. They only do that once or twice a year, to cast out demons. Welcome to Liberia."

Almost alone in Africa, Liberia had never been colonized, leaving its twenty-eight tribes and hundreds of sub-tribes living more or less as they had for centuries—even in a capital city with paved streets and a twelve-story hotel. A month after the devil dance, I went with Bestman, our house-boy, to his tribal court to watch a trial by ordeal: the flat of a red-hot ma-chete was put closer and closer to the suspect's calf; if he flinched—guilty!

Liberia was a U.S. pawn in the Cold War contest for Africa. The coun-try's currency was the U.S. dollar and the cops in Monrovia wore discarded Ohio State Patrol uniforms. We kept Liberia pliant with a huge aid pro-gram, with enough spillover to line the pockets of the ruling elite—the descendants of returned American slaves. In 1964, we'd built a lavish pal-ace for their leader, a squat, cigar-smoking dictator named William V.S. Tubman.

In addition to foreign aid, the country ran on revenues from rubber and iron ore, mined by American and European firms. English may have been the official language, but the 95 percent of the people who weren't in the ruling clique spoke dozens of tribal tongues. The climate was a steam bath. Envelopes stuck themselves shut on the shelf, mold grew in shoes over-night, and when you wrote a check the sweat ran down your hand to smudge the ink.

The Foreign Service put all its new officers through a two-year training rotation, meaning I would transfer every six months to different parts of the Embassy in Monrovia. As a political officer, I wrote biographic reports on President Tubman's cabinet, then did an analysis of the potential for unrest among the tribes that was quietly shelved because it called too much attention to the corruption of the dictator and his cronies. In the Embassy's Economic Section, I tracked down the details of Liberia's foreign debt and projected the future of the iron ore mines near the Sierra Leone border. I worked for half a year for the Voice of America station in Monrovia, host-ing a talk show broadcast in West Africa. My last six months in country I replaced the Vice-Consul, issuing visas to Liberian students headed for U.S. universities and bailing Americans out of local jails.

One of those jailhouse missions of mercy involved an American PanAm employee who'd run over a tribal boy on the road near the airport—the third fatality that year on Liberia's tiny network of paved roads. Many trib-al people coming to the coast for the first time had never seen a motor ve-hicle—let alone a paved highway; they'd wander in amazement down the middle of this dark, smooth trail, then stand and stare at a metal monster flying toward them at 80 miles an hour. This boy had never known what hit him.

The Liberian Government-—which had over the years turned extortion into an art form—automatically charged any foreign driver in a fatality case with first-degree murder, the penalty for which was death by firing squad. The terrified driver was thrown in jail, often in some small jungle town, and left to reflect that Liberia was the last country in Africa to outlaw cannibalism. After a few days of this, the driver's company was ready to pay for an acquittal, with the size of the bribe determined by the size of the company. PanAm was a big company.

As American Vice-Consul, it was my job to advise PanAm on the size of the bribe needed to free their man, and to arrange for the company to hire the Honorable C. L. Simpson, the bag man who would deliver it. Simpson had been Vice-President of Liberia in the 1930's until forced to resign when accused of dining on the liver of a political opponent—a case that had become a political embarrassment, even in Liberia. His hair now graying into white, Simpson had run a small law office in Monrovia ever since, surviving on the fees he charged for his access to the Tubman regime.

On the day of the trial, I drove with Simpson and the local PanAm manager down the coast to Buchanan, a small town east of Monrovia. In the trunk was a suitcase full of twenty-dollar bills. At the courthouse, Simpson took the suitcase into the judge's chambers, then into the jury room.

As it turned out, the senior class of the University of Liberia Law School was in the courtroom in Buchanan that day, to observe. The judge invited Simpson, one of the country's most famous figures, to speak to the students, which Simpson did, for almost an hour. His voice soaring and plunging like a Baptist preacher's, Simpson charged the students with the nobility and sanctity of the profession on which they were embarked. They looked up at him in awe. I looked over his shoulder at the jury box, and saw at least two men with the tips of twenty-dollar bills protruding from their shirt pockets. The jury took five minutes to find the driver innocent. I took him back with me to Monrovia, and mumbled some platitude in response to the tearful thanks of his wife.

None of my jobs at the Embassy was demanding, and Mimi and I went upcountry as often as we could, trekking into jungle villages with anthropologists and missionaries. For the anthropologists, Liberia, relatively undisturbed by Europeans, was a living laboratory. For the missionaries, it was a chance to convert real "heathen," still pretty much untouched by radios, Levi's and fast food.

A bloody coup and an even bloodier civil war would rip Liberia apart years later. A friend of mine named Cecil Dennis, who'd become Foreign Minister by then, was tied to a pole on the beach and shot. I've heard the story from many people that, with a dozen bullets in him, Cecil had refused to die until he'd completed the Lord's Prayer.

In my time in Liberia, ending in the spring of 1968, I saw none of that unrest. The best I can say for my tour there was that I learned the trade.

I also learned what the trade did to people. With a few exceptions, the officials above me at the embassy in Monrovia were the dregs of the Foreign Service. They'd been sent there to end their careers, or to get a grip after a drinking problem, or as exile for transgressions hinted at but never revealed. Most of them were pleasant people, more than willing to help Mimi and me adjust to Foreign Service life. A few were nasty, eager to take out their personal failures on ambitious underlings; I learned quickly to stay out of their way as best I could.

The fact was—I'd been sent to start my career in a Foreign Service graveyard. This raised the uncomfortable suspicion in me at the time that the Foreign Service didn't think much of me or what I could do. In retrospect, I was giving the Foreign Service too much credit for thinking. Some harried personnel officer in Washington needed to match a hole with a peg, and I, as the most junior peg at hand, had been pressed in.

I have few memories of my life with Mimi then, other than the occasional trips upcountry and one R&R visit to East Africa. It isn't because the memories were so awful that I repressed them; it's just that very little happened between us. We had no dreams together. We did no planning for our future as a couple and no planning for a family. We quickly settled into a numbing embassy social routine that minimized the time we spent with each other.

As I expected, Mimi kindled none of the passions that had driven me from Jean.

I know that there have always been people who've wed for reasons other than love, and some of them have built decent marriages. Mimi and I, however, were playing house, almost as small children do, without the sharing and affection and vulnerability that might have allowed a relationship to grow. Instead, our charade slid that first year into mutual blame for the loneliness we both felt, and that blame began to feed a quiet contempt and anger. We were creating a black hole from which no light could emerge, and we both lacked the courage, the will and the tools to do much about it.

Nonetheless—Liberia was where our daughter Malory was born, delivered in the middle of the night at a small clinic near our apartment, down a rutted dirt road in the jungle. Mimi and I were both as excited by this new life as any new parents. The excitement brought us together, at least for a time, and dealing with all the usual trials of new parenthood took our minds off our marriage.

Both sets of grandparents came to see the baby. Mimi and I were as respectful and affectionate with each other as we could be in front of them. Certainly there was no way I was going to confide the sadness and frustration I felt. I was then twenty-four, embarked on an unworkable marriage and a career that didn't look at all like the romantic pictures I'd concocted around that campfire near Tennant Creek. The career, at least, would dramatically improve, thanks to ambitions in the desert to the north.

In the summer of 1968, the State Department transferred us to Libya, then a feudal kingdom on the north coast of Africa. Run by a corrupt elite, awash in sudden oil wealth, stretched by rising expectations—the country was a political time bomb whose fuse had already been lit. In the vast and empty desert that began just south of the Mediterranean beaches, a group of young Army officers had begun plotting the coup that would change their country, and the Middle East, forever.

My job at the American Embassy in Tripoli, the capital, was liaison officer to Wheelus Air Base, a huge U.S. Air Force and NATO training base seven miles east of the city. For the first year of my tour, while old King Idris sat on his throne, I spent a good part of my time solving minor problems and bailing drunken American airmen out of the Tripoli jail. After two dull years in Liberia, this wasn't much of an improvement. Still, it was hard to complain. Libya, because of the oil boom, was at least a modest blip on the international horizon, and the U.S. Embassy there was staffed by first-rate professionals. Unlike Liberia, there was a livable climate and a large and interesting international community.

Mimi, Malory and I lived in an old Italian house on the coast road to Tunis, with thick stuccoed walls and a gnarled grape arbor shading a courtyard overlooking the Mediterranean. The house even had a name, painted on a ceramic plaque at the gate—Villa Fiorella. We spent most weekends picnicking with friends on white sand beaches, spreading our blankets among the columns and mosaics of ruined Roman cities. Other times we'd explore the farms and villages in the hill country south of Tripoli, a narrow band of fertile land between the Sahara and the sea.

This sweet life did not keep our marriage from spiraling further downwards. By now we scarcely talked, and it was evident to both of us that our "responsible" marriage had been a horrible mistake. For a time, we each (separately) saw a psychiatrist at the Wheelus base hospital, a pleasant blond midwesterner named Sherman Franz. Sherman kept quietly asking me why I stayed in a marriage that produced so much pain. I didn't have the courage even to listen to him, let alone attempt an answer. Instead I mumbled unfounded hopes that somehow, someday, the marriage might improve. Divorce would have been very difficult, not just because we were from Catholic families, but because of the expectations those families had. And for me, at least, divorce would have been an admission of failure that I could not bring myself to make.

Not even when it became clear we wished each other dead.

A year after we'd arrived in Libya, I went with a group of geologists by plane and truck deep into the Sahara, to look at Neolithic cave paintings. After the truck had left and when the plane missed the coordinates for our pickup, however, the trip threatened to become a disaster. Eighteen of us were stranded in a trackless waste somewhere near the border with Chad. We shivered through the desert night and watched with foreboding the coming of the dawn. It soon was 110 degrees. There was no shade, and we had almost no water. We made reflectors out of empty beer cans and discussed the odds of making it on foot to an oasis thirty miles away.

Luckily, we never had to try. Twenty-six hours late, the plane appeared. When it landed to refuel at Kufra Oasis, on the way back to Tripoli, everyone but me rushed to the single phone, to tell their wives that they were safe. I didn't bother; for Mimi, that would not have been good news. When I walked into Villa Fiorella late that night, her disappointment that I was alive was undisguised.

Mimi's reaction to my surviving the desert trip was logical—only death, it seemed, could get us out of the mess we'd made. I returned the favor. When Mimi almost died of a burst appendix a few months later, I had to make an effort to seem properly anguished in the hospital waiting room.

Malory somehow learned to survive in this soap opera, a shy, quiet child. I have a photograph of her in a little blue and white dress, standing in a narrow band of shadow on the porch of Villa Fiorella, her small face solemn and sad. Given how much I avoided going home, she got more attention from her nanny than she did from me.

But there was more afoot in Libya in 1969 than the sadness at home. The coup plotters had by late summer completed their plans. The Embassy was blind to the threat; our expectation was that the old King eventually would be eased out by a junta of U.S.-trained Army colonels. The country would keep its pro-American tilt, and the oil money would simply flow into a new set of Libyan pockets. In the meantime, there were those picnics among the Roman ruins, and belly dancers at lavish parties thrown by oil barons and arms merchants who'd joined the feeding frenzy in a country that had more money than it knew how to spend.

At work I spent most of my time trying to break all records for advancing in the Foreign Service. It was just like Tacoma, with commendations and promotions replacing straight A's, scholarships, and Scouting badges. I found dozens of things I could do at the airbase or the Embassy for "extra credit." I worked harder and later than anybody else, and I was quickly promoted past the bottom ranks.

One of the skills I excelled at was ferreting out political information my Embassy wanted, even if it meant abusing the few friendships I had. Once, when the Embassy needed to know about a top-secret shipment of tanks the British were sending to the Libyan Army, I tricked my British counterpart, over a boozy barbeque, into telling me what I wanted to know. I got a pat on the back from the Embassy and lost a friend.

In those days, the quest for manhood that dominated my life kept me from questioning the trade-off. My relationships with rivals or potential rivals were nearly all *mano a mano*. That, I thought, was how real men were. My real-life heroes were still tough guys like Roy on the *Golden Bear* or the Legionnaires I'd met in Algeria. The concept of developing trust as a means of solving political problems—at the core of what I teach now—seemed totally naïve then. I saw the world as tough and unrelenting, where only those willing to meet it on those terms survived.

After six months of working like this, I got constant, crippling headaches. Dr. Franz diagnosed stress. I began taking tranquilizers so that I could function. I was popping pills when the revolution came.

During the night of September 1, 1969, a young Army lieutenant named Mu'ammar Qadhaafi and a small band of conspirators took control of Libya. So cleverly planned and executed was their coup, and so welcomed by the people of Libya, that it was essentially bloodless. King Idris was sent into exile in Egypt. A handful of his ministers ended up in jail, and the rest were allowed to flee.

It all came as a complete surprise to the United States and, for that matter, to everybody else. In hindsight, there were abundant signs that a revolution was coming, and that it would be led by junior officers—not the well-heeled colonels already on the U.S. payroll. But so well was America's bread buttered by our cozy relationship with the old king and his oil that we ignored or misinterpreted every sign that it would end. Before September 1, we had never even heard of the coup leaders. After two weeks of frantic sleuthing, we cabled Washington that Qadhaafi was a Muslim zealot, not a Communist dupe. In those days, that information was received as good news.

My headaches vanished as fast as the old regime, even though I was working harder and under more apparent stress than before. It's not hard now to see why. Before the revolution, my stress was self-induced, created by a furious ambition at work and a disastrous marriage at home. Now, suddenly, all that personal *angst* was overwhelmed by a real political crisis that threatened important U.S. interests and the stability of the entire Middle East. When Wheelus Air Base became the first political target of the new leaders of Libya, as liaison officer to the Base I suddenly found myself in the middle of a very big and dangerous game—one I was sure I knew how to play.

Coping with the risks of a revolution demanded focus, toughness and courage—qualities I'd pushed myself hard to develop. For the first time, my romantic images for a Foreign Service career were not a joke. The violence and danger that unnerved some of my colleagues at the Embassy did exactly the opposite for me. I felt more comfortable with the howling mobs outside the Embassy that September than I had with the cocktail party guests inside in August. When I saw the first burning automobile on the streets of Tripoli, I was back in contact with a part of me I'd begun to fear I would never use again, a part that lived on danger and risk, a part that still heavily defined who I thought I was. The worse things got in revolutionary Libya, the more calm and competent I became.

Two weeks after the revolution, Qadhaafi demanded that the United States turn over Wheelus Air Base to his new government. Since the Base had been put there under the friendly king, its only defense was a chain link fence that kept camels off the runways. We could have ferried in troops to protect it, but that would have started a war and cut off the supply of Libyan oil. And trying to operate a training base in a hostile environment would have been insane.

Grudgingly, the U.S. agreed to the Libyan demand. I was named part of a team that met weekly with members of Libya's new ruling junta—the Revolutionary Command Council—to negotiate the terms of the transfer of the runways, barracks, hangars and hospital.

The talks promised to be tough. The young Libyans on the RCC resented America's support for Israel, and for a corrupt feudal regime in their country that had let very little of the oil wealth trickle down to ordinary people. The Americans were outraged that a bunch of twenty-something hotheads were "stealing" our air base and blaming us for every real or imagined wrong in their world.

Still, there was some hope that the base could be transferred quickly. While it was clear that Qadhaafi would never be an ally, cooler heads on both sides realized that, if the talks over Wheelus bogged down or blew up, it could fatally damage the chance to salvage even a minimal relationship between the United States and the new Libya. The stakes were high—keeping up the flow of oil to Europe and the United States, in return for oil money, spare parts for the U.S.-supplied Libyan Air Force, and irrigation technology that was already starting to make the desert bloom.

The Libyans also wanted to raise their flag over this prized turf as soon as possible, as a symbol of their triumph and for bragging rights in the Middle East. The U.S., for its part, had no idea what Qadhaafi would do next, and wanted the 5,000 Americans at Wheelus out of harm's way as soon as possible. We also thought the talks might move quickly because the Libyan negotiators were mostly young Air Force officers who'd been training and working with American counterparts for years.

Fat chance. From the first session, Americans and Libyans went at each other like junkyard dogs. We fought over everything; there was even a screaming match over who would get the bedpans and other items of small equipment from the base hospital. We praised others on "our side" for pettiness that should have been greeted with embarrassed silence. After the battle of the bedpans, whenever American military were forced to leave some equipment behind, they did their best to break it first, right down to the light sockets. The Libyans weren't pleased.

Negotiations that should have taken two months took nine. Finally, we ran out of things to fight about. On a hot cloudless day in July 1970, the Stars and Stripes was run down the pole at the main gate for the last time, and I watched the last planeload of U.S. Air Force people disappear into the summer sky. My job at that moment was to call the Pentagon and tell them the exact time when Wheelus became Iqba ben Naafi Air Base, re-named after one of the Prophet's most bloodthirsty lieutenants.

Near the flight line I reached for a telephone that I'd been using for almost two years—and this time felt a gun in my back. "No America phone!" a voice barked. I turned around slowly with my hands in the air and saw a

Libyan soldier, his face twisted with anger and his carbine pointed at my chest. "Libya phone!" the man said. I wasn't about to argue. I backed away, got into my car, and drove off the base for the last time, heading down the coast road toward Tripoli.

My knuckles were white on the steering wheel but not from my run-in with the soldier. I was still steaming from the soul-numbing wrangling over the base, wrangling that had not only prolonged the inevitable, but also degraded all of us as human beings.

In retrospect, the rancor unleashed at Wheelus was also an important reason why relations between the United States and Qadhaafi's Libya started off as badly as they did and continued to worsen. Maybe nothing we did in 1969-70 could have kept Qadhaafi from becoming a major sponsor of world terrorism. Personally, however, I think the fate of PanAm 103, blown up over Scotland by Libyan agents in 1988, was determined as much by what happened at Wheelus in 1970 as it was by a Libyan bomb-maker eighteen years later. A respectful effort to build a bridge to the young revolutionaries when we had the chance at Wheelus, before Qadhaafi's course was set, might have at least tempered what happened next. Instead, after the bitter fighting over Wheelus, the U.S. shut off the flow of spare parts to the Libyan Air Force. Within months the Libyans scrapped our planes and carried on with Russian MIGs and advisors. It all went downhill from there.

I couldn't see that future, driving down the road to Tripoli. All the same, I felt an overpowering sense of defeat. How could so many people on both sides at the Wheelus talks have acted so poorly, letting anger and frustration turn what should have been difficult but manageable talks into a bitter battlefield?

And what about me? Sure I was a junior officer, but I was also the Embassy's liaison to the base. If I'd been uncomfortable with the way my seniors were handling the talks, I could have said something. I hadn't. Instead, I'd joined the sniping. I felt angry, confused and ashamed. Now I had to drive back to the Embassy because the Libyans wouldn't let me use the damn phone. It was already late afternoon. I'd call the Pentagon from my office, and then I'd go home.

But Villa Fiorella was no home. It was a house with three lonely people in it. In my mind I saw Malory's sad little face. I felt the stiffness of Mimi's greeting and my own. And I realized with a start that I felt very much the same way about my failing marriage as I did about my role in the brawl at Wheelus—angry, confused and ashamed.

But what if that was no coincidence? *What if I felt the same way about these two failures because my roles in each of them were linked?*

I pulled the car off the road at the edge of a deserted beach, where shallow waves lapped onto the sand. The Pentagon could wait a little longer for news of America's failure. Right then, I needed to contemplate my own. A shepherd boy and two scrawny sheep walked up the beach on the hard wet sand at the edge of the ebbing tide. The boy waved. A soft wind blew foam off the tops of receding waves and scattered it inland on sand that had already dried.

The parallels between Wheelus and home quickly became clear: trust destroyed; behaviors sunk to embarrassing lows; any hope of finding common interests undermined by anger and fear…

The parallels were so exact, the two situations *had* to be linked. And if they were, then the ill wind connecting them, I thought then and still do, blew from home to Wheelus, more than the reverse. I'd been taking the anger and confusion and shame I felt in my personal life out to the negotiations at the base, and it had corrupted my behavior there.

I was not the only one.

I pictured the Libyans and Americans who'd clashed around that negotiating table. How many of them were letting a political feud unleash personal rages or depressions that had been silently deepening in them for years? How many failed husbands, fathers and sons were taking out their home-grown anger on the people across that table, now ready targets because our countries were at odds? How many people, incompetent to deal with the relentless stress of the revolution, were now focusing their frustrations on people with different-colored uniforms? For how many of us were these talks the perfect, sanctioned release of poisons we could not deal with in our personal lives?

Because we represented governments, it was easy to side-step personal responsibility for what we said and did at that table. And me—I'd chosen a career in the Foreign Service, in part because I wanted to be connected, to be part of something with a context and significance that was bigger than me. What I began to see that afternoon outside of Tripoli was that that connection came with a price: in a larger pond, I needed to take more responsibility for my actions. Yes I was a junior officer, but because of my key role at Wheelus, my actions at those talks *mattered*, not just to me, but to a course of events whose importance I sensed then but could not see.

These were painful, half-formed thoughts that afternoon—understandings that would finally come home three years later at the height of a battle on the other side of the world.

I watched the boy and his scrawny sheep disappear down the lonely beach. The sun was getting low, and the Pentagon was waiting for my call. I put the car in gear and rolled back onto the road. In the near distance, the minarets of Tripoli shone against a darkening sky.

Two weeks later, I was transferred to the State Department's Vietnam Training Center in Arlington, Virginia, where for the next six months I would struggle through a Vietnamese language course. I'd asked for years to be sent to Vietnam. I was delighted with the assignment—and fought hard to be posted where the action was, someplace far from Saigon. The adventure in Libya had only whetted my appetite—and I knew that a good performance under fire would rocket me further up the State Department's promotion ladder.

Mimi welcomed the assignment as much as I did. She and Malory would live in Bangkok, a comfortable State Department "safehaven." And Vietnam meant that she and I would have to deal with our disastrous marriage only every other month, on my short R&R visits. In fact, the assignment could separate us for as long as two years. That anticipation temporarily warmed the cold war between us, and amid that relief, our second child, Jason, was conceived the day the language course ended.

Chapter Ten

Hué, 1971

In January 1971, I arrived in South Vietnam to work for CORDS, a country-wide command of American civilians and military, described back home as the "pacification program." The acronym stood for Combined Operations Rural Development Support. The "R" had meant "revolutionary" until some Pentagon flack decided that made us sound too much like the Viet Cong. The military in CORDS were almost all Army. The civilians came from the State Department, the Agency for International Development (AID) and the CIA.

The withdrawal of American troops from Vietnam had begun the year before. By the time I arrived, U.S. troop strength had been cut by half, to 280,000, and it was going down every week. It was clear to most Americans in Vietnam—and to most Vietnamese on both sides—that military security in South Vietnam was deteriorating as fast as American troops were going home. But in order to keep justifying the withdrawals to the American public, the Nixon White House did whatever it could to support the fiction that South Vietnam could win the war on its own. Handing over the war to the South Vietnamese was called "Vietnamization" and it was a fraud from the beginning.

I think I knew this even before I got to Vietnam. I didn't care. I wanted to be in the adventure of a real war and now I was. I wanted to keep moving swiftly up the Foreign Service ranks, and this was the surest way to soar. As I'd hoped, my record in Libya had convinced the State Department to send me to a place both difficult and dangerous; I was appointed American advisor to the City of Hué, a political tinderbox only fifty miles south of the Demilitarized Zone (DMZ) that separated South Vietnam from the North. As part of that job I would also lead a joint civilian/military team responsible for all the economic development projects in both the city and the surrounding province. Like most CORDS officers, I was stunningly unprepared for my job. I was twenty-eight years old, spoke only pidgin Vietnamese, and had no training or experience whatsoever in either economic development or public administration. But CORDS was the channel for millions of dollars of U.S. aid—and our hand on the purse strings gave people like me influence we would never have gained otherwise.

Saigon, where I landed first, was stinking and ugly, nothing like the delicately beautiful city I'd first seen in 1964. In seven years, a huge American presence had overwhelmed the tree-lined boulevards and trim white buildings. As that presence now receded, it was leaving behind moraines of bars, brothels and black markets. The American economic strategy for winning the war included burying South Vietnam in western consumer goods. Levis had become the pants of choice. Radios and tape decks blared from even the most squalid shops. Thousands of motorbikes filled once quiet streets with the earsplitting roar of little engines, and wrapped much of downtown Saigon in a pall of acrid blue smoke.

I signed papers and sat through Embassy and Army briefings for three days. The Army then flew me north to the regional command center at Danang and the next afternoon on into Hué.

The tiny airstrip in Hué was wedged just inside the south wall of the Citadel, a huge nineteenth-century fortress of stone and brick, modeled on the Forbidden City in Beijing. The small single-engine plane circled the walls, wrapped on the south and west by the Perfume River. As the plane banked, I stared out the window at the fortress, the river, and a line of whitewashed French colonial buildings on the far bank. It was like seeing Iloilo from the deck of the *Golden Bear* again. It was like riding the taxi into Harvard Yard. I looked down at the battlements and at the sampans on the river and I knew beyond doubt that this was another place where my life would turn.

The plane set down on a dirt runway and taxied to a stop next to a long line of South Vietnamese Army (ARVN) tanks. Bob Wenzel, the Province Senior Advisor and my boss, met me as I clambered down the ladder. Bob was a senior Foreign Service Officer, tall and thin, with short curly hair and wire-rimmed glasses. I would learn very quickly that his shy smile and boyish looks belied his competence.

He took me straight to dinner at the CORDS mess, in a sprawling head-quarters building across the river that had once been a private school. We reached the mess hall in time for the first course—a traditional beef noodle soup, heavy on cilantro, called *phu*—which I came to love and still do. Bob interrupted the slurping to introduce me to his crew.

In January, 1971, there were forty Americans—half of them civilians, half military—on the CORDS team that served the city of Hué and its quarter-million inhabitants, as well as the surrounding province of Thua Thien. The CORDS command structure alternated between civilians and military. Bob Wenzel, with the equivalent rank of colonel, was in charge. His deputy was Lt. Colonel Don Zurbriggen, an artilleryman, built like a wrestler, who struggled daily to mesh twenty years of Army spit-and polish with the distinctly looser CORDS culture. I was third in command, with the equivalent rank of major. I had four deputies, two Army captains who handled logistics and two civilians—Howard Lange, another Foreign Service Officer who was also my housemate, and Gene Niewoehner, an affable, overweight Kentuckian who directed CORDS social welfare and refugee efforts.

To Americans, Hué was the capital of Thua Thien, a second-rate province fifty miles south of the DMZ. But Hué remembered better times. Five hundred years before, it had nurtured the revolt which had finally freed Vietnam from Chinese rule—then played a major role in the civil wars that ripped Vietnam apart for the next four centuries. In 1802 Nguyen Anh, a local warrior known for pulling his prisoners to pieces with elephants, had unified all of Vietnam, proclaimed himself emperor, and made Hué his capital. His first imperial act had been to build the Citadel and, at its center, a great palace. From the dark, wood-paneled throne room in this palace, the mandates of heaven had gone forth across the land.

But not for long. Nguyen Anh's heirs were not his equals. Eighty years later, weakened by corruption, the Nguyen dynasty had meekly fallen to French invaders, who then placed a series of puppets on the throne. The last of them, a chubby, tennis-playing womanizer named Bao Dai, had fled to France in 1955.

The people of Hué, however, were tougher than their emperors, and puppets for no one. From the beginning of French rule, the city had become the center of the struggle for independence. When the Vietnamese had finally forced the French out and the country had been partitioned in 1954, the citizens of Hué continued to rebel—first against the rule of Ngo Dinh Diem, and then against the series of inept generals who succeeded him as leaders of the Republic of Vietnam.

The military despots in Saigon consistently misread the opposition from Hué as a Communist plot. While the Viet Cong underground no doubt added what they could, the fact was that rebellions in Hué were fueled by an enduring passion to throw off *any* form of outside control. Tough, independent, and naturally given to plotting, the citizens of Hué hated with equal intensity the corrupt politicians in Saigon, the American occupiers, and the Viet Cong.

Geographically, Hué lay exactly halfway between Hanoi and Saigon. In temperament, however, the people of Hué resembled their tough northern cousins much more than they did the less disciplined southerners, whom they regarded with open contempt. This attitude, which the citizens here hardly bothered to disguise, only made Saigon regimes more suspicious of anything to do with Hué. They ignored the city—except when they were ruthlessly crushing the plots that eternally sprouted here.

The Viet Cong treated the city even worse. Determined to teach the "fence-sitters" of Hué a lesson, the Communists murdered 3,000 civilians when they overran the city during the Tet Offensive in 1968; many of the victims were intellectuals who opposed domination by either the right or the left. The bloodbath did not push Hué toward Saigon. It simply left the people there more fearful of the Communists and less trusting of the Saigon government's ability to protect them. Doomed by their sheer orneriness to remain isolated and vulnerable, what the people of Hué wanted most stayed out of their reach. What they wanted most was to be left alone.

In this setting, the U.S. government had launched a massive campaign to win the political support of the citizens of Hué and Thua Thien for a war effort the citizens never wanted, led by a Saigon elite they detested, and supported by foreigners they considered crude and ignorant.

I was joining that campaign—a hopeless effort to win the hearts and minds of people who'd been spitting on interlopers for seven hundred years. CORDS' job—in Hué/Thua Thien as throughout South Vietnam— was to build a political and economic infrastructure strong enough to win popular support for an anti-Communist government in Saigon, and to deny that support to the Viet Cong. The effort was total; it included everything from brutal counterintelligence operations to economic development. CORDS advisory teams operated in all ten rural districts in the province, with a larger headquarters team in Hué. Everything in CORDS was on a short fuse. With the American withdrawal from Vietnam due to be completed by 1973, CORDS had just two more years to pull off its miracle.

The State Department hadn't sent me to Vietnam to fight, but I hadn't been in the province a week when I learned that the word *noncombatant* didn't mean much this far north of Saigon. I got the message when a sniper's bullet whistled past my ear on the main highway twenty miles south of Hué. Joe Jackson, the burly major who was driving, yelled at me to hold on and duck as he gunned the jeep out of range, zigzagging to spoil the sniper's aim.

"That's the second time this week," Jackson growled when he finally slowed down. "We think it's an old Viet Minh not spry enough to travel with a VC squad any more. They set him up on one of those hilltops a half-mile off and let him bang away. He hasn't hit anyone yet, but this was too damn close; now we got to get the fucker." I slowly loosened my grip on the sides of the seat, wondering that my first brush with death in Vietnam might have been at the hands of a pot-shotting Viet Cong reject.

Snipers or not, it was the U.S. Government's policy not to issue weapons to civilian advisors in Vietnam, even to those of us in distant and dangerous outposts. The reason was not principle, but PR. Nixon and Kissinger had promised the American people that handing the war off to the South Vietnamese was an honorable exit for America—we would supply the arms and the South Vietnamese would win the war. One way of reinforcing the lie that Vietnamization was succeeding was to get pictures on American television of unarmed American advisors shaking hands with happy peasants in the hamlets and paddies—and walking the streets of Hué.

On the ground, we understood the reality very well. Without American troops, the question of the end of South Vietnam was not "if" but "when." Every civilian advisor I knew north of Danang had "borrowed" at least an M-16 and a .45 from Army depots and knew how to use them. My housemate, Howard Lange, and I maintained our own private army of four guards; we were under no illusions that they would defend us, but we did expect at least a warning shot. I kept a field telephone and a case of grenades under my bed, and I slept with an M-16 propped against the bedstead. As the very visible U.S. advisor to the city, I was an easy target for assassination or abduction, anytime the Viet Cong chose to take me out.

So it wasn't just for fun, on a blue-sky day in March, that I drove out to practice shooting in a gully just west of town. I went with Graham Fallon, a Navy doctor attached to CORDS. Fallon ran public health clinics and did surgery at the province hospital. Like many young doctors called up to military service in Vietnam, his uniform went no deeper than the cloth. He had a bright, irreverent Irishness that kept him in constant trouble with the brass. We quickly became good friends.

Fallon and I threw our M-16s and two boxes of ammunition in the back of my truck, then left both doors open while I climbed in and turned the key. We knew the primitive fusing in Viet Cong car bombs made a buzz before the charge went off—we had a half second in which to fling our bodies out of the car. I turned the key. The engine purred.

I threaded the little truck down narrow streets crowded by shabby villas with tin roofs, whitewashed walls, and heavy shutters of dark wood. At the Perfume River we turned right, dodging potholes filled with brown water left by a morning rain. A convoy of ARVN trucks passed us going north, the young soldiers sitting in the rear looking sullen and bored. Behind them, a large sampan moved slowly upstream, with the family wash hung on a line like battle pennants. On the far bank stretched the walls and battlements of the Citadel.

Schoolgirls in black silk pants and white flowing dresses called *ao dais* walked hand in hand on a broad promenade along the near bank. The dresses were split from the hip down the sides, and a soft, spring breeze moved the light material and played with waist-length tresses of jet-black hair. Most of the girls wore low, conical straw hats, fastened with ribbons beneath their chins. The picture belied the convoys, the soldiers and the war.

At the Nguyen Huong Bridge, we turned west, away from the river, past the three-story white colonial buildings of the University of Hué. Mildew had discolored large patches of stucco in the walls; some of the plaster had crumbled, exposing brown bricks underneath. The hundreds of smaller scars were bullet holes, left from the Tet Offensive three years before.

The streets near the university at midafternoon were crowded with students on bicycles and motor scooters. Housewives hurried along the pitted sidewalks, most of them carrying plastic net bags filled with vegetables and parcels wrapped with newspaper and string. Street vendors sat on low wooden chairs behind tables of black market radios, cheap jewelry and blue jeans. From somewhere in the bustle, a radio warbled Vietnamese music, the high, shrill tones sounding to Western ears like fingernails across a blackboard.

No one except very small children waved at us as we passed, and they were scolded when they did. Older people either looked down or simply stared at us. Honking to clear a path would not only have been useless—it would also have changed dozens of those blank looks to angry glares. To the people of Hué, Republic of Vietnam, the U.S. emblem on the doors of my truck was the symbol of yet another unwanted and unworthy occupier of their land.

Three miles from the city the tarmac ended and the road narrowed. With the rains over, the water in the rice paddies was low, glinting from under masses of green shoots. The paddies ran west another ten miles to a line of low brown hills which pushed into larger hills and finally into the Annamite Chain, a north-south range of forbidding crags that hid the A Shau Valley, the border with Laos and the Ho Chi Minh trail.

Small clusters of tin-roofed huts crept up on the road from either side. Women with loads of vegetables or firewood balanced at the ends of shoulder poles walked with a practiced glide that somehow kept the poles from bouncing on their thin shoulders. Small boys with sticks drove water buffalo along the edges of the paddies. The sky was cloudless and the air warm and nearly dry.

The road we were taking had been the main route for Viet Cong forces attacking Hué during the Tet Offensive. The wall of the village store we'd just passed was pockmarked with bullet holes. Ahead was a tree broken off by an artillery blast. From a helicopter we could have seen a random pattern of craters in the paddies, lasting scars from moments of flame and flying steel. The Viet Cong, shattered by a month of heavy fighting with U.S. Marines, had finally fallen back along this road to the safety of the jungles and mountains to the west.

CORDS charts that spring showed the city of Hué and the surrounding area as "secure." The local Viet Cong were still forced to work at night, and were mostly limited to harassing the city with rocket barrages from afar. The main danger Fallon and I had to fear on this narrow road in daylight was hitting a buffalo, or an ARVN jeep careening down the wrong side of the road.

A mile past the last in a string of three hamlets, the road narrowed to a track, and the paddies began to give way to a crumpled carpet of nearly barren hills. I pulled the truck off the road and bounced fifty yards up a shallow gully, stopping near a slight bend. Fallon and I took our guns and the ammunition boxes from the rear seat and walked a few more yards to an area already littered with shot-up beer cans and shards of broken glass.

An M-16 rifle has a switch along its side, just to the left of the rear sight, that allows the shooter to either fire one bullet at a time, or to fire bursts from the sixteen-shot magazine. We set out bits of metal and glass at different distances and squeezed off one shot at a time, sending geysers of dirt into the air. When we'd each fired three or four clips, we put the rifles down and banged away with our .45s, holding the big pistols in both hands. The .45 was accurate for only thirty feet or so, but its large bullets, especially if you notched the tips with a pocketknife, could tear a body almost in two.

Fallon used up his ammunition first. I had one more M-16 clip. I slammed it into the rifle and blasted away at a nearby bush on full automatic, holding the gun at my waist. In two seconds, the bush disappeared.

I stood in a cloud of gunsmoke, not moving, my ears ringing. When I finally turned toward the car, Fallon was staring at me, not a muscle moving.

"What are you looking at?" I asked him.

"Do you know how you looked when you were firing that gun?" Fallon asked, his voice flat.

I stopped short. "What do you mean, how I looked?" I answered. "I was shooting a gun. How was I *supposed* to look?"

"You looked," Fallon said quietly, "like a maniac. A real maniac. Your teeth were bared and your eyes were slits. You looked like you can't wait until it's people instead of bushes. You looked like you *enjoy* what's going on here. Sometimes you scare the shit out of me."

I don't remember what I replied. It doesn't matter. What mattered was that I knew instantly that what Fallon had said was true. I hadn't seen a bush in front of me. I'd seen a squad of Viet Cong thrown backwards by the force of the bullets, their arms flung over the heads, blood spurting, brains and bone flying, death-cries trapped in their throats. Then I'd seen them on the ground, muscles twitching for an instant, then still.

Fallon's comment had shattered that reverie. It was as if he'd shot a flare into my soul and in that sharp, phosphorous light I could see demons there. I was silent all the way into town.

That evening I sat alone in my room, getting drunk on Johnny Walker Black. Somewhere in the night a dog barked. The soft sound of sandals on a graveled walk, and a muffled cough, told me the guards were still awake. I refilled my glass, then flicked the switch on the tape recorder by my chair. I'd bought the machine at the PX only the week before, and I had only one tape; Gordon Lightfoot sang my favorite cut on it for the hundredth time:

> *I'm standin' in the doorway, my head bowed in my hands*
> *Not knowin' where to sit, not knowin' where to stand.*
> *My father looms above me, for him there is no rest.*
> *My mother's arms enfold me and hold me to her breast.*
> *They say you've been out wandrin'; they say you traveled far.*
> *Sit down young stranger, and tell us who you are.*

Lightfoot was in the room, talking straight at me. I moved my head and watched my shadow shift on the wall.

Who was I that afternoon, blowing away bushes and wishing they were Viet Cong? Had I really become some kind of maniac, as Fallon had said, ready and eager to kill?

In retrospect, by 1971 I'd spent most of my life storing up anger I'd never dealt with. The Viet Cong in my fantasy that day were stand-ins for the bullies who'd taunted me as a kid, and for the "in" crowds that had kept me out. I was angry at my father for not being the man I wanted him to be, angry at an unloving wife, and angry at me for trapping myself in a disastrous marriage. But anger had no place in the repressed, tightly-wired person I'd become. So I'd kept it buried along with the rest of my emotions— unspoken and unspeakable. For long periods, I'd even forgotten it was there.

Then the botched negotiations at Wheelus had pushed some of it to the surface, and given me an official excuse for letting it fly. But Wheelus had been just a shouting match. Vietnam was a shooting war, and it had suddenly provided a new sanction for the violence in my heart and given a voice to my anger I'd never had before.

The power and ugliness of that voice had shocked Fallon and it had shocked me. He'd been right, firing that burst from my M-16 that afternoon, I'd wanted my dark fantasy to be real. It was now OK for me to kill.

In time I would accept that what *was* real was the gentleness I'd inherited from my father, that it was his gift, and that it was more powerful than the anger generated in my youth. But I didn't know any of that then, not that evening, and the uncertainty frightened me. The glass of Scotch slipped from my fingers and shattered on the tile floor. I twisted up in the chair and turned out the light.

Chapter Eleven

A Dangerous Game, 1971

In March, 1971 the ARVN had launched an attack into Laos in an attempt to cut the Ho Chi Minh Trail, the main supply route for North Vietnamese Army troops (NVA) fighting in the south. Two South Vietnamese divisions had tangled with the NVA near Tchepone and been badly mauled. The attack had been staged through Hué. One week we saw an endless stream of ARVN tanks and trucks and cheering troops heading west. Three weeks later, a smaller stream came back. There were coffins on some of the trucks, and none of the troops were cheering.

The ARVN First Division, mostly recruited from the sons of Hué, had suffered huge losses. The funerals had a far more powerful effect on local people than the propaganda that a "great victory" had been won. Worse, the ARVN's poor showing in Laos greatly increased the doubts of citizens that South Vietnam could survive without American troops. Not only had the ARVN been outfought in Laos, but as soon as they'd left their positions around Hué to attack the NVA, Viet Cong guerillas had immediately stepped up their assaults on small garrisons and outposts west of the city. They'd gained little, but only because the U.S. 101st Airborne Division, stationed at Phu Bai just outside the city, was still a significant force. What would happen, in less than a year, when the 101st was gone?

Only the wildest optimists, among the Americans I knew, believed that the South Vietnamese could win this war on their own. Those of us in CORDS who would outstay the 101st had more personal concerns. Hué was only fifty miles from the DMZ. The North Vietnamese were certain to attack the city. But when? And what would keep us alive when they did?

One night soon after I'd arrived in Hué, two drunk American military advisors warned me not to expect a helicopter rescue if Hué came under fire. They bragged that they'd hidden a canoe on the riverbank near the old French sporting club, and stocked the canoe with weapons and a radio. If Hué fell before their tours ended, they'd save themselves by paddling the seven miles out to the South China Sea.

It was not just doubts about the ARVN that convinced us the country was doomed. It was also the slow and steady unraveling of the country's political fabric. By 1971, the little glue that still bound the country together was dissolving in the low-level panic created by the American withdrawals. In Hué, the same people who had cursed us for coming now cursed us doubly for leaving.

The Saigon government, as usual, reacted to rumblings in Hué by stepping up its harassment of political activists in the city—which provoked more unrest. Even the clumsiest moves from Saigon, however, did not increase popular support for the Viet Cong; people remembered the massacres committed by the Communists just three years before, and they clung to their perch on a desperately thin fence.

In early April, I took my first R & R visit to Bangkok. Mimi and I had not seen each other for almost four months. She met me at baggage claim with an uncertain hug.

CORDS had put Mimi and Malory in a two-story tropical bungalow, with verandas, hardwood floors, a pond in the entranceway, and a garden exploding with orchids and bougainvillea. Mimi had started a course in Thai art at a local university. Malory was then four and a half, and delighted at the prospect of a new brother or sister arriving in the fall. She seemed much happier than she had in Libya; playing with her on the lush lawn in front of the house was the high point of the trip.

Mimi and I were both determined to make the four days as pleasant as we could. The excitement we both felt at the prospect of a second child helped cushion the re-entry, but we were still very cautious with each other. We talked about the new baby, about Malory and about the house. The three of us went sightseeing. It didn't take long for Mimi and I to realize, however, how much we'd enjoyed our time apart, and to confirm that nothing fundamental in our relationship had changed. Even before Mimi took me back to the airport for the flight back to Saigon, I was thinking about my war. It was a pattern repeated every time I came.

A month after I returned to Hué, on May 9, 1971, a young Buddhist monk named Thich Chon The sat in the middle of a busy Hué intersection, doused himself in gasoline, and struck a match. When I got there his charred corpse was still upright, his hands clasped in prayer. Observers said he had not cried out. A note said that he had died to protest the war.

I looked at the blackened body and saw the smiling dead face of the girl VC looking up at me in the Delta six and a half years before. And I wondered what I'd wondered then—what must it be like to believe in something so much you would die for it?

I knew I'd risk my life for an adventure, but I couldn't see myself doing that for any other cause, at least none that I could see then. I had no religious faith. I was in Vietnam not to serve my country but for the adventures and promotions the war would provide. I'd joined the Foreign Service, in part to provide a larger context and significance for my life, but that was less about public service than about becoming powerful, about beating the bullies. My family meant little to me then. The only thing I knew I believed in was *me*—but now the dark side that Fallon had seen on our practice shoot had raised new doubts about who *I* was.

Should I believe in something beyond myself? Did that girl in the Delta or this monk have something I should want?

I still carried that distant niggle from the McKinley River. If my narrow escapes from death were not luck, then that must mean I was being spared to do *something*, to serve some purpose beyond my own needs. But if that was so, then why didn't I know what that purpose was, so I could believe in it? How could I even start such a quest with no map and no signs?

Within an hour the monk's suicide catalyzed a protest march, led by students, which was put down with tear gas and clubs. Three more monks would immolate themselves in Hué before the end of the year.

Suicidal monks and radical students were not the only protesters. One morning in June, a group of disabled war veterans, angry that the government had failed to deliver promised benefits, blocked traffic for three hours with a sit-down strike on the Nguyen Huang Bridge. Two days later, they staged another sit-in, this one along the interior staircase at city hall. Each man sat on a step, holding a grenade with the safety pin pulled. All each had to do to explode his grenade was let go the spring-mounted handle on its side. Their hand-lettered signs, I was told, proclaimed their readiness to die.

The civil servants had clustered in the courtyard, unwilling to enter the building. At nine-thirty, Mayor Le van Than, a tough young ARVN colonel, drove up to the front of the building in his jeep, spoke briefly to an aide, and strode toward the lobby. He beckoned, not to his own employees, but to me to follow. I understood what he was doing: if the Mayor and his American advisor refused to be intimidated, then the vets' bluff was called. They could only kill themselves—or leave.

Understanding Than's strategy was one thing, but risking my life for it was another. I hesitated a half-second, then followed him toward the stairs where the veterans waited, watching us with cold eyes. There was no way I'd risk my life for my country's dubious stake in this war—but I gave almost no thought to risking my life for the sheer adventure of Than's gamble. Why shouldn't I still be invulnerable? Avalanches on McKinley, raging rivers, gunners in Cyprus, Viet Cong snipers, live grenades in angry fists—my life, I was sure, was not going to end in violence.

Than gave a short speech to the veterans, answered a couple of questions, and started up the stairs. Understanding my role in Than's gambit, I followed two steps behind, smiling and nodding. To my surprise, the vets smiled and nodded back. I almost put my hands together in the traditional Vietnamese greeting, then thought better of it because of the grenades. If any vet had responded to my gesture, we'd all have been blown to hell.

Mayor Than never looked back. At the top of the stairs, I went to my office. The veterans sat on the hard marble steps. At mid-afternoon they finally left.

After work I drove across the river, then north two miles on a rutted dirt road to Linh Mu, a sixteenth-century pagoda where I came often, especially if the day had been tense. I walked up a low set of stone steps to the pagoda grounds, listening as a breath of wind caught the prayer bells hung from a nearby eave. Bright red and yellow pennants moved in the same breeze. The smell of incense and the sound of monks chanting drifted from the main hall. An old monk was sweeping the courtyard with a handmade broom. Two others were trimming shrubs in the gardens that flanked the courtyard on three sides. On the fourth side, to the west, was a low wall looking out over a bend in the Perfume River.

I walked to the wall and sat down, straddling the worn bricks. A light mist lay over the river, softening the picture of a fisherman casting his net from a small boat anchored near the far bank.

> *They say you've been out wandrin'; they say you traveled far.*
> *Sit down young stranger, and tell us who you are.*

Gordon Lightfoot was taunting me. The anger that Fallon had seen had raised serious doubts in me about who I was. Issues of belief and purpose raised by Thich Chon The's suicide circled in me like the eddies in the river below, appearing, then disappearing in the current. There was no resolution to any of it.

The sun blinked out behind the mountains to the west. Slowly the near hills faded to purple as night came. And with the night came the war.

A flare arced into the sky only a few miles away. A machine gun opened up across the river, every tenth round a red tracer curving into the night sky. Once, the whole skyline jumped in white light and the still air shook with a sound like thunder. This was ArcLight—a bombing raid by B-52s flying so high that they could not be seen or heard. After the war, Communist veterans would say they feared the B-52s most of all. With no warning, a swath of earth a half-mile long would turn into a fiery heaving hell. Anyone there not blown to pieces or incinerated was killed by the concussion.

The pinpricks of light to the left were the 105mm howitzers at Firebase Bastogne, searching for Viet Cong patrols setting out on their night missions; to the right were the guns at Firebase Normandy. I counted the seconds between the flashes and the reports, giving the rough distance from this wall to the killing.

I would keep coming to this wall until, a year later, the war closed in and the danger from snipers became too great. I came to find peace, and found instead a front seat on the war. The war that I wanted to be a part of, as Fallon had observed.

Another flare shot into the sky, this one on a parachute, floating earth-ward in a red phosphorous glow, illuminating treetops.

In June 1971, the 101st Airborne stopped patrolling in the hinterlands and prepared to go home. In another eight months the last American com-bat presence north of Danang would be gone. One by one, U.S. military advisory teams in the rural districts also began to withdraw. Predictably, security in the province deteriorated further. A few outlying police posts were overrun. Rocket attacks on Hué increased.

On June 13, my twenty-ninth birthday, Fallon and I drove out to Nam Hoa, the most westerly—and least secure—district outpost in the province. Nominally we both went to inspect CORDS projects we were responsible for—a housing project in my case and a new health clinic in his. But the fact was we both went because it was a part of the war neither of us had yet seen.

The road went north from Hué for a few miles, past the tombs of the Nguyen Dynasty emperors, then followed the Perfume River upstream as it bent toward the mountains.

Fallon insisted on stopping for a cigarette at a viewpoint where the road hairpinned through a set of low hills above the river. Below us, the V's of a sampan's wake etched the flat water, dispersing in the tangled under-growth that crowded both banks. Blue smoke from a cooking fire on the far bank struggled up through the heavy air.

Fallon had barely lit up when we heard three shots in quick succession. One of the bullets ricocheted off the boulder where he was sitting, missing him by an inch. We grabbed our guns but could see nothing in the dense brush. Fallon crouched behind the boulder and covered me while I ran for the truck and started the engine. When he threw himself in the other side,

I hurried the truck down the small hill in front of us. We drove the rest of the way to Nam Hoa without incident.

Hard against the foothills and the jungle, Nam Hoa was a frequent target of small-scale Viet Cong assaults. The district compound was a grim, low fortress of heavy timbers and sandbag walls, perched on top of a small hill. The land around the compound was cleared of jungle for a hundred yards in three directions, and much more than that to the east, where the hill fell away into a broad, gently rolling expanse that had long since been cleared by local farmers. A minefield circled the compound at the base of the hill, bordered by three-foot-high coils of barbed wire.

We followed the District Advisor, a soft-spoken major from Oklahoma City, up the short, steep trail to the compound. His team of eleven Americans started drinking by three in the afternoon. Just before dinner, they began target shooting at tombstones in a nearby cemetery, laughing and clapping with each hit. I asked the major to stop them—ancestor worship is central to Vietnamese life and pot-shotting at tombstones was incredibly stupid. He and I were of equivalent rank, however, and he wasn't about to listen to any complaints from me about his men's games.

When night fell, I saw that two perimeter lights on the southwest corner of the compound—nearest the jungle—were out. The major said they were supposed to have been fixed, but, well, tomorrow would have to do. We ate dinner in the team mess, an underground room with a ceiling of metal runway planking held up by sandbags and heavy timbers. The still air stank of cigarettes, mold, and sweat. After dinner the drinking began in earnest, over a card game that went on until after midnight. I felt like I was on the wrong side in an old Errol Flynn movie, where the evil king's minions carouse in the castle while the good guys silently scale the walls. Neither Fallon nor I slept well.

This night in the castle was uneventful. I reported the major to the Army brass when I got back to Hué, but nothing came of it.

Two days later, I flew on a helicopter mission west into the Annamite mountains, a rugged land whose only inhabitants were Montagnards—native people pushed into the mountains centuries before by invaders pouring in from southern China, the ancestors of modern Vietnamese. It was a quick, routine trip to pick up an ARVN reconnaissance team and its U.S.

advisor. It was against the rules for a civilian to go on what was technically a combat mission, but there was no rule that wasn't broken in Vietnam.

We flew low. Skimming the tops of the trees might draw a stray round from an AK-47, but it also meant that any Viet Cong below would have less time to aim and fire heavier weapons. I steadied myself in the canvas and metal seat as the pilot banked and turned around massive ridges covered with thick jungle. To anyone on a neighboring height, our helicopter would have looked like a single deft brushstroke in a Chinese painting, a bird dwarfed by steep green hills and occasional crags of gray rock. The only people we saw were small groups of Montagnard women walking on narrow trails, carrying wicker baskets of firewood on their shoulders.

Two thousand yards from the pick-up zone we spotted a plume of purple smoke rising from a small clearing. The pilot approached warily. The door gunner's trigger finger tightened as he swung the barrel of the .50 caliber machine gun from side to side, looking for any sign of an ambush. The Viet Cong knew we had only a few colors of signal smoke. If they had wiped out the team, a lucky guess now with the color of smoke and they could be luring us into a trap.

Then an American voice with a deep Southern drawl crackled over the radio: "Lightnin' Foh Ninah, this is Hurricane Alpha. Do yew read me? Ovah." The identification codes were correct, and the accent could not have been faked. A few seconds later we could see the team in the clearing, waving. The pilot set down quickly and kept the rotors turning while six ARVNs and a U.S. Army captain ducked under the blades and piled aboard.

On the ground, the bright day we'd been flying through had turned to gloom. Thick brush ringed the clearing. Through it rose the trunks of huge trees arching into layers of branches that met in layers of sun-proof shrouds. We couldn't see five feet past the clearing edge. The men we picked up had been in this jungle for three days, in a game of ambush and counter-ambush, where half the casualties were caused by booby traps buried in the forest floor or hidden in the dense brush. There could be an entire NVA regiment watching us land and we wouldn't know it until the bullets flew.

The hair on the back of my neck was standing. I felt my body lean forward, one part of me hurrying the pilot's hand on the throttle, but the other loving being there, hearing the pilot bark commands to his crew, feeling my pulse quicken, straining to see movement in the jungle. Two minutes later, the chopper lifted clear and picked up speed heading back to Hué.

The gunner stared out the open door, watching for a muzzle flash or a puff of gunsmoke below. Listening to the rotors thudding above my head was hypnotic. I leaned back in the canvas seat and closed my eyes. I heard Lightfoot again:

> *The room has all gone misty, my thoughts are all in spin,*
> *Sit down, young stranger, and tell us where you been.*

This day, the question was not just *where* I'd been but *why*. I was the only person in that chopper who'd not been ordered to put himself in harm's way. The risk for me was totally unnecessary. What was I doing there?

My answer was immediate. I was there because armed combat was an adrenaline rush. When the hair on my neck had stood up in that clearing, I was both scared and high in ways I'd never felt, except, in a smaller way, when I'd walked the Wall in East Berlin, with guns trained on my back.

In mountaineering, danger is impersonal—no mountain had ever *tried* to do me in. And risking accidental bullets in Cyprus or Algeria or Libya, or potshots in Vietnam, was not the same as being on a combat mission. Even the patrol I'd been on in the Delta in 1964 was the kind of "safe" outing the U.S. Army reserved for the press. Had our luck been different this day, however, other human beings would have been trying to kill us. And I felt then, watching the jungle speed by underneath, that a mortal showdown with a human foe was the highest adventure there was. And the chance to play, if only for a moment, in this most dangerous game, was why I was in that chopper that afternoon.

What did that mean for what Fallon had seen on our practice shoot? Had we been attacked on this mission, I knew I would have shot to kill, and thought nothing of it. But I also realized, hanging on to the steel frame of my seat as the helicopter banked and turned, that the chance to kill was not my purpose for being there. *Being in the game* was my purpose and I would have killed only because killing—and avoiding being killed—was how the game was scored. Fallon had seen the face, not of an angry, eager killer, but of an angry adrenaline junkie, for whom being in a war was now the only fix that worked.

I didn't take much comfort from this thought. Maybe I wasn't a socio-path, now unleashed to kill. But how much better was it to be hooked on adrenaline to the point where I now needed to get my next fix through a gunsight? And if it took bigger and bigger risks to get me high—where would it end?

Chapter Twelve

The Cauldron Boils, 1971

The helicopter from the pickup mission continued east into Hué. On the outskirts of the city, red earth had been scraped off the hilltops to make level platforms for batteries of heavy guns. Thin pools of water in bomb craters glinted in the late afternoon sun. Sandbag walls protected check-points at bridges and police posts.

The chopper circled the southeast corner of the Citadel and landed just inside, at 1st ARVN headquarters. I clambered out, then walked past a line of tanks to my truck. If I hurried, I could get back to CORDS in time for dinner.

But I was in no mood to rush. Halfway to the Citadel gate, I stopped to watch a fisherman cast his net in the moat that surrounded the imperial palace, a huge square building with thirty-foot walls of polished black wood, curving eaves, and an enormous high-peaked roof of red tile.

The fisherman flicked his wrist as he threw, so that the net opened and floated down softly, making hardly a splash as it settled on the still water. At the man's direction, a small boy threw pebbles into a patch of lo-tus blossoms floating to one side of the net, hoping to frighten a carp out from under the roots. A wisp of white smoke rose from a cooking fire in a hut at the edge of the palace grounds, as the fisherman's wife prepared for his success.

Less than fifty yards from the fisherman's net was the Citadel main gate, one of half a dozen openings in fortress walls that were almost twenty feet thick. For the twenty-six days that the Viet Cong had held the Citadel during the Tet Offensive, the area just behind the gate had served as a field hospital, and the battlements above it as protected points of fire. The fight for the Citadel had been fierce, with the Viet Cong finally driven out by U. S. Marines and helicopter gunships.

I drove through the gate, the sound of the truck's engine reverberating off stone walls that had protected, for a time, the wounded and dying. As I passed into sunlight on the other side, I looked into my rear view mirror, through the open gate, past its memories of torn flesh and shattered bones; I could see the fisherman, now standing in a tunnel of light, raise his arms and cast his net again.

At the river I turned left, and the fisherman disappeared from view but not from mind. What would his family talk about at dinner, in a land that had been at war as long as the parents had been alive? How many people they loved had been killed by Japanese, French, Viet Minh, Americans, ARVNs or Viet Cong? How many times had they heard the shrieks of the dying and trembled for their own lives?

And what was *I* doing here, in this family's life, part of a war I'd never believed in? After the brawl at Wheelus, I thought I'd accepted that what I did in these important places mattered, that I had to be more...*responsible.*

I *was* responsible in Vietnam, I told myself, in the sense that I did my jobs well. I was smart, courageous, hardworking and tough. But that wasn't the kind of responsibility that challenged me then and I knew it. I'd just come back from a combat mission that for me had been just a game, an adrenaline rush. From the first day, I'd treated this whole war as a game—the best stop yet on an endless road of high adventure—another place I would take risks, survive, and then move on, protected by an invulnerability I accepted but did not understand.

But in Vietnam I wasn't climbing some crag where the only people depending on me were tied to the other end of a rope. I was in a brutal war, not as a *voyeur* and no longer as an underling. What I did made a difference in people's lives, including that fisherman and his family.

Making a difference in people's lives was one of the reasons I'd decided to join the Foreign Service, sitting around my campfire at Tennant Creek. But that reflection had been not about service but about power. Now, six and a half years later, the moral emptiness of why I was in Vietnam—and the moral emptiness of my life—began to grate on me like a barking dog in the night.

In the summer and fall of 1971, the political disintegration of South Vietnam accelerated.

Exhausted by its sally into Laos in March, the ARVN stayed near its bases in the province the rest of that year and licked its wounds. The U.S. 101st Airborne Division at Phu Bai, just outside of Hué, continued to send its battalions home. Each departure ratcheted up the fear and unrest within the city. The Vietcong and the North Vietnamese were content to watch and wait, knowing that time was on their side.

In June, the Thieu government, in an effort to create a fig leaf of legitimacy, announced national elections and the no-holds-barred electioneering that followed put even more heat under the political pot in Hué. With each demonstration or riot, Washington became more interested in what was going on. Given that Hué was the major source of opposition to a Saigon regime on which the U.S. had now bet the farm, the Nixon White House was particularly sensitive to anything that could challenge its carefully orchestrated lies that the South Vietnamese could survive on their own.

In order to support the lies, the liars needed to know the truth. In July 1971, I was ordered to begin filing secret reports on the politics of Hué directly to Washington through a special channel in Danang. I was given freedom to report what I actually saw and thought, without it being filtered through the sanitizing layers of the American bureaucracy in Saigon.

Politics in Hué in 1971 were a witches' brew of Confucian tradition, government corruption, student radicalism, Buddhist maneuvering, right-wing posturing and Communist subversion—all made worse by the fears generated by American troop withdrawals and salted by the local predilection for intrigue, egomania and sheer cussedness.

What made Vietnamese politics especially hard for many Americans to understand was the ease with which most Vietnamese could hold multiple, conflicting loyalties. The cold-warrior types on the American side never saw this as anything other than duplicity and they treated it with contempt. To the Vietnamese, however, family ties, religion, education, social status and business connections could all play roles more important than political ideology at any given time. And with many people of Hué, the mix of allegiances could shift almost from week to week.

The Viet Cong quickly learned of my new political role through their network of agents in the city and asked to meet, through an intermediary at the University of Hué. The meeting took place in early August, about midnight, at a minor pagoda on the western edge of the city. Dinh van Kinh, my interpreter, came with me. A member of the city's privileged class that had been decimated during the Tet Offensive, Kinh sweated all the way to the meeting. I told him I was sure we'd be safe. The Viet Cong didn't need midnight meetings to take us out; they could kill us in broad daylight any time they chose. He wasn't reassured.

The pagoda was built on a small rise, so even on a still night there was chance of a breeze. The only sound was from the soft movement of bells and the only scent, a slight smell of incense left from the evening prayers.

Kinh and I were met by the abbot and taken to a covered porch facing a small courtyard, surrounded by wooden pillars that cast clean shadows in the moonlight. A monk brought tea, placing a circle of small cups on a low wooden table in front of us.

A few minutes later, a well-known radical monk named Thich Chon Thuc appeared from the left side of the courtyard and with him, three men in black pajamas. The four of them, who were all about my age, sat on benches on the other side of the low table. After the bare amenities, they delivered the standard Communist line: Thieu was a corrupt puppet; with Thieu and the Americans gone, a neutral government could establish lasting peace. They showed little interest in anything I had to say. After an hour, they rose, bowed once, and left as quietly as they had come.

After months of probing and thinking, I sent a long message to Washington on the politics of the war.

The Viet Cong gained support in the countryside, the message said, not because people believed that living under Communism would be so good, but because so many knew that living under the Thieu government was so bad. South Vietnam was a house built of bricks without mortar. From the outside it looked impressive; in fact, there was very little holding it together. The report ended:

> "It makes little difference if Hué radicals are card-carrying Communists or not. They would act scarcely different if they were. In many ways it would be more reassuring if they were, for we would be dealing with a devil we know. It does seem clear that many Hué radicals and radical groups have evolved their politics on their own, with no wish to serve an ideological master.… Radical politics in Vietnam *do* represent a very real body of non-Communist political thought. Many Vietnamese *are* tired of the interminable foreign presence, *are* sick of the war, *are* disgusted with corruption and *do* wish to see a more flexible, responsive government not dangling on the end of a U.S. string.… It is this voice that must be taken into account in any strategy which purports to predict the future of this nation past the next few years.… And who can be sure who will own Hué in 1975? Why shouldn't the people here hedge their bets?" [The full report is now part of the John Graham Collection of The Vietnam Project at Texas Tech University (www.vietnam.ttu.edu).]

My report arrived in Washington at a time of intense efforts by the White House to paint the war as a simple struggle between good guys and bad, with the good guys winning. The report was not welcomed, and, at least in official Washington, it sank without a trace. I got a half-dozen private messages of praise from senior policy-makers who couldn't or wouldn't support me openly.

I value that report, not because of what it said about the war but because of what it said about *me*. For all I knew at the time, in telling the truth about the war I saw in Hué, I was risking a career that was very important to me. It never occurred to me to sugarcoat that report, although I easily could have. I still would have been praised for my hard work and diligence, and would have avoided the risks.

I sent that report unvarnished because I realized, I think then to my surprise, that telling the truth was more important than my career.

Sending it was the first genuinely responsible thing I'd done in Vietnam; it showed me that I *did* believe in something beyond the game, beyond self, at a time when I was seriously beginning to question the moral emptiness of my life. Reading it thirty-six years later, I still feel proud.

There were other important lessons. The first was that the risks I took in sending that report were just as exciting as flying on a combat mission into the A Shau Valley—kill-or-be-killed was not the only way to get a charge. The second lesson, clear only later, was that bold acts of principle were possible and worth doing, even in the cesspool that was Vietnam. While the report failed to change policy, it was widely read—and the notoriety it caused boosted my career rather than the opposite.

In the last half of 1971, anti-American riots made Hué a more dangerous place for Americans than at any time since the Tet Offensive. The left attacked us for propping up the Thieu regime. The right accused us of selling the country out. No one trusted American promises to keep up the flow of military supplies once our soldiers were gone. In late July, laid-off laundry workers at the fast-disappearing U.S. Army base at Phu Bai started a work protest that quickly turned into a brawl. On August 16, a U.S. Army truck hit and killed a student near the university; the students then firebombed the truck, burned Nixon in effigy, and scrawled anti-American slogans on walls throughout the city. On September 12, an American soldier shot and killed a Vietnamese "cowboy" who was trying to steal his watch, setting off two more weeks of rioting. More firebombs were thrown at U.S. vehicles. CORDS officers moved around the city under armed guard. At my favorite restaurant, somebody threw a heavy glass ashtray at my head, then fled; the other patrons just looked down at their bowls of soup. It became too dangerous for CORDS Americans to go into the countryside, effectively shutting down our economic development projects.

Some of the unrest was fueled by the Viet Cong underground, although it was hard to see how they could be making things worse. Even the die-hard optimists among the remaining Americans were shaken. We hadn't been harassed by the Viet Cong in months—but now the people we were risking our lives to help were trying to kill us.

This made for less than cheery conversations around the CORDS bar. Bob Wenzel, our leader, was the exception. I never figured out whether he was a perennial optimist, or thought he had to be for the rest of us. Lt. Colonel Zurbriggen, watching the city disintegrate around him, cursed his counterparts. Gene Niewoehner, the social welfare coordinator, was the most vocal. His job sent him into every corner of the city and he was prob-ably more aware than the rest of us of the depth of anti-American feel-ing—and the danger it posed. His voice had a bad tendency to turn into a whine after a couple of drinks.

At the height of the chaos I left on another R & R. I was in Bangkok on September 26, when our son was born, red and bumptious, at a small clinic not far from the house. I stayed ten days, getting to know Jason and playing with his sister on the lawn.

Mimi and I were totally focused on the baby, and that made our lives together seem less empty and more congenial than on my earlier visits. Halfway through the visit, I'd even renewed my naïve hopes that the mar-riage could somehow improve. But Mimi, it was clear, did not share those hopes. She was the realist. In retrospect, Jason's arrival had simply taken our minds off the emptiness of our marriage and the utter unwillingness of either one of us to do anything about it. Nor did I trust her nearly enough to share the introspections and doubts that were beginning to challenge the self-absorption of my life. Our cold kiss at the airport sent me back to my war, with all of that unvoiced.

Tensions were even higher in Hué when I returned. More barracks at the American base at Phu Bai were empty. Fewer and fewer helicopters clattered over the city. Whatever political cohesion there may have been in Hué when the year began was gone, undermined by relentless infighting among dozens of political factions. When leftist candidates swept the local elections in August, the city's right-wing parties howled in protest.

One element in Hué that remained stable was the level of official corruption. In early November, the wives of the Mayor and of the ARVN First Division commander were caught stealing U.S. flood relief supplies and selling them on the black market. Less than a week later, every member of the City Council was implicated in a scheme to steal land that had been set aside for low-income civil servants. Public outrage shredded whatever public trust remained in the city's leadership. For the Americans in the city, anti-American rioting and corruption further undercut any rationale for more U.S. commitment and sacrifice, and for continuing to put our own lives at risk. Even the most gung-ho lieutenant on my team could see that this unraveling made the city ever more vulnerable to Communist subversion and assault, and an ever more dangerous place for any American to be.

Chapter Thirteen

The War in Earnest, 1971 – 1972

The rainy season in Hué began in October and lasted until January. The water fell in sheets, drumming off corrugated iron roofs and sluicing down muddy streets. Even when there was no wind, the downpours were so heavy they could knock an umbrella out of your hands.

The storms lasted half an hour. When they passed, the air was fresh for a few minutes, and a skittish sun drew clouds of steam back into the sky. Then the low clouds closed again, a gray shroud pressing wetness under every door, through every window, into the fabric of every jacket and sweater and coat. Shoes not worn were covered with mold in two days. Underwear and bedsheets were never quite dry. The air temperature hovered in the fifties, but the constant wetness created a bone-chilling cold that the little CORDS space-heaters were powerless to dispel.

But the heavy rains and the cold did what the ARVN and the police could not. Riots and protests in the city stopped. And in the countryside, the Viet Cong stayed in their lairs. Sodden and sullen, the enemies in this war endured the same gray skies and waited for the rains to end.

In late October, Typhoon Hester hit the city, and howling winds ripped off roofs and uprooted trees. Two feet of water fell in less than two days. At the height of the storm I got a frantic call that the province's entire store of rice was about to be flooded out. When I reached the warehouse, water was already spreading onto the floor and lapping at the bottom of the three-inch-high pallets on which the burlap bags of rice were stacked.

Mayor Than was already there, sitting on top of a six-foot stack of bags, gently kicking them with his heels, looking like a little boy waiting for a bus. A soft shadow passed back and forth across his face, as the dim bulbs hanging from the warehouse ceiling swung back and forth with each blast of wind outside.

"If the rains don't stop," I yelled above the storm, "the water will reach the bottom row of bags by the end of the afternoon."

Than stopped kicking the bags and looked at me. "I'm sure you are right, Mr. Graham," he says, "but what can we do? The culverts are backed up. There is no place for the water to go. And we have no more sandbags. Perhaps," he added with a small, nasty smile, "we should ask the United States Senate. If they don't want to help us win this war, maybe at least they can stop the rain."

"Maybe they can," I answered, "but in the meantime it wouldn't hurt to get some soldiers here with shovels and buckets. We can do *something*."

Than continued to stare at me and smile. Then he began kicking his heels into the bags again. He was still kicking when I finally gave up and left.

Than was dealing with the floods just as his people had done for centuries—he accepted them. For him, as for most Vietnamese, fatalism was no moral failure; it was their way of staying in balance with forces and destinies they believed they had no power to control. Needless to say, this attitude drove all the "can-do" Americans nuts. We saw it as a sign of weakness, and it only confirmed our doubts that the South Vietnamese could or would ever defend their country on their own.

To my annoyance, the rains stopped just before the water reached the rice.

The monsoon pushed some Americans well past the point of annoyance. Reynard Jones, a sergeant attached to CORDS, had been brooding for weeks, drinking heavily every evening. Every gray, clammy day his suspicions grew that his wife, somewhere in Montana, had left him for a rival. The day after Typhoon Hester passed, Jones came to work with his .45 drawn, took Lt. Colonel Zurbriggen hostage, and demanded to be flown home. Provided with an Army helicopter, he got as far as Danang before he handed over the gun to Zurbriggen and broke down in sobs.

Jones never knew how lucky he'd been. Two soldiers attached to CORDS had climbed to the roof and taken a bead on the back of his head as he'd marched his hostage out the door. Had they been given the order to fire, Jones would have been a victim of the rains, as surely as if he had drowned. Watching those gun barrels follow Jones to the jeep, I thought of Colonel Than and the rice. For Sgt. Jones, a little fatalism would have helped.

During the monsoon, the pace of U.S. troop withdrawals gathered speed. By February, the few battalions of the 101st Airborne now left at Phu Bai were marking time, no longer a serious military force. CORDS continued to stand down. Six of the ten district teams in the province had been dismantled. The other four were soon to go, leaving only a small team of Americans operating out of province headquarters in Hué. Because the Army members of CORDS were being sent home as part of the escalating military withdrawal, it was mostly CORDS civilians who were left behind, even as the security situation deteriorated. It didn't make sense. But there was not a lot in Vietnam that did.

I had now been in Vietnam one year. My orders said I had one year to go, but at the rate the U.S. pull-out was accelerating, I doubted that any of us in CORDS would be here that long. Whether Hué would be in friendly hands for another year was another question.

The rains ended by mid-February. Puddles that had been standing for months in the roads outside of town began to burn off, leaving geometric patterns of cracked red mud.

Tensions grew as the sun dried out the roads and fields. The youngest schoolchild knew that the beginning of the dry season was the time when the enemy attacked. And this year, the NVA and the Viet Cong had been resting and resupplying for eight months, waiting for the Americans to pull out.

It had now been four years since the Tet attacks. Would the Communists make another all-out attempt to overrun the country? Hué was only fifty miles south of the DMZ, and less than thirty from NVA divisions hidden in the mountains to the west. The people of Hué cleaned up after the monsoon, looked uneasily at the sun—and waited.

The small CORDS team in Hué watched too—but we lacked the temperament to wait. Before the rains stopped, we built sandbag bunkers around our compound and installed machine guns on the roof. We may have been sent here to win hearts and minds, but our headquarters was day by day looking more like the Alamo.

With the ARVN now deployed north and west of Hué to blunt the expected NVA attack, security in the lowlands behind the ARVN screen was left to local militias. They were tested by a series of hit-and-run attacks by the Viet Cong, shooting up guardposts and police stations, laying mines, and kidnapping local officials. One after another, villages marked "secure" on CORDS maps became "contested."

We had plenty of time to contemplate our predicament. "Lemme see if I've got this right," Howard, my deputy, said one evening after a couple of drinks. "We're here to pacify Vietnam. But after seven years we can't go five miles outside of town. We've just spent the afternoon hauling sandbags up to machine guns on the roof, so we can fight a battle around our own typewriters. Might that not suggest," he continued slowly, looking at the life-size painting of a nude that Lt. Colonel Zurbriggen had brought back from his last R & R in Manila, "that we aren't doing very well?"

"Hey you Ha-wood," said Twi, the bar girl, "you want 'nother gintonic?"

If our lives in Hué had become unreal, it was nothing compared to the craziness in Saigon. Every day, the Embassy and the U.S. military command pumped out reports telling Washington how well the Vietnamization of the war was going. The Embassy called me down for consultations every month or so; I never understood why, since I never told them what they wanted to hear.

I had by now come to thoroughly hate Saigon, or rather what the American war effort had done to it. Now we were leaving behind, not just the trash of war, but also massive unemployment and a war economy that would quickly collapse without outside support.

The pimps on Tu Do were part of that economy, and they'd gotten much more aggressive in flagging down what little business remained. A small boy shouted to a G.I. ahead of me that his sister was a virgin. The soldier bantered with him, then moved off. A traffic light changed, and a gaggle of motor scooters filled the street, belching fumes and noise.

I walked on, remembering that I was part of this obscenity. Someday the beauty of this land might return, I thought, but it would happen only very slowly, like the green things in a forest that push through blackened earth after the passing of fire.

By the end of February, NVA main-force units, no longer deterred by American helicopter gunships, began to probe closer and closer to Hué. North Vietnamese bulldozers were spotted making a road only thirty miles from the city. Firebase Angel, on the outer defense line, fell on February 27, 1972. At CORDS, the only thing between us and the NVA now was the ARVN and local militias—not the stuff of a good night's sleep. We started regular drills to defend the compound. The thought of a handful of CORDS types holding off the NVA was stupid, but the effort made us feel good. During the Tet Offensive four years before, there had been no evacuation of CORDS and one of our predecessors had been killed and another captured.

Outgoing artillery boomed and small arms chattered every night. B-52 strikes shook the earth. Some of the city's more skittish citizens fled south. Everybody else, including CORDS, waited for the NVA's other shoe to drop.

There was an alert within the city several times a week now—a staccato rattle of small-arms fire and sometimes the whump of a incoming rocket or bazooka round, then flares and a siren. Howard and I drilled our four guards, hoping that if the house was attacked at night, they would at least fire a few shots before they broke and ran. I practiced rolling out of bed, grabbing my rifle, then putting on my flak jacket and helmet without raising my head above the mattress. Howard and I made sandbag walls behind at least one window on each side of the house, with gaps in the top layer of bags we could use for firing ports.

I was still excited to be playing in this dangerous game, but the game was getting nastier by the day, and the novelty was wearing off. Unlike the helicopter mission into the mountains the year before, this was no quick sally into harm's way, but a slow, exhausting escalation of danger. As part of its continuing efforts to hide the deteriorating security situation from the American people, the U.S. Government was leaving what remained of the Hué CORDS team out on a limb, and the chance that the NVA would saw it off was very real.

March 3 was Howard's birthday, and I invited Bob and Gene over for dinner. The small arms fire started just as we were sitting down, followed by a warning siren. I got the lights; Howard checked the guards. Bob and Gene grabbed their rifles and crouched behind the sandbag walls. Ba Pho, the cook, sat quietly in the darkened kitchen, tapping her feet nervously on the tile floor. Suddenly there was a pair of loud whumps close by, and the night sky was lit by explosions. Small arms barked for thirty seconds more, but the sound of firing then moved away from us as the attackers fled. My radio crackled: a VC squad had fired two B-40 rockets into the Quang Duc police post, half a mile away. I gave the code names for all the Americans in the house, and reported that we were OK. Ba Pho collected the bowls and reheated the soup.

The Communists would get bolder. On March 30, NVA main force units smashed directly south across the DMZ into Quang Tri Province, just to the north, heading straight for Hué. For the next two days, the NVA rolled over ARVN defenses, finally stopped only by reinforcements rushed from Hué and Danang, and by massive support from American aircraft and naval guns. The "Easter Offensive" had begun.

For the next two weeks, the ARVN held its own in Quang Tri. A few more citizens of Hué fled south, but most stayed, encouraged by positive news from the battlefront. Seventy thousand refugees, fleeing the fighting in Quang Tri, streamed into the city. CORDS was at the center of a huge relief effort; with our help, city agencies set up refugee centers, dug latrines, provided immunizations and delivered food. A week of unseasonal rains turned everything into a sea of mud. But the immediate challenge was met, and the stream of refugees slowed as the NVA drive into Quang Tri stalled.

In mid-April, the North Vietnamese opened a second front directly to the west of Hué. Soon there were skirmishes being fought less than ten miles from the city—so close that U.S. Air Force Phantoms began their bomb runs over my office. ARVN heavy artillery from Camp Eagle, just south of Hué, boomed around the clock. Sticks of 500-pound bombs from B-52s were now falling so close to the city that the explosions shook the ground like earthquakes.

While the North Vietnamese attacked Hué from the north and west, Viet Cong guerillas began an all-out attempt to blow the two main bridges on the road south to Danang—the city's last ground link to the outside. Each night for over a week their attacks grew more ferocious. Their targets were predictable, however, and the defenders were ready. On April 12, seventeen VC, most in their teens, were killed in a suicidal attack on the main bridge just south of the city.

CORDS' normal work was essentially shut down, except for a few construction projects within the city limits. We did what we could to improve our own defenses, but that was more about keeping us busy than bolstering any realistic chance we could hold off the NVA if the city fell.

I didn't need the busy work—my role as a political reporter became more important the worse the situation became. Who in the city would fight and who would flee? Was the Viet Cong underground getting bolder? How was the local government reacting to the crisis? I moved around the city, talking to people and watching, then filed reports through Danang to Washington. None of them were optimistic that the government could keep the city under control as tensions mounted.

There was a strange lull in the fighting for the last week of April, with both armies dug in on battle lines north of Quang Tri City and west of Hué. During this pause, I flew with a U.S. Army captain to a small fishing village on the coast, to pay reparations to a family that had been all but wiped out by friendly fire. Five people had been blown to pieces by a rocket jettisoned by a damaged U.S. Navy jet just seconds before the pilot ejected himself from the plane.

Our helicopter flew north, beneath naval gunfire from American warships just offshore. Shells exploded on a ridgeline to the west of us, small puffs of bright white smoke appearing suddenly like cotton balls on greenbrown hills. A few miles farther and the ground beneath us changed from the rice paddies to a desolate strip of coastal sand flats and marshes named by the French troops who fought there in the 1950s, "The Street Without Joy."

We set down on the beach, and several hundred people led us to the village through a forest of fishing nets draped on towering tripods of bamboo. A few of the children smiled and waved; the older people greeted us with blank stares. There was no sound in the heavy salt air, save the crunch of our own footsteps through the dunes.

The house was a pile of charred timbers. Inside the wreckage were scraps of aluminum and steel, a twisted knob from a kerosene lamp, and a fragment of a family altar. The sea was not more than seventy yards away. I wondered why the pilot couldn't have waited another half second before letting go his rockets—or why they'd been armed—or why he'd had to jettison them at all. A year before I might have asked these questions. This day I didn't bother; I knew the captain's answer would be a shrug.

The surviving family members, in white headbands of mourning, were waiting for us. The captain gave them $200. Through an interpreter, he read a short statement that said the accident was regrettable collateral damage in a war against the Communists and that the money was in full payment of the U.S. Government's obligations. I watched the faces of the survivors. They were expressionless, like old posed photographs on family altars.

No one else spoke as we turned and walked away. Only the small children followed us to the helicopter, calling "Hey GI" and looking for candy. Most of them seemed about Malory's age. She was probably also barefoot today, running through lush green grass, well out of reach of a war where death came quickly from the sky.

That afternoon, back in Hué, my interpreter Kinh took me to meet Trinh Con Son, whose ballads of the sadness and futility of war had made him the Bob Dylan of Vietnam. The singer lived in a little apartment near the west edge of town, his small living room crowded with books and cheap knickknacks. A family altar sat on a table near the far corner of the room, a

1970 PanAm calendar tacked to the wall behind it. The only light in the room came from a single bare bulb hanging from the ceiling.

Trinh greeted us and offered tea. His criticisms of the war were not new, but he was quietly eloquent, which was why the Saigon government kept throwing him in jail. When he asked me what I thought, I told him that I saw little hope for either a negotiated settlement or a military victory. He did not appear surprised. "Hué," he said, "is a place that does not permit happy endings."

I drove Kinh to his house, then went down to a restaurant on the riverbank. Evening sounds began with Buddhist gongs in nearby temples and the slap of wooden shutters closing in market stalls. When the sun disappeared, the river ran black, its slow current rippling reflections from the bridge lights above. Almost immediately, the thunder of artillery from Camp Eagle began and the first parachute flare arced into the night sky. There was Lightfoot again:

> Now will you try and tell us… that power does not rule,
> That war is not the answer, that young men should not die?
> Sit down young stranger; I'll wait for your reply.

Chapter Fourteen

The Easter Offensive, April – June 1972

For most of April, the skies over Quang Tri were clear—perfect weather for an ARVN counterattack, supported by airstrikes. But the cautious and incompetent ARVN generals in charge of the northern defense line did not move, giving the NVA time to regroup and resupply. On April 27 a weather front moved in, and the North Vietnamese renewed their attack under the cover of clouds. This time they quickly overran ARVN positions and, within a day surrounded Quang Tri City, trapping eighty-eight American military advisors, including my friend Fallon, who'd been transferred there the month before. Unless they were evacuated by helicopter, it was only a matter of days, perhaps hours, before the garrison at Quang Tri City would be over-run.

Thousands more people from Quang Tri poured south into Hué, swelling the refugee population to over 100,000 and swamping the fragile support systems we'd struggled to maintain. The refugees added their panic to that of a crowded city already terrified by the new assault. A few tough-minded citizens started organizing a local militia—they remembered that many of the civilians who'd fought for their lives during the Tet Offensive had survived; it had been the docile ones who'd been herded out into the sand flats and massacred, their hands tied behind their backs.

At CORDS, we knew that if the ARVN defense of Hué crumbled, this time there would be no U.S. Marines to the rescue. There would be scattered shooting as a few armed civilians fought for their lives—but the prospect of holding off the NVA with a local militia was not real.

Quang Tri City fell the afternoon of May 1. Fallon showed up at CORDS headquarters in Hué that night, plucked out by helicopter under heavy fire. He was furious, both at the ARVN units who'd cut and run at the first salvo, and at the U.S. command for waiting so long to evacuate Americans. His stories made for plenty more brooding around the CORDS bar. Fallon was certain that his experience would be repeated in Hué, only worse.

He also brought me a present—a pair of cufflinks he'd made from bullets taken from the body of a Vietnamese child on his operating table. He'd cast the lead in small seashells he'd picked up on the beach. I told him that he should keep the cufflinks, but he refused to listen. He was heading to San Diego in the morning. He hated this war, he said, and he wanted no mementos of it.

Firebase Bastogne, the anchor of Hué's western defense line, fell on the night of May 1, and the news whipped through the city like a squall. The next morning, NVA armored columns pushed south along the coast from Quang Tri City, rolling over the shattered remnants of the ARVN division that had crumbled the day before. By May 2, the battle line arced fifteen miles north and ten miles west of the city. To the east was the South China Sea and to the south, the road to Danang—Hué's last ground link to the outside world.

Another 100,000 refugees poured into Hué. There was no shelter for them and almost no food. Desperate people fought for scraps of garbage and looted houses and shops. Among the refugees were hundreds of deserters from the ARVN divisions shattered in Quang Tri, still wearing their uniforms and carrying their M-16s.

It was finally too much. At about noon on May 2, the city cracked.

Almost as if on cue, 150,000 people from Hué joined 200,000 refugees from Quang Tri in headlong flight south, jamming the two-lane road to Danang. Thousands more rushed the landing craft unloading ammunition at the nearby seaport of Thuan An, crippling the flow of ARVN supplies and creating an enormous security threat. Most of the city's leaders and civil servants fled, effectively shutting down city services and government.

Law and order collapsed; gangs of deserters fired their weapons into the air, smashed storefronts, and looted at will. A mob of drunken ARVN soldiers torched the main market at Dong Ba; the city's firemen had long since fled, and the fire quickly threatened to engulf the surrounding acres of shacks and small shops. The black smoke did not rise but spread in a pall over streets now jammed with terrified people and echoing with the sounds of gunshots and the shattering of glass. Somewhere nearby a grenade exploded and a woman screamed. Hué was not waiting for the Communists; Hué had begun to destroy itself.

The four CORDS civilians still left in Hué stared, stunned, from behind the iron fence surrounding the province headquarters compound. There was nothing Bob, Howard, Gene or I could do but watch the shouting, shoving mass of people stream past us toward the Danang road.

Navy F-4s screamed in low over our heads, racks of black bombs and napalm shells hanging from their wings and bellies. The ground shook as the bombs fell on NVA tanks now only ten miles away. Outgoing ARVN artillery crashed and boomed. And off the coast, the guns of an armada of American warships sent tons of high explosives raining down on the enemy.

As night fell, the main bridge over the Perfume River was backlit by the flames from the burning market. Silhouettes moved slowly across—cars and trucks piled high with people and furniture, and walking figures pushing wheelbarrows or balancing shoulder poles. In that mass a child was wailing loud enough to be heard over the guns. There was another staccato flash of explosions from the B-52s. A parachute flare drifted downward, and in its light I could see a pair of sampans, jammed with people, moving quickly downstream.

As far as any of us knew, the battle raging just north and west of Hué that night—May 2, 1972—was the turning point of the entire war. If the city fell, the road to Danang was open to the NVA.

The consequences would also be personal. It wasn't as if the four of us left in CORDS that night were in some safe headquarters, watching symbols move on a map. None of us believed we would be pulled out in time if the city fell. The choppers would be mobbed by Vietnamese eager to save their skins too. We'd have to shoot people off the skids—and some of them would be shooting back.

Over a cold dinner, we agreed that the fate of the city—and our own lives—could depend not just on South Vietnamese and American firepower, but on how fast order could be restored. We also agreed there was no way the Vietnamese were going to pull the city back together on their own; those officials who hadn't run away were disorganized and ineffective. It was up to us.

Colonel Khien, the new mayor, would be a major obstacle. A corrupt hack who'd replaced Mayor Than the month before, he was now hiding out in his house with a few cronies, overwhelmed by the crisis. By reputation, the one thing he cared about was saving face; whatever we did in the next twenty-four hours had to make him look good, or he would spend more energy undermining us than fighting the Communists. We made a plan, then caught a few hours sleep.

By dawn on May 3, several things had shifted in our favor: NVA advances from the north and west had stalled, thanks to American aircraft and naval guns. The timid ARVN generals who'd lost Quang Tri were replaced by better men, including local hero and former mayor (now General) Le van Than—the same man who'd led me up a staircase of grenade-toting vets six months before. In the city, the concrete walls of the market had contained the flames, and the fire at Dong Ba was burning itself out.

The exodus south had slowed; in one day, the city's population had plummeted from 400,000 to fewer than 100,000. Some of those remaining were refugees and some were deserters—but most were citizens of Hué who, for whatever reasons, had chosen to stay.

As the morning sun began to light the pall of smoke still hanging over the streets, the four CORDS Americans began pulling together the Vietnamese needed to form a martial law government and re-establish order. I reached a few of my contacts by phone, but Kinh and I had to drive to the others' houses, maneuvering the truck through streets full of broken glass and possessions thrown or fallen off overloaded cars. For the first time in sixteen months, I carried a .45 on my belt within the city limits—concerned less about the Viet Cong than about ARVN deserters willing to kill us for the truck. Kinh and I worked as fast as we could; the battle lines outside the city were still holding, but no one could be sure for how long.

The message to the officials we could find was simple: help save the city now, or risk being trapped here and killed. Most of the people I reached were happy to see some initiative and agreed to cooperate. But I literally pulled one terrified civil servant out from under his bed. At another house, I found a key power plant engineer in his underwear, sitting cross-legged on the floor of his living room, playing his flute.

By early evening, we'd pulled together enough Vietnamese to restart city services—now all we had to do was get Colonel Khien to take charge. When we went to his house, however, he told us that he would follow our plan only if we agreed to postpone launching the new government until 9:00 the following morning. He needed the rest of the night to set up a meeting of his own for 8:30; when the people we'd organized showed up at 9:00, Khien could then "invite" them to join his meeting and the whole enterprise could appear as his idea.

We had no choice but to go along with Khien's plan—even though it meant leaving the city unglued and leaderless for another twelve hours. After the meeting, Nuoc Cuong, the deputy mayor, walked with me out to my truck. He thought that delaying until morning could not make that much difference.

Cuong was a reasonably good man, and brave enough to have stuck around. But I'd had too little sleep and I turned on him.

"I don't know whether twelve hours will make a difference or not," I told him, "but it might. What I do know is that some Americans risked their lives to pull this plan together today—something Vietnamese should have done but didn't, either because they'd run off or because they had their heads in the sand. And now we're told to let the city stay lawless for another twelve hours, to make time for the bureaucratic bullshit of a man who got his job only by kissing President Thieu's ass for years."

Cuong's face went blank, but he was in the wrong place at the wrong time, and I was just getting started. I pointed across the river to the orange glow from the fire at Dong Ba. "Your people burned down their own fucking market and damn near torched the entire town," I almost shouted at him. "Do you think the people in Hanoi would have done that? Would Hanoi have collapsed the way this city has, if your army was at *their* gates? Would their officials have cut and run? Or would every last man, woman and child be out digging anti-tank ditches? How long are you going to use America as an excuse for losing this war? What part of your goddam survival is *your* goddam responsibility?"

Cuong glared back at me. "Maybe you are on the wrong side," he replied evenly.

"Maybe I am," I growled. "All I know is this city is destroying itself. The deserters are the problem. You need to set up a firing squad and shoot some of them as a lesson. And you should do it now, tonight."

I was in Cuong's face. Two veins bulged on the side of his neck, but there wasn't the flicker of expression on his face. Neither one of us moved for what seemed a very long time. Finally I turned away, walked to my truck, and drove back to CORDS.

There was an intrepid CBS reporter at the compound when I got back. In the mood I was in, I should have avoided him. Instead, I gave an honest and angry interview that was broadcast all over the world. My mother told me later I looked haggard. The Embassy in Saigon told me to keep my mouth shut.

After the interview I went to my office and sat in the dark for over an hour thinking, not about what I'd said to CBS, but about urging Cuong to set up that firing squad.

I realized, sitting there, that I had no idea if shooting some deserters would stop the looting or not, or if there were better alternatives. What I *did* know was that the deserters were almost certainly scared kids who'd been conscripted into the ARVN off their rice paddies the month or even the week before. I also knew that I'd never believed in America's aims in Vietnam and that I'd long since known that the war was a lost cause. I was in Vietnam only for the adventure and promotions.

The key thing was—I knew all these things and up until that moment I didn't care. Vietnam was a self-centered game for me, and those farm boys were pieces on the board.

Now some of them might die.

Another F-4 screamed in over my head, rattling the dirty coffee cups on my desk. The question for me, I understood very clearly that night, wasn't whether setting up that firing squad was militarily a smart thing to do or not. The question was, how had I treated this life-and-death responsibility so lightly?

The chair pushed the pistol in my holster against my hip until it began to hurt. I took the .45 out and laid it on the desktop. The perimeter light behind me glinted off the black steel. Artillery and bombs crashed and boomed.

Suddenly, for me the war was no longer a game.

But how could I have thought for so long that it was? How could I have allowed my life to become that shallow, that irresponsible?

My report to Washington six months before had been both responsible and brave, but it had also been impersonal, like bombing from 30,000 feet. This day the challenge had been in my face and it seemed very much that I had failed.

I thought of the moment on that beach outside Tripoli when I first began to see the connection between the failures in my personal life and my role in the disastrous talks at Wheelus. In Libya, I'd been a junior officer. In Hué, I had far more power and I was using it to play with people's lives. Now it had come to this night, and I saw the war for the first time not as my playground, but as the first circle of a hell created not by the NVA, but by the irresponsibility of my own life. In the darkened CORDS office, I watched the dull reflections off my gun and listened to the sounds of artillery. Then I put my head down on the desk and closed my eyes.

I couldn't put it in these words then, but what was missing for me in 1972 was any moral context for my actions—any overarching view of why I was on the planet, a view that would have given me better guidance than did the unmet needs of an unfulfilled life.

What I *did* realize that night in Hué was that I had no such broader, deeper view. It seemed my life had drifted about as far as it could from the thought at the McKinley River that my survivals might carry a *quid pro quo*—that I was being saved for purposes higher than my own. My context in Vietnam was that of a self-absorbed adventurer, a hot-shot Foreign

Service Officer heading for the top. Beyond that, I didn't know who I was. I felt exposed and empty. My body shuddered, and it wasn't from fear, or the dampness of the night.

Three large execution poles were erected on the riverbank that night, on the Citadel side, near the bridge. I don't know if anyone was ever shot there.

Truckloads of ARVN MPs arrived from Danang the next morning, and by noon had stopped the worst of the rioting and looting. The new martial-law government restarted key city services by the end of the day, and made plans to evacuate the remaining refugees. That night, Viet Cong radio broadcast a long diatribe condemning the new government in Hué and the role of Americans, "posing as advisors but in fact secretly controlling the government, propping up the people of Hué as cannon fodder for the imperialist war machine." There were thumbs up at CORDS. If the Viet Cong were this mad, we must have done something right.

The whole first half of May we waited for an all-out NVA assault that never came. On May 12, three NVA companies and six tanks drove south in a suicidal probe; the sky was clear and U.S. jets caught this small force in the open just short of the city and obliterated it. On May 15, ARVN units re-took Firebase Bastogne from a surprisingly small NVA force, pushing back the threat from the west. We didn't know it then, but the NVA had already made their decision to pull back, convinced that attacking into the teeth of American airpower was fruitless. Over the summer of 1972, they slowly abandoned their positions in Quang Tri. Their final assault on Hué wouldn't come for another three years.

By the end of May, citizens began to trickle back into Hué. President Thieu came to the city, and his casual stroll down the main street convinced more people that it was safe to return. On May 25, I was told that my tour of duty in Vietnam would be cut short by six months—I could leave by mid-June. As a reward for my work in Hué, the State Department was sending me to Stanford to study decision theory for a year, all expenses paid.

June 13, 1972. My thirtieth birthday. The Embassy car crawled through the outskirts of Saigon, headed for the airport. Swarms of motorbikes belched black smoke. Market women swinging their carrying poles stepped in front of us, forcing the driver to brake repeatedly, pitching me against the front seat. It was the hottest, noisiest, dirtiest day I ever spent in Vietnam. It was also the last.

I checked in for Thai Air Flight 997 to Bangkok, to help pack up my family and head back to the United States. When the flight was called, I walked across the tarmac and up the rear gangway of the Caravel. Sinking into a lavender seat, I savored the cold as the sweat on my shirt began to evaporate in the air-conditioned cabin. I closed my eyes. The engines started. The plane lumbered out to the runway, then down the concrete and up. I opened my eyes to see the airport buildings swing out of view as the plane banked sharply to the left. I heard Lightfoot again:

> *They say you've been out wandrin'; they say you traveled far.*
> *Sit down young stranger, and tell us who you are.*

Maybe in California I could do that. Maybe I could find in myself a hunger for more than the next adventure. Maybe I could find someone who could do more than play games.

But what if playing games was all I knew?

The wings of the Caravel leveled and it headed west, into the setting sun.

Part Two

Amazing Grace

Chapter Fifteen

California, 1972 – 1973

The State Department gave me a year at Stanford, all expenses paid, as a reward for my eighteen months in Vietnam.

Mimi, Malory, Jason and I spent a week in India and another week in France on the way home. Mimi and I circled each other like wary boxers, not sure what to expect after a year and a half apart. Money from Vietnam bonuses was a temporary balm. In Paris, we went to the Moulin Rouge and the *Folies Bergere*. We spent more on one meal than I'd spent in a month on the road in Europe ten years before. We bought a new car and shipped it to California.

What we couldn't buy was honest talk about our marriage. I know I hoped things would be better. Mimi, as always, was more realistic. During the performance at the *Folies*, when I put my hand on hers, she pulled away and would not meet my eyes. I shifted in my chair to watch the showgirls, and quietly sucked for air. Absence had not made our hearts grow fonder. What it *had* done was let each of us get used to life without the other and to see from that perspective just how bad being together really was.

While Mimi and the kids continued on to Tacoma, I spent ten days in the other Washington, trying to convince whomever would see me that America's strategy in Vietnam had failed. The CIA gave me a thoughtful hearing. The State Department, the Pentagon and the White House closed one door after another in my face. People were still talking about "light at the end of the tunnel." One assistant secretary called me a quitter.

A correspondent friend arranged for a secret meeting with Ben Bradlee, editor of the *Washington Post*. He listened to my accounts of America's failures in Vietnam but, for reasons I never knew, did not pursue what I told him.

Neither did I. I didn't go to the Congress nor join uniformed vets, like John Kerry, then protesting the war. The Foreign Service was still my life, and I was afraid that if I rocked the boat any more than I already had with my views on the war, I'd be thrown over the side. I finally flew out to join my family.

Tacoma was relentlessly the same. Both Mimi's father and my own were strong supporters of the war, so politics became another taboo for conversation, joining religion and the state of our marriage. I annoyed everyone by going up in the mountains by myself for a week, walking most of the way around Mt. Rainier.

From my Cub Scout days, this mountain had been a totem place. Often I'd see faces in the patterns of dark rock and white ice, and sometimes the faces seemed to talk to me. Sitting, staring at the volcano, I would lose myself for hours in private reveries. This time, in the summer of 1972, all I sought was some peace of mind, some resolution to the questions that had followed me home from Vietnam. Instead, all I heard was Gordon Lightfoot's taunt, from behind every ridge, on every breath of wind:

> *They say you've been out wandrin'; they say you traveled far.*
> *Sit down young stranger, and tell us who you are.*
> *The room has all gone misty; my thoughts are all in spin*
> *Sit down, young stranger, and tell us where you been.*
>
> *And will you gather daydreams or will you gather wealth?*
> *How can you find your fortune when you cannot find yourself?*
> *My mother's eyes grow misty; there's a tremblin' in her hand.*
> *Sit down young stranger—I do not understand.*

I'd come back from Vietnam a stranger to myself, uncertain and afraid for the future. The week on Mt. Rainier gave me neither insights nor support. Instead, things got worse.

I started having violent nightmares. Walking down city streets, I'd cross to the shadowed side to avoid sniper fire. I jumped at sudden noises. The sound of a traffic helicopter would instantly space me back to Vietnam. But the thing that bothered me most was the memory of shouting at Cuong to set up a firing squad in Hué, and the moral emptiness I felt behind not just that night, but behind my whole participation in the war and the life-path that had led me there.

The questions from that night continued. What should I, could I, believe in beyond myself? I wasn't looking for the kind of messianic goal that had driven that dead guerilla girl in the Delta or the immolated monk in Hué. But surely there was something deeper than adventure and ambition. What was it?

I didn't know. Whatever conviction that had led me to tell the truth about the war in my report from Vietnam, and to risk that meeting with Ben Bradlee, had been quickly eroded by the opposition and apathy I'd met in Washington DC. Failing to score in the first inning, I'd quit the game, carrying with me idle anger and empty ideals.

Mimi and I rented a pleasant house in Palo Alto only a mile from the Stanford campus. For the kids it was heaven; our neighbors were relentlessly friendly and those across the street even had a pool that attracted every kid on the block. Malory started school. Jason took his first steps. Every morning I biked down quiet streets and through groves of eucalyptus trees to class. There were no clouds of motorbikes belching fumes, no shrill music blaring from loudspeakers, no tropic heat pasting my clothes to my body. I played a lot of tennis, took up distance running, and went rock climbing in Yosemite with the Stanford Mountaineering Club.

I studied decision theory and created computer models for making foreign policy. I knew there was no chance my models would ever be used, but I didn't care. California was a timeout. My life was a mess, and this year was time I needed to pull it back together.

In California Mimi and I quickly settled back into the pattern of isolation and blame we'd created almost from our wedding day. It never again became as bad as it had in Libya—by now we could both deal better with the void. But we were also both still young, and we hungered for something more. We saw other couples who seemed genuinely in love, who fully shared their lives, who liked being together. Both of us, I think, ached for that kind of connection.

We would never find it in our marriage. Neither of us was ever willing to make the other a priority. My career and my adventuring were more important to me than Mimi would ever be. And when she'd cut short our honeymoon to finish her private pilot's license, she'd set a pattern that never changed. Throughout our marriage she filled her life with projects—in the arts, in small business ventures—that were always more important to her than I was.

It wasn't the kids that kept us together. Mimi and I were both too selfish to have stuck it out for them, even if we'd been convinced that staying together was in their interests.

Inertia, the expectations of our families, the Catholic culture we'd grown up in, our own stubbornness—all these things kept us together. And for me, at least, there was wishful thinking. Almost until the day the marriage finally ended, I clung to the fantasy that it might get better—that I could say or do something that would turn it around, that I could take the picture of Ideal Family we projected and make it real.

So we stayed together—two active, overachieving people, making no moves on a matter of core importance to both our lives and finding no way to even talk about it. The garage of our house had been converted into an office; we said it was my place to study. In truth it was a place where I could be apart, and I spent most evenings there.

Then Mimi, my unloved and unloving partner, set in motion the first of two events that reshaped my life.

Halfway through the year in Palo Alto, she brought home a brochure from a group, the Creative Initiative Foundation (CIF), that ran workshops helping people gain "deeper perspectives" on their lives. These perspectives, as far as we could tell from the brochure, depended not on religion, but on honest introspection. Mimi asked me if I wanted to go to an introductory meeting at a house not far from where we lived.

I never knew what her motives were. She may have thought CIF could improve our marriage (although she did not say that), and was trying to do something about it. She may only have been curious. Whatever her intent, since CIF worked only with couples, the only way she could go to the meeting was if I came too.

For my part, I'd been in California five months and had made no progress in answering the questions that had pursued me from Vietnam. I was still a stranger to myself. The nightmares from the war continued. I saw nothing to lose by trying something new.

The CIF message we heard that night was basic: take charge of your life... stop reacting to the expectations of others... be honest and compassionate. I was hooked immediately, not so much by the message, but by the honesty, caring and self-confidence of the two forty-something couples that delivered it. Sitting on a sofa listening to them, I saw their lives as such contrasts to my own that my body shuddered with despair. I was trapped in an awful marriage and riddled with the self-doubts raised in Vietnam. I presented so many false fronts to the world, especially about my marriage, that I'd lost track of what was bullshit and what was real. Now I was looking at four people who were what I longed to be.

After several more evening meetings, Mimi and I signed up for a week-long retreat, held at the CIF center at Ben Lomond, a collection of simple cabins deep in the Santa Cruz Mountains, southwest of Palo Alto.

The first evening, each of the fifteen couples there was asked to introduce themselves. When our turn came, Mimi and I went to the front of the room. Mimi said that she was miserable, and little else. I pasted on an uncomfortable smile as she spoke. When she finished, everybody clapped loudly.

Then I told everyone that I was fine. I added a few war stories, leaving out every nagging question from Vietnam, every corrosive doubt. The clapping was polite. I stood awkwardly for a second or two, then followed Mimi back to our seats.

I sat down, puzzled and angry that I'd somehow failed to communicate to these people who I was. I looked straight ahead, pretending to listen to the next couple. Of course, I told myself, how could they possibly know? None of them had ever faced bullets or avalanches. They were academics, lawyers, housewives, accountants… The biggest adventure any of them had ever faced was probably running out of gas in the Yucatan. How could they possibly know what it meant to have done what I'd done?

And what was *I* doing, spending a week with people whose lives were about research papers and balance sheets and diapers? What could I possibly learn from them? And what right did they have to turn their noses up at a life that was so obviously richer than any of theirs?

I hung in for the next four days, listening to lectures and sitting through small-group sessions where we were supposed to bare our souls. In the beginning, I told more stories of danger and risk, then sat uncomfortably as others wept or raged about unhappy childhoods, sour relationships and personal failures.

I couldn't help noticing that the people who honestly shared their lives seemed to benefit from it. I longed for that catharsis, but the part of me that had written wooden travelogues from the *Golden Bear,* stared straight through the famine in Ethiopia and run from the emotions lit by Jean in Australia now screamed at me to maintain the armor around my heart.

But this time the pain of wearing that steel screamed back. I was tired of living an emotionally constipated life, tired of the loneliness, and scared for the future if nothing changed. Cautiously I began sharing some of the doubts and questions raised in Vietnam. As the facilitators prodded, I pursued some of the threads down to first causes. I began talking about my gentle father, the bullies of my childhood, and the dark side of my adventuring. The others listened, and the questions they asked and the comments they made were intelligent and caring.

I was nowhere near as open about my marriage. When Mimi described her pain and frustration, I responded with platitudes that surely it could and would get better and that I would try harder.

For the final morning of the retreat, men and women met separately to talk about stuff, mostly sexual, they wouldn't share with their spouses in the room. Rob, a CIF leader, began the men's session by reminding the fifteen of us that each gender contained the opposite, and that men weren't complete without learning to acknowledge and use their "feminine" side. Then we dutifully listed on a blackboard all those "feminine" qualities that men tended to shortchange, such as caring and gentleness. When we'd filled the board, Rob asked us whom we thought, from our observations over the last week, was the man in our group with the strongest innate "feminine" qualities.

Tough choice, I thought, with all these wimpy guys. Maybe it was that mathematics professor with the nervous laugh. Or maybe the little accountant who kept getting teary. But that wasn't what the others thought.

Every other man in the room picked me.

I thought it must be some kind of joke. It wasn't.

When Rob asked the others to explain their choice, they all said the same: they saw me as a naturally gentle and caring man so afraid of acknowledging that part of himself that he'd crafted a public image that was almost the opposite, that I was drowning in my own macho bullshit.

An image? I stammered that all the stories I'd told were true. And they hadn't heard the half of them.

I was missing the point, said Alan, an English professor. Nobody doubted my stories, or the fact that I was adventurous and tough, at least in a physical sense. But everybody there sensed I was more than my stories.

"I think your stories are like a screen," said Angelo, a graduate student from Italy, using the English words carefully. "You are using them to hide who you are, not just from other people, but from yourself."

"Yeah, and where did you get your degree in psychotherapy," I said, glaring at him. "I thought you were an engineer."

Rob could see an explosion coming, and he jumped in, suggesting that I see the group's choice as an honest and well-meaning assessment. Just think on it, he said.

But it was too late for peacemaking.

I didn't have to think about it, I said. The group's view of me was laughable. Maybe it made them feel better to try to take me down a peg, but I wasn't buying. It was clear that I'd just wasted a week of my time with people whose lives were so insular they had no way of judging what they were attempting to judge. How could they know what a "man" was supposed to be if they'd never tried to be one? None of them had ever had midnight meetings with the Viet Cong. None of them had climbed McKinley's north wall.

Then I stood up and left the cabin, slamming the door behind me.

Trails headed off in all directions, winding through groves of eucalyptus and across open hillsides of brown grass and manzanita. I hadn't intended to walk more than a short loop while I cooled down, then go back and pack up for the drive back to town.

But I was gone for over three hours.

My guts unclenched. It wasn't just the anger of the moment I felt lift, but something more. My body began to feel light as if I were walking on the moon. I began to run, faster and faster, until I was hurtling down the trail in long, leaping strides. Sure that no one was watching, ever so often I'd jump into the air and float, it seemed, for Olympic distances.

Finally out of breath, I slowed to a walk. The world was quiet, except for the soft crackle of dried eucalyptus leaves beneath my feet, and the quick cries of birds I had disturbed.

Thoughts rushed in of what had happened in that cabin. Had the judgment been from only two or three, I could have continued to dismiss it. But all fifteen men had the same opinion, reached quickly, with no chance of collusion.

I replayed what each man had said. The message was not that I was unmanly—but that the manliness I projected was only part of me, hiding another part. They saw me not as a wimp, but a dissembler. And the whole CIF refrain, from that first meeting in Palo Alto, was that if I acknowledged what I was trying to hide, my life would work a lot better than it did.

"You just don't get it," I heard Paul, a real estate broker, yell at me as I'd headed out the door. "We're trying to pay you a compliment. We're trying to tell you that beneath all your bullshit there's somebody you ought to get to know. And you take it as an insult. Grow up, man."

So—what if these men were right? What if they'd found the stranger in me I yearned to meet?

Images crowded in. Not of dodging bullets—but of loving a rag doll named Sammy until I was almost ten and of learning to sew Sammy's yarn hair back on myself whenever the old stitches failed…

Not of going eagerly to war—but of refusing to join schoolyard fights…

Not of climbing the Wickersham Wall—but as a kid bringing toys to an orphanage at Christmas and writing poems for my mother on Mother's Day ...

Not of the "sensible" marriage to Mimi—but of the passionate affair with Jean...

I sat down in the middle of that trail and cried for almost an hour.

When I returned to the cabins, Mimi was angry that I'd made us late in getting back to town and picking up the kids from the neighbors. Part of me wanted to tell her about what had just happened. A wiser part feared that her response would be an unbelieving sneer. I sensed that what had happened to me was an epiphany that could change my life, but I also sensed that it was very fragile, like the starting wisps of flame of a campfire in the rain. For now, I needed to protect myself. I mumbled to Mimi that I'd gone for a walk and lost track of time. I apologized for making us late, and said little more all the way back.

In Palo Alto, my mind fought a rear-guard action for weeks until it surrendered to what my heart, I think, had accepted as soon as I'd stormed out of that cabin. The men at Ben Lomond had been right. More memories crowded in from my childhood, confirming their view of who I was.

What had happened to that gentle, feeling boy? How had I let him disappear?

Taunted by bullies, not fighting back, the boy was terrified that his gentleness was his father's genes. In Palo Alto, I could still hear the bullies' taunts, still see my father backing off from a fight at work and hear my mother's blaming, "Oh Al..."

No wonder I'd tried so hard to hide a side of me that I saw as responsible for so much unhappiness. No wonder I'd set my course to be tough and powerful, even at the cost of burying my heart.

The adventures that began aboard the *Golden Bear* had been my path to manhood. Danger became the perfect toughening ground and adrenaline my drug of choice. And because I could never get high enough, it was inevitable that someday I'd be drawn to war as the only test left worth facing. War became the ultimate adventure, the most dangerous game, and the ultimate pursuit of an ideal of manhood that could never be attained.

For a time, I'd gambled only with my own life. But in Vietnam the adventurer had become the willing agent of organized violence in which there were many more lives at stake.

Now it seemed that if I broadened my definition of manhood past the cartoons in my head, if I became comfortable and secure with the man I really was—my life would become more genuine, less driven. I'd be able to reclaim a softer side of me without fearing that I was undermining my life.

It wasn't, of course, that easy. My experiences with CIF provided not finished answers but a map for the search. I poured myself that summer into these explorations with the same intensity I'd applied to every other trek into the unknown. I talked with Rob, the CIF leader from Ben Lomond, a couple of times and read every "self-help" book I could find.

As my insights grew stronger, I tried to talk to Mimi about what I was struggling with, but she was unwilling to listen. I remember one sunny Saturday afternoon sitting with her in our backyard. The kids were splashing in the pool across the street and we were enjoying a quiet drink, talking about the house, about the neighbors, about whatever. I started to tell her that I thought my life had changed, that I was wiser about the things that had stood between us. She laughed in my face and made it clear she wasn't interested in my flailings. Then she took her glass and went back into the house. The screen door slapped like a rifle shot.

There was another issue the experience at Ben Lomond forced me to grapple with that summer—and that was my fierce commitment not to be my father's son.

When bullies had been making my life miserable, my father was coming home scarred from office battles in which he'd been outmaneuvered or outfought, and I had to watch him sort the peas on his plate as my mother nagged him for his failures. When the high school in-crowd had been taunting me as a nerd, my father was showing off my report cards as if A's were all that mattered. When I'd been struggling as a teen to keep up hope that my life would change, my father was a picture of unfulfilled ambitions. At a time of my life when I'd been searching for models of manhood, I knew with certainty and with shame that I didn't have one at home. If my father was a loser, then wasn't I destined to be a loser too? Every time I'd felt softness in myself—his softness—the fear grew that I was more his son than my tough Croatian mother's.

So I'd used my father as a model of what I *didn't* want to be. He'd made it easy for me to be disappointed in him because he was so disappointed in himself. And the more he'd attempted to live his own failed dreams through me, the more I'd held him in contempt.

In Palo Alto I finally saw the injustice of that contempt. In demanding that my father be someone he could never be, I'd lost sight of who he was— a quiet, caring man with a right to live his life unbounded by my needs. In disowning his gentleness, I'd disowned a part of me. I'd deprived myself of a complete life, a life with an open heart and a capacity for loving and being loved.

I flew up to Tacoma to see him in July. He was surprised, but agreed to go off with me for the weekend to one of his old fishing haunts on the Olympic Peninsula. We stayed at a run-down fishing camp on the coast the first night, then pushed on into the rainforest the next morning. By midday, we were sitting on a warm rock on the bank of the Bogachiel River, watch- ing spray break in bright beads as the clear water rushed down from gla- ciers upstream.

When I started blurting out the thoughts that had been consuming me since Ben Lomond, my father seemed genuinely surprised. He was silent for a moment, then said that, to him, I'd always seemed a happy and well- adjusted kid. And when I apologized for my angry and unfair judgments, my father just looked at me and said that he didn't know what I was talking about. Then he checked his lure, and cast it expertly into an eddy where he thought a fish might be.

Whether he'd really been that blind to my struggles as a youth, or whether he just couldn't open that door, I never knew. But the trip at least brought some closure for me. When I apologized for my blaming, the anger that flowed from that blaming eased. And when I told my father that I loved him and then hugged him, I was also, finally, putting my arms around myself.

My father died seven years later. Long after that, I found a faded pic- ture I wished I'd had before. The picture is of my father in the late 1920s, before booze and failure had killed his spirit. He's on a beach, looking buff in one of those chest-covering bathing suits of the day. He's staring into the camera with all the confidence and expectations of a young man at the top of his game, ready for action. I keep that picture on my desk, in a place where I see it every day.

I found a telegram with that picture. Dated April 3, 1926, it was from the publisher of the *Honolulu Herald* offering him a job as a reporter. It was sent at least two years before the picture was taken. Given the chance for the adventure of his young life, he'd turned it down and never talked about it. I've put that telegram away. I prefer to look at the picture and think that's who he was.

I stayed at Stanford through August, completing a master's degree while Mimi and the kids lived with her parents in Tacoma. By the time I flew north to join them, I was worn out with introspection and aware that I needed to make some serious commitments to change my life.

The cost of closing off my heart had already had been enormous. I'd given up the first real love of my life rather than lose control over my emotions. I'd lived with loneliness in a marriage rather than risk the vulnerability and compassion that real partnerships demand. From Ethiopia to Vietnam, I'd walked through some of the worst suffering on the planet without a backward glance. In Hué my failings may have cost others' lives.

What I was doing with my life wasn't working, but the difficulties of changing seemed enormous.

I thought of Fallon, staring at me, asking me if I knew how I looked, blasting away at a hillside in Vietnam. He'd looked into a place in me I'd tried to hide, and what he'd seen was dark.

But those fifteen men at Ben Lomond had looked into the same place and seen light.

Could I learn to live in the light?

I didn't know. All I knew was that I had to try.

The night I made that commitment, the nightmares from the war stopped.

Chapter Sixteen

Washington, 1973 – 1975

Rain flew against my office window at the State Department in long, punishing streaks, its drumming rising and falling with the wind. The line of broad-leafed trees on the far side of the street lurched back and forth, as if in pain. I watched a man in a dark blue Navy overcoat hurrying up the sidewalk, bending low into the weather, one gloved hand keeping his white uniform hat from spinning off his head.

The gray sky and numbing rain matched perfectly how I felt inside. When I'd left California, I'd been sure my life would change. But now, after two months in Washington, D.C., the cocoon I'd begun to open at Ben Lomond had been stripped away, and inside I'd found no butterfly. The new commitments I'd sworn to make were far harder than I'd expected, and the forces pulling me backward more powerful.

Mimi and I had bought a plain brick house on a cul de sac in Falls Church, Virginia, a half-hour west of Washington. We had two kids, a mortgage, a dog and a lawnmower. I spent Saturday mornings at the mall at Tyson's Corner, buying garden supplies. That first year I put in a goldfish pond, a rose garden, and a barbecue in the back yard. We slipped into suburban living as if we'd been there all our lives.

The introspections in California challenged me to create an honest and balanced life. I found that easiest with my kids, now seven and two. In Palo

Alto, I'd been so consumed in trying to figure out my own life that I'd barely noticed theirs. But in Falls Church, spending time with them quickly
became natural and comfortable—they were no longer some little visitors
who called me "Daddy." I started coaching Malory's Little League baseball
team. In the beginning it was something Mimi insisted that I do. Very
quickly the "Penguins" and the fast-food celebrations that followed every
game created a link with my daughter that was as important to me as it was
to her.

While what had happened at Ben Lomond had changed my perspectives on myself and brought me closer to my children, it had done nothing
to improve my marriage. For a time after the retreat I believed with the passion of the newly converted that opening my heart would open Mimi's as
well, and that belief fed my hapless fantasies about our marriage like new
twigs on a dying fire. It had been Mimi who had got us to that retreat, but
it was also she who rejected that anything important had happened there.
Trying to restart that conversation nearly always meant getting hurt. I could
still hear the screen door in Palo Alto slapping shut.

What discouraged me most that miserable first autumn in Washington,
however, was the thought that I could never mesh the insights from Ben
Lomond with the adventuring that had consumed my life since the *Golden
Bear*. I now accepted that the extremes to which my narrow quest for manhood had led were deadly. But did that mean there were no adventures left
at all? I knew I couldn't go backward, but huge parts of me resisted going
forward, especially as I could see no middle ground. In Palo Alto, I never
dreamed that the choices would be as stark as they now seemed—from
stemming the chaos in Hué to taking tickets at a PTA fair. The shift terrified
me more because it seemed not that my life as an adventurer had been tempered—but that it was over. Every day I spent pushing papers or potting
plants depressed me just a little more.

The rain continued to lash against my office window. The pencil on top
of my desk rolled onto my lap and then onto the plastic pad beneath my
chair. I stared out into the storm and felt a level of despair that matched
anything I'd ever felt in Vietnam. What was the point of trying to change
my life if I was only exchanging one set of miseries for another?

Then some things started to improve.

Just as the men at Ben Lomond had said, behind the John Wayne bullshit was a person that others seemed pleased to meet. I quickly fell in with a group of other young officers at the State Department and we met regularly to talk shop, play baseball and exchange dinners in each other's homes. Many of the neighbors in Falls Church, and people we met through Malory's school, were young professionals with interesting lives. As I learned to listen, the social stiffness I'd always felt began to ease, and I could now get through a cocktail party or a neighborhood klatch without looking at my watch.

In my own house, I finally accepted that, no matter how much I thought *I* had changed in California, nothing had changed my marriage. Mimi and I settled back into a living arrangement that was minimally respectful, unloving and flat as a glass of beer left overnight on the porch. Lowering my expectations reduced the pressure on Mimi to raise hers and, in an odd sort of way, the tensions between us eased. Privately, however, I kept my fantasies that the marriage would someday improve; I would continue to press my nose against that cold glass for another seven years.

What *did* improve was our life as a family. Mimi and I took short trips with the kids and often spent the weekend at a farm near Charlottesville, owned by the parents of Foreign Service friends. The couple, a retired doctor and his wife, liked to have younger people around, and we loved the quiet beauty of the fields and ponds and barns. We picked vegetables from the farm garden, shared the cooking, and helped with farm repairs and chores. Mimi and I each found the place a wonderful break from Washington and Falls Church. Malory and Jason loved running through the fields with their friends, and splashing in the pond; I loved showing them how to shuck corn or bait a hook.

Things also were looking up at work. Foreign Service Officers like me were normally posted to the State Department in Washington for one tour after every two or three tours abroad. Because of my record in Vietnam, I'd been given a plum three-year assignment as a planning officer in the Bureau of Political-Military Affairs. "PM" was the Department's principal liaison with the Pentagon, responsible for advising the Secretary of State on the political implications of any military issue, from selling arms to planning nuclear war. Our offices were on the seventh floor of the State Department, next to those of Henry Kissinger, at the top of the Department's food chain.

Through PM, I began to find plenty of adventures in Washington. The arenas weren't icy cliffs or jungle battlefields, but conference tables and briefing rooms. The weapons weren't bullets and bombs, but option papers, negotiations and artful backroom deals. When I arrived, PM was involved in debates within the U.S. government over the use of nuclear weapons, with America's allies over sharing the costs of NATO, and with huge corporations over bids to build the next generation of fighter aircraft. I wrote papers, argued positions, and helped build coalitions with other agencies and countries. I was a newcomer to Washington, but I quickly learned that succeeding in that world demanded brains, stamina, strong nerves and will—qualities I knew I had. The higher stakes made everything more exciting. True, it wasn't kill-or-be-killed, like a combat mission in Vietnam. But at the end of the day the prize was the President's ear and the chance to influence policies that affected millions of people.

What I failed to appreciate, at least at first, was that Washington politics often were just a bigger form of the same shallow game I'd criticized myself for playing in Vietnam. I saw testosterone and ambition sway important decisions on the national security issues I dealt with, and always at the expense of far-sighted solutions and sometimes even common sense.

You kept score in this game by how far you outdistanced the competition. Because individuals always acted in the name of some agency or country, they could and did easily sidestep personal responsibility for any messes they made. The game was unresponsive to human suffering, and if it destroyed or impoverished innocent lives, that was a regrettable part of the playing. The big difference from Vietnam was that, in the game played in Henry Kissinger's Washington, the whole world was the board.

After the initial months in Washington of gloom and doubt, however, I'd been so grateful that there were adventures left in my life that I played this new game willingly, even after I began to see its dark side, and despite the fact that I increasingly disagreed with the policies being made, especially those that I saw contributing to poverty and injustice in the Third World. Then (as now), America supported dictators who waved our flag, and pushed trade and aid policies that only widened the gap between the world's haves and have-nots.

The more my heart had opened after Ben Lomond, the more aware and concerned I'd become about the suffering of the world's poor—suffering I'd seen first-hand. Acknowledging that pain and America's role in causing it, however, didn't lead me to seriously challenge the decisions that kept it in place. Worse, in the hardball world of Washington, even attempting to give my heart a voice in my actions seemed impossible—if I wanted to stay in the game. The excitement was too attractive for me *not* to play—and I wasn't about to flush my career.

The assumption in Washington was that you were tough and dispassionate enough to play—or you sought a lesser game. The best I could do was to tell myself that, with my insights from California, I could play in this game and not be tainted, or perhaps even that I eventually could tweak the rules.

The State Department was smart enough to recognize that young officers often could not be pounded into its mold overnight, and it cut us a surprising amount of slack. On arriving in PM, for example, I found that my dissenting reports from Vietnam had helped push me on the Department's fast track, rather than the reverse.

This official tolerance, however, did not extend much above the middle ranks. By then, the Department figured, you were either a team player or you weren't. The top levels of the Department were completely hierarchical, especially under Kissinger. Even for the young mavericks, the Department's apparent flexibility was often more an attempt to defuse opposition than to tolerate it. The Department's *Dissent Channel*, for example, was a monthly publication created less out of principle than as a safety valve for the anger and energy of people who might otherwise have voiced their opinions in more embarrassing ways. We argued in the *Dissent Channel*, for example, that the trade ban on Cuba should be lifted. Our arguments never changed policy; our reward was the satisfaction of seeing in print something deeper than the dry calculus of most of the Department's formal decisions.

But there were plenty of times when ideals and *realpolitik* clashed, with no *Dissent Channel* to cushion the impact.

In early 1974, for example, PM assigned me to write a policy paper on international arms sales. I quickly discovered that hundreds of millions of dollars of U.S. arms went to emerging Third World nations in Africa and Asia where the rationale was not politics but profit. Automatic weapons, artillery pieces, armored vehicles and land mines were being sold to countries who'd fought their last wars with castoff World War II rifles and, not too long before that, had made do with spears. The effect was catastrophic: modern weaponry had changed the nature of Third World skirmishes as fundamentally as the machine guns at Verdun had changed the nature of warfare in Europe. Not only had casualty rates soared for the combatants— many of whom were barely in their teens—but the butchery had included women and children as well.

Other than a small blip in their GNPs, it was hard to see any gain for the countries selling the guns, even if "their" side won. Arms often slipped through loose Third World controls to terrorist groups and rogue states who then used or resold them in ways that came back to bite the seller.

Nearly every country that sold arms to the Third World publicly regretted it, but none did anything about it. The smell of money was too strong. "If we don't do it," went the refrain from Washington, London, Moscow and Paris, "then somebody else will." If that hypocrisy wasn't enough to fuel some outrage, meeting some of the human slime who controlled the arms trade was. A thoroughly drunk executive from Rockwell International once collared me at a cocktail party to tell me how his company's latest plane, modified for jungle warfare, could fly slow enough to allow pinpoint napalm strikes on even small villages. He wanted the State Department's blessing to flog his wares. He probably got it, assuming he was smart enough to remind the Department that the dictator who wanted the planes had graduated from Ohio State and that the Soviets were already arming the country next door.

So my policy paper on arms sales soon became a serious test of how far I was willing to go for my ideals, not in the *Dissent Channel*, but for real. I'd already learned enough about the Washington power game to know that expressing moral outrage was bureaucratic suicide; it let your opponents discredit your entire argument by dismissing you as "soft." So I built a case that the modest economic benefits weren't worth the political risks—no one could guarantee where arms sold to Third World states would end up.

But I'd made a fatal error. On the last page, I'd used the word *moral* just once, to describe what I felt was the U.S.'s obligation to restrict sales. That paper ricocheted back from Henry Kissinger's desk with every suggestion for restricting sales rejected. A very large "Bullshit — H.K." had been scrawled across the paragraph with the word *moral* in it, the writing so emphatic that Henry must have broken his pen.

I didn't fight the decision, at least not then. The Foreign Service was my life, and there was no way I was going to risk my career by taking on the Secretary of State.

If my first attempt in Washington to fuse ideals with foreign policy fell short, at the next opportunity I didn't even try.

In the late spring of 1974, as part of my job in PM, I was appointed to the small U.S. delegation to NATO's Nuclear Planning Group (NPG), a top-secret body that planned strategies for nuclear war in Europe. If I understood the dangers of selling conventional arms to the Third World, I certainly understood the dangers of planning for the use of nuclear weapons that could incinerate the planet. But the NPG was one of the hottest tickets in the Foreign Service, and its power and prestige completely overmatched whatever misgivings I may have felt about what I would be doing there.

The NPG's planning was more complex than just deciding where to aim the warheads. In those years, NATO's strategy was to counter a Soviet invasion of Western Europe with the limited and precise use of small nuclear weapons against the invading army. The United States had spent billions on developing such weapons. Early in my assignment to the NPG, the State Department sent me to a nuclear base in the New Mexico desert for a week just to see the hardware. Some of our nuclear weapons could fit into a backpack. Some had minimum radiation effects and were good for knocking down buildings. Some had maximum radiation effects, and were designed for killing people while minimizing the damage to buildings. The NPG advised not only on where the warheads should hit, but how much and what kind of damage each should cause.

With this fine-tuned arsenal, NATO was armed and ready to answer a massive Soviet conventional attack with a wide array of small, surgical nuclear strikes. And if the war escalated, then the U.S. was prepared to use air- and sea-based nuclear missiles and bombs against Soviet cities.

The Soviets had exactly the opposite strategy. Their warheads were huge and inaccurate. They declared over and over that *any* use of nuclear weapons by NATO would automatically mean a full nuclear response by them which would end life on the planet.

So the two sides toyed with the fate of the world. NATO intended to call the Soviets' bluff, betting that, in the event of a conventional Soviet attack in Europe, we could use limited, accurate nuclear strikes against Soviet military targets. Unable to respond in kind with their inaccurate, city-busting weapons, the Soviets—we thought—would absorb the blows rather than start World War III.

Nobody, of course, really knew what would happen if even a single nuclear warhead went off, but that deterred neither the game nor the gamesters. Some writers at the time glorified nuclear war-planning by comparing it to chess, or at least poker. It was nothing of the kind, for in those games the risk and struggle result in a clearly better result for at least one of the players. What we and the Soviets were doing was much more like a teenager's game of chicken—driving cars straight at each other until somebody swerved—or didn't.

In retrospect, there's no question in my mind that the NPG helped deter a Soviet attack in Europe that could have led to World War III. The problem I saw, from the belly of the beast, was that the NPG increasingly believed its own propaganda. Its planning went beyond deterrence. The NPG really thought that a nuclear war could be fought and won just like any other war and it counseled NATO governments to that effect.

As part of my work on the NPG, for example, I was assigned to a multinational task force designing nuclear strategies called TIPAR—Targeting to Impede Post-Attack Recovery. TIPAR was based on the assumption that if NATO's efforts to limit nuclear war failed, and most of the planet was a smoking, radioactive ruin, NATO could still "win" World War III if it got back up off the mat first. TIPAR was a strategy for keeping the other side down. It made sure that no matter how destructive the initial exchanges, NATO would still have some missiles and warheads left, and the spy satellites and communications necessary to spot any resurgent sign of life in the

Soviet Union—and destroy it. We joked that TIPAR could take out the last radioactive cow in the Ukraine.

In the NPG, we were driven to treat lunatic plans like TIPAR as rational policy by the same testosterone highs that fueled much of the power game in Washington. It was no accident that not a single NPG planner was female. The NPG told itself that this was too steely-eyed a game for women to play. The "feminine side" I'd acknowledged in Ben Lomond traveled with me to NPG meetings, but it had no voice there

In the NPG, we played with the fate of the entire planet—but we did it so *respectably*. Nobody ever got their hands dirty. Most of my NPG colleagues would have recoiled at the idea of killing anyone face to face. We never saw any blood nor heard any screams of pain. But we all spent sixty hours a week planning moves we all knew would end life on the planet, and, for many, end it with the agonizingly slow wasting of radiation poisoning and starvation.

In the NPG we all wore dark blue suits and silk ties and drank sherry in the evenings. Most of our meetings took place in Europe. Once we met at a sheep farm in Sussex, and between sessions played croquet. Another meeting, in Norway, ended with a lavish banquet in a twelfth century castle, in a torchlit room lined with suits of armor, and liveried servants bearing roasts on silver trays. If the meetings were at NATO headquarters near Brussels, I'd stay with a British diplomat friend of mine, and we'd blow all the *per diem* I saved in four-star restaurants. And if the meetings lasted through Friday, I'd spend the weekend in London or Paris or on a ski slope in the Alps.

Neither I nor any of my NPG colleagues questioned what we were doing at the time. The NPG was simply too hot, too rewarding, too seductive to let any serious reflections surface. What could be more exciting than playing with the fate of the world? Besides, the peer pressure to keep silent was too strong. Had any one of us suggested that what we were doing was crazy, he would have been labeled behind his back as "losing his nerve," and would soon have found himself in another job.

I did not discount what the men at Ben Lomond had seen. I was glad that I'd replaced the macho cartoon of me with something that made my life more livable and more complete. I was glad now to accept that I was my father's son. But I short-changed all those insights in order to play in the NPG. Whatever moral courage had supported that dissenting report from Vietnam and the secret meeting with Ben Bradlee was overwhelmed by the thrill of jousting in a much bigger game than I'd ever played. It wasn't that the ideals I'd discovered in sending that report or meeting with Bradlee—or in trying to limit arms sales to the Third World—were phony. They were real and they were important. But in those first years in Washington, my ideals were bobbing like balsa on the surface of my life, easily pushed aside by the pressures and temptations of a soaring career.

I needed a moral anchor, a context deep enough to give my ideals meaning and weight.

Chapter Seventeen

The Strangest Path, 1975 – 1977

Mimi had never accepted that anything in me was different after Ben Lomond, or even if it was, that it could improve our marriage. So I was surprised, in the late spring of 1975, when she suggested we explore another path to change.

She'd heard a radio spot advertising a lecture by a group called the Inner Peace Movement (IPM), held at a Holiday Inn in Arlington, not far from our house. We'd rarely talked about spiritual matters with each other, but we each could certainly acknowledge a lack of inner peace. Our marriage was in a permanent state of low-level tension. And at work, the gap between planning nuclear war and the ideals trying to surface in my life was growing like a fault in the earth.

We found a sitter and went.

We arrived ten minutes late, and the speaker, a squat, plain-looking man named Francisco, had already begun. The first words I heard got my attention even before I'd found my seat. "You are all here," Francisco said in a thick Puerto Rican accent, "because you are seeking meaning in your lives and have not found it anywhere else."

Well that's a jump, I thought. Then I remembered Rusty, the Harvard teaching assistant who'd erased my Catholic faith but left nothing in its place. For years, consumed by my adventuring and content with my faith in myself, I'd felt no loss. I hadn't been much interested in larger questions of "meaning." The insight from the McKinley River that there might be a larger purpose to my life—something that would make my life more meaningful—hadn't disappeared, but at best had sputtered weakly like a broken neon sign.

That complacency had been eroded in Vietnam by doubts about who I was and what I was doing with my life. The reflections in California had begun to address those doubts but had focused on welcoming a kinder, gentler part of me, not on raising primal questions.

Recently that focus had begun to shift. There were woodlands just behind our house in Falls Church, and I began taking quiet walks there in soft Virginia evenings. Looking up at the night, I knew I didn't have any satisfactory sense of meaning for my life and this time felt the absence. Was being a fast-track Foreign Service Officer with two kids, a rotten marriage and a barbecue in the back yard all I was? If my deliverances from violent death meant I was being "saved" for something, I still had no idea what that something might be. Especially as I got swept up in bureaucratic power games and the Nuclear Planning Group—watching my ambition trump ideals at very turn—I felt like a fast ship without a rudder. Now this guy seemed to be talking straight to me. He was Gordon Lightfoot in a bowling shirt. I still knew the words:

> *I'm standin' in the doorway, my head bowed in my hands*
> *Not knowin' where to sit, not knowin' where to stand…*
> *They say you've been out wandrin'; they say you traveled far.*
> *Sit down young stranger, and tell us who you are.*

Francisco then said that there was no way we could understand the meaning of our lives without understanding the ultimate context in which our lives were set—the stage on which our personal dramas played. This context, he said, was "God." God was not a personality, but an over-arching and inclusive consciousness. God had no religious identification—not Christian, Jewish, Muslim, Hindu, Buddhist or anything else.

The surest way to know God, to understand this ultimate context, he continued, was not through religion but through direct transcendental experience—plugging into levels of consciousness that surpassed ordinary thought, and doing it without the help of priests, preachers, rabbis or gurus. The aim of the Inner Peace Movement, he said, was to help people find the meaning in their lives by helping them meet God on their own.

I liked that. I'd never replaced Catholicism in my life because I needed neither the guilt nor somebody else's opinions of my life's path. Now Francisco was saying, find God—find the context in which my life had meaning—and find it without a go-between.

He then announced a demonstration. A woman in her mid-thirties, one of his group, sat on a chair in the front of the room. Without any prompting or hypnotic suggestion that I could see, she soon seemed to doze off. Then suddenly she began to move heavily in the chair, as if she'd gained a hundred pounds. She began to speak, but in a man's voice. The voice said that it was an entity who had lived many lives, and who was now functioning as a spiritual guide—"Those of you brought up as Christians may think of me as an angel," it said.

For the next twenty minutes the "angel," speaking through the woman in the chair, talked about the power of love—eloquent stuff, but nothing a good flesh-and-blood preacher hadn't said before.

When it seemed that the "angel" had finished, Francisco clapped his hands once, and the woman acted as if waking from a fitful sleep. She rubbed her face for a few seconds and answered a few questions, her voice and body movements the same as before the "angel" had come.

If in fact there had been an angel. After the program had ended, I challenged one of Francisco's lieutenants, a plump middle-aged woman named Sara Bassett. "Any modestly skilled actress could have created that scene," I said. "Yes," Sara answered, "but why would she want to do that?" If I really wanted to find out more about what I'd seen, and to learn more about what Francisco had said, Sara suggested I join a meditation group sponsored by IPM. She gave me her card and suggested I call.

Mimi and I drove home confused as to what we'd seen, for once sharing the same thoughts. What were the group's motives? Francisco didn't ask for money. If IPM was a cult, it had a very uncultish clumsiness about it. And if Francisco was supposed to be a guru—nobody could have seemed less likely in that role.

Both Mimi and I were skeptical, yet agreed there'd been something compelling about the evening that neither of us could put into words.

The next day I forgot about the Inner Peace Movement and buried myself in drafting arguments for selling a new American fighter plane to NATO. Whatever had happened at the Holiday Inn—it wasn't important.

That night, however, I awoke about 2 A.M., hearing my name called repeatedly by someone whose voice I did not recognize. Jerking upright, I was startled to find the room full of smoke. I roused the family, then watched them watching me as if I'd lost my mind. The smoke had disappeared. None of them had called me, and a thorough search revealed no one else in the house.

The next night, I awoke again, called by another voice. This time, as I sat upright, I found that I literally could not open my eyes. Panicking, I finally pried them open with my fingers, and turned on the light. Only Mimi was there, again looking at me as if I was crazy. My pajamas were soaked in sweat.

The experiences continued for a third night, then a fourth—clearly more than just bad dreams or the war-induced nightmares I'd had in California. Then I remembered something Sara, from IPM, had told me after the lecture at the Holiday Inn. Some people, she'd said, had a special facility for transcending normal consciousness, but such people had to be very careful. Not every entity "out there" was an "angel." Opening the door into these realms without training—even a crack—could result in nightmares or worse.

It seemed nuts, but I was at a loss. The experiences weren't going away. I found Sara's card. She was as unlikely a spiritual guide as Francisco, but she was my only contact to that night at the Holiday Inn. I called her and told her what was happening to me. Did it have anything to do with what I'd seen at Francisco's lecture?

Maybe, she said. Twice before she'd met people who were natural psychics, but unaware of their powers; suddenly, given an awareness of the possibility of other planes of consciousness, they'd found themselves "out there," but out of control. If that was what was happening to me, then we needed to talk.

I asked her why she'd used the world "psychic," since nobody was less psychic than I was. I couldn't bend spoons with my mind, had never picked a winning lottery number, and had a hard time believing in anything I couldn't prove with my mind.

"That's what the other two said," she laughed. Then she suggested I join an IPM group that helped people explore their psychic potentials. The purpose, she continued, was not to bend spoons or guess lottery numbers, but to learn to safely visit those higher planes of consciousness—the ultimate context that Francisco had talked about. A group would start in two day's time at her house in Rockville, Maryland, about forty-five minutes from Falls Church. Other than an evening or two, she said, what did I have to lose?

Desperate to understand what was happening to me, and knowing nowhere else to turn, I said I'd come. When I told Mimi what I was going to do, she said she wanted to come too. Two days later we both found ourselves in Sara's living room, with four other people, three women and a man. All of them were about our age, worked in government agencies, and had been attracted by the lecture at the Holiday Inn. None of them was waking up in the middle of the night.

That first meeting Sara taught us to meditate—quieting thoughts, and following breaths in and out. Mimi had spent a year in India in college, so meditation was not strange to her. For me, however, deliberately shutting off my mind seemed dumb. Sara pulled me aside at a break and urged me to stick with it. It might, she said, be the way to end my nightmares.

Mimi and I got home about eleven. When I started hearing voices a few hours later, I sat up and began to "meditate" as best I could. Whatever had just woken me stopped calling. Within a few nights after that, the phenomena stopped entirely.

Mimi and I kept going to weekly meetings at Sara's house. With each session, I found less trouble getting into a meditative state than getting out. My consciousness kept wanting to slip deeper and deeper, not into sleep, but into some other state I'd never experienced, something that was neither sleep nor wakefulness, some void I instinctively feared. Sara taught us to control our descent by counting breaths—the tighter we focused on counting, the more conscious we remained.

A month after the first meeting, Sara told us that, one at a time, we were to stop counting breaths and to let the meditation go as deep as it would go; she'd bring us back with a clap of her hands. We could trust her. She wanted me to go first.

I settled back in my chair and closed my eyes. At first I started counting breaths, afraid to let go, not knowing where I was going and not sure I'd come back. When I paused in the counting, I picked up speed. Suddenly to my horror I was heading over a cliff. I tried to count my breaths again, to pull back, but it was too late and my momentum carried me past the edge. For an eternity, I hung by my fingertips over a void.

Then I dropped like a stone. The wind tore at my clothes and pushed a scream back in my mouth. I closed my eyes, waiting for the instant of annihilation.

Then, suddenly, the falling stopped, and I began to float, weightless. The cliff disappeared, and I was back in the living room, but in a corner of the ceiling, looking down at my own body sitting in a chair, with Sara leaning toward me and the others staring.

I found I could control the float with my mind, up and down, left and right. I moved around the room, but nobody noticed the me who was not the me in the chair. I moved through the wall of the house into the suburban night, then back inside. It was like no dream I'd ever had. I was in total control of my movements.

Suddenly I heard a clapping, and it was as if I'd landed heavily back in the chair. I opened my eyes, pinched the tops of my knees, and touched my face. Sara asked me how I felt and I said fine, but what I really felt I couldn't express. If what had just happened to me was not a dream, then every definition of reality I had was suddenly incomplete. Mimi and two other people that evening had what appeared to be similar experiences. I had a degree in science from Harvard and one in decision theory from Stanford, and both of them were screaming foul. What had happened couldn't have happened.

Mimi and I talked nonstop all the way back to Falls Church—the longest conversation we'd had in years. Clearly we'd each entered some kind of trance—but how? Meditation was not that strange in America in 1975, but no meditators we knew had ever described anything like what had happened to us. Had we been hypnotized? If so, it had been remarkably subtle, and to what end? When we reached home I waited in the car while Mimi went inside and paid the sitter. In those brief moments I created a whole new fantasy of how our marriage would improve. Sharing the powerful weirdness of IPM would bring Mimi and me together.

The next morning I took a vacation day and spend five hours in an occult bookstore in Georgetown, reading in a back corner where nobody I might know could see me from the street. I quickly found that what had happened to me in Sara's living room was not uncommon. There were references to the same phenomenon in the mystical literature going back millennia. It was called an "out-of-body" experience, and it was a manifestation of the existence of the soul—an aspect of being transcending the physical body, the personality and the mind. The soul was eternal and timeless; it left the body at death, but could be reborn into multiple lifetimes. The soul could also leave the body temporarily as a result of deliberate shifts in consciousness—which seemed to describe what we were doing in Sara's living room. So said the books.

If that wasn't the explanation of what had happened to me, then what was? I was sure it hadn't been a hallucination. I'd taken no drugs. All I'd done was meditate without the brakes—and entered a state of consciousness that went beyond anything I'd thought possible.

That evening, when I told Mimi what I'd learned in the bookstore, she seemed strangely uninterested. We'd both shared the same experience but the curiosity that was consuming me barely seemed to touch her. She asked a few questions, then said it was time to put the kids to bed.

I counted the days until the next session. When it came, Sara told me that, as I began to float outside my body, I was to look for a pair of bright lights and to follow them. On cue, the lights appeared, dazzlingly bright but somehow not causing me to squint. They came up to me, then went forward a short distance and stopped. When I began to follow them, they kept moving forward steadily, always in sight, leading me down what appeared to be a bright tunnel that soon opened up into what was not so much a place, as an extraordinarily peaceful state of being.

I was surrounded by a diaphanous white light, as if walking in a damp meadow, watching ground fog burn off in the morning sun. Except that there were no sights and no sounds, no dimensions to it, no physical elements of any kind. I felt the presence of other beings, floating as I was floating, communicating greetings without spoken words. It was not the "heaven" of my Catholic youth, and it certainly was not the "hell." The overall feeling was of profound peace and joy.

Mimi and another woman in Sara's group described similar experiences. It was not reassuring to listen to each other afterwards and realize how much we sounded like the accounts of people who'd been tripping on LSD.

But we'd taken no drugs. Yes, Sara had suggested following the white lights, but she'd said nothing about what the lights would lead to; we'd discovered that on our own. And if these experiences were all just dreams—they felt far more real than any dreams any of us had experienced before—and certainly just as real as the waking state to which we kept returning.

Mimi and I kept going back to IPM sessions at Sara's house, back to the place of light. We talked some about what was happening, but as our experiences deepened, they also became increasingly personal and difficult for either of us to share. Mimi had no wish to open up that part of herself to me. And I was afraid that if I gushed everything I thought and felt, she would challenge me or laugh at me and I was unwilling to take that risk. Instead of pushing us together as I'd hoped, IPM sent us down separate tracks, and we talked less and less about the journeys.

I read more books—everything from the early mystic texts of Christianity to the Tibetan Book of the Dead. I read works by savants and scholars, from St. John of the Cross to William James. And I studied the reports of "life after death" experiences of people who'd "died" on operating tables and then come back to life after moments in other realms.

Virtually all these writings described worlds of consciousness beyond the normal waking one, descriptions that very closely matched what I was experiencing. If I was crazy, then it was a remarkable coincidence that so many other people had been crazy in just the same way over four thousand years.

There was also the fact that, whatever they were, these trips out-of-body were profoundly educational. I came back each time with insights that I know I would never have reached with my conscious mind.

What I learned was that there was indeed life after death, but not the one the nuns and priests of my childhood had described. I didn't see my great grandfather or meet St. Peter. What I saw was that each of us existed on three planes at once. The first was the normal waking self, the part of me that walked into Sara's living room and would someday cease to exist. The second was the soul, a timeless entity that underwent continual rebirths, each life a series of opportunities for spiritual growth. The soul was the part of me that traveled in an out-of-body experience.

The third plane, and the hardest to fathom from a waking state, was not so much a plane as a totality in which all souls melded, each being part of the whole, not as a petal is part of a flower, but as a wave is part of the ocean. And that "ocean" was God, the ultimate context for our lives, and the intelligent, organizing force for everything. God was not the separate, anthropomorphic Almighty of my Catholic youth, on whose whims I was punished or rewarded, condemned or absolved. I—and everyone else—was part of God, part of this totality. Our connectedness at this level was a core aspect of creation and—if we chose to acknowledge it—a strong basis for compassion and co-existence in our earthly lives.

These insights didn't come in through my brain, as if I'd read a brilliant new book. I directly experienced these understandings without filtering them through my mind. I saw what I saw, I learned what I learned, by being in the middle of it. The closest comparison I can make is how you learn that your body will float in water. You learn by floating.

The out-of-body trips I took, beginning in the middle of 1975, were the most extraordinary experiences of my life. They were, exactly as Francisco had promised, meeting God face-to-face. I know my reports of them seem outrageous or even insulting to some. But these things happened to me, and I'm relating them with as much honesty and accuracy as I can.

I understood almost from the beginning that if these experiences were not hallucinations, dreams or madness, then I'd found much more than just a metaphysical primer, a kind of user's guide to the universe. The discoveries I made out-of body filled fundamental needs in me that, unmet, had confused and crippled me for decades.

Most immediately, the experiences gave me a practical framework for living a responsible life. Humans were not abject beings, too sinful and weak to master earthly challenges without the help of some distant and capricious God. The reality I saw was governed far less by divine whim than by earthly cause-and-effect. That design demanded that we accept far more responsibility for the choices we made; because we were each a part of the same whole, every choice we made affected everything else.

I learned through IPM to see my own life as a constant series of moral choices, with unavoidable consequences for every choice. If I made them to serve others, to heal, to bring people together—then I deepened my links with the totality, with God. If I made self-serving choices that promoted division and suffering, I carried the confusion and pain created by those choices on with me, confronting the same choices again and again until I got it right, in this life or a future life.

This framework is the opposite of what I'd been taught as a Catholic— that we're all born sinners and need God and His priests to save our damned souls. It's much tougher to accept the truth that our spiritual destiny is entirely up to us.

Twenty years later the movie *Groundhog Day* would describe this system precisely, showing the Bill Murray character living the same day again and again and again until he gets it right. But I'd been given a huge advantage. In *Groundhog Day*, the hero has to figure out his moves without ever being told how the process works—or even that there *is* a process. In trance, I was shown precisely how it works and then invited to use what I'd seen to improve my life.

The lessons from Wheelus and from Hué now became clearer. I *was* responsible for my actions—but in an even more profound way than I'd thought; the choices I made could shape not just events and situations in this lifetime, but for lifetimes to come. And the lessons of Ben Lomond— acknowledging who I was, opening my heart—now were not just personality adjustments for this life, but crucial lessons for my soul's journey.

My experiences through IPM at last sharpened the vague sense from the McKinley River that my deliverances from violent death were not luck, but signs that I was meant to find and fulfill a purpose higher than satisfying my own needs. What I saw out-of-body was that what I'd felt on the riverbank was true— that I *was* being saved for a higher purpose: that purpose was not to pursue power and status (as I'd hoped, sitting by my campfire in Tennant Creek) but to heal and to serve, to use my life to help bridge conflicts and solve public problems, and to support others in doing the same. I would carry out this purpose not as the cartoon superman I'd tried for so long to be, but as who I really was—a gentle, caring man, my father's son, inspired by the ideals that had begun to rise in me beginning with that dissenting report I'd sent from Vietnam.

Finally, the "ultimate context"—God—I found through IPM became the guiding framework for my life, the framework I'd seen lacking that terrible night in Hué, listening to the bombs, wondering how many men I'd sent to their deaths because of the games I'd come to Vietnam to play. I now saw myself as part of a reality much bigger than me, with roles to play that would put my ideals into action and give my life the deeper meaning I sought, walking in the woodlands on soft Virginia evenings.

These revelations were huge. They encompassed every aspect of my life, answering questions and sharpening answers that I'd wrestled with for decades. Still, knocked from my horse, I became no Paul. My mystical experiences did not heal my marriage, nor give me the courage to stop planning nuclear war, nor instantly make me a better person. What I gained was an incentive and guide for growth, not a sudden remake of who I was.

At home, Mimi and I—who'd both completely ignored any spiritual education for our children—tried to tell them about what we'd learned from IPM. The kids would have none of it. Their two-week summer indoctrinations by Catholic grandmothers proved more than enough to send them running whenever Mimi or I tried to explain anything beyond Sunday School. We made a few clumsy attempts to explain to them what we were doing with meditation and trances, but they were too young, and all we did was scare them.

At work, my boss, a hang-loose academic who knew what I was doing, kept asking me with a grin when I was going to show up for work in a white robe with light shining out of my ears.

Mimi and I kept going to trance sessions. Despite the repeated experiences out-of–body, despite the obvious importance of the revelations, I still had doubts that any of this was real. The doubts hung around like a bad cold, even though by now I was in so deep I knew that if what I was experiencing was *not* really happening, then the only other possibility was that I was insane. I wanted a sign. In the late summer of 1975, it came.

We were at our friends' farm in Charlottesville on a lazy Saturday afternoon in July. A lone hawk circled the south field, riding the hint of a breeze. The only sounds were insects buzzing, and the shouts of kids riding in a hay wagon pulled by a snorting tractor that hadn't done a day's work in years. The rest of us were sitting on the farmhouse porch, drinking fresh lemonade and talking.

Suddenly a four-year-old boy, the son of another couple, came running toward the house, holding his left hand and shrieking. The other kids were quick at his heels, shouting that the boy had just put his hand on the hot tractor exhaust pipe. A quick look showed serious burns. The owner of the farm, a doctor, went inside for his first aid kit. The boy's mother held him, but the pain was intense and the frightened child wailed even louder.

What I remember next is a feeling of immense personal calm and confidence. I quietly asked the mother to give the boy to me. When she did, I put the boy's burned hand between my hands, closed my eyes, and imagined myself back in the place of light. The boy stopped screaming. When I took my hands away, his hand showed no signs of being burned.

It was impossible for me to pretend it hadn't happened. The mother took her son back, looking in my eyes without speaking. The others stared. Mimi didn't say a word; to this day, I have no idea what she thought had happened.

While I've by now had hundreds of mystical experiences, that boy was the only person I ever healed with my hands. In retrospect, his healing was less about him than about me. Given the skepticism of my science-trained mind, I needed that physical proof and the universe—God—provided it. Since the incident at the farm, I've never doubted that what I learned and did through IPM was real. As real as climbing the north wall of Mt. McKinley or fathering two children. Healing the boy was like pushing my fingers into a light socket. The voltage shattered my skepticism, re-ordered my mind and left me free to accept what I would have never discovered on my own.

After the experience at the farm, the final year of my three-year tour at the State Department was a remarkable straddle. I was promoted to a higher grade in the Foreign Service at the same time I was spending hours every week out of my body. I continued to work in the Nuclear Planning Group. I would lead a meditation on a Sunday afternoon, then catch a night plane for Brussels and spend the week plotting how to turn Leningrad into glass.

I understood very well that seeking God and planning to incinerate the planet were in direct counterpoint, and I struggled with the inconsistency. I didn't want to give up my career in the Foreign Service. I told myself I could have it all—that I could use my new insights to promote policies of peace. This was a gross rationalization, and I think I knew it then. Challenges to the State Department's *realpolitik* had gotten no easier since my aborted effort to cut arms sales.

Just as my frustrations with the NPG were mounting, however, my tour at the Department ended and, in the fall of 1976, I was thrown into a new arena where Henry Kissinger was not in charge. I was awarded a "Congressional Fellowship"—a one-year program that immersed fast-rising FSOs in the legislative process, preparing us for senior assignments where that experience would be important. Most of the Fellowship was on-the-job. For the first half of the year, I worked as an aide to Don Bonker, a young congressman from Washington State. For the second half, I was a foreign policy advisor to Senator John Glenn, a straightforward man who won my respect forever by spending forty-five minutes on a busy day telling stories of his flight into space to Malory's Brownie troop—eight little girls in brown beanies sitting on the floor of his office, staring, wide-eyed.

Senator Glenn also encouraged me to resurrect my ideas on restricting arms sales. I drafted legislation and the senator pressed his colleagues to support it. In the end the bill failed to pass, but, by raising the issue in a way that shifted some attitudes in the Senate, it came far closer to changing U.S. arms sales policy than the doomed paper I'd written at the State Department two years before.

The near-miss convinced me that powerful institutions—with the right leadership and tactics—could be moved to do good things and that I could help them do it as I gained experience and skill. The arms sales bill also showed me I could find and do important work on public policy that served my ideals instead of forcing me to ignore them; I didn't have to lead two lives. These discoveries were like watching the clouds lift and seeing the summit of Mt. McKinley for the first time. The goal may have been distant and difficult—*but it was there* and I would reach it.

Finally, working in Congress to limit arms sales showed me that not all adventures had to involve risking my life on icy cliffs or in distant wars. Realizing the stakes, countering the arms sales lobbies, drafting last-minute amendments—all of it got my blood running, only this time my goal was saving lives.

The Congressional Fellowship ended in mid-1977. After five years in the United States, Foreign Service procedure said I must now go outside the country for my next series of assignments. But I'd discovered another option, one than was perfect for me, and fit the Foreign Service rules.

Jimmy Carter had come to the White House in January 1977, promising a global campaign for human rights. Knowing that Washington insiders would dismiss his effort as naive, Carter centered the campaign at the U.S. Mission to the United Nations in New York, America's embassy to the world body. He put the Mission under the direction of civil rights leader Andrew Young. Carter made Young not only Ambassador to the UN but a member of his Cabinet, and, as a further sign that he meant business, gave him more power and autonomy than any UN ambassador had ever had before.

Any Foreign Service Officer paying attention saw that joining the small U.S. Mission staff during Carter's presidency would be a rare chance to influence American policies toward two-thirds of the planet. For someone like me, struggling to close the gap between what I did for a living and what was in my heart, working on a human rights campaign backed by the President of the United States was ideal. And since the Foreign Service considered the UN Mission a "foreign" assignment, a posting to New York also met the Service's requirement that I go abroad. I lobbied the State Department for two months for a job at the Mission. When I was successful that summer, Mimi, Malory, Jason and I prepared to head for the capital of the world.

First we went home. My parents were impressed with pictures of me and Senator Glenn hunched over papers on his desk. I went up to the Elks Club with my father so he could show me off to his cronies, and I gave an interview to the local paper that all my parents' friends were sure to read.

Around the dinner table, the Inner Peace Movement joined the long list of taboo topics. The kids had blabbed enough to ring alarm bells in my very Catholic mother. There was no way, however, I could talk to her about trances or even meditation, and I laughed off her attempts to probe.

That summer of 1977—with Malory now almost eleven and Jason nearing six—I took my kids into the mountains for the first time. These trips into the wilderness—which continued until both Malory and Jason were grown—would be fundamental to shaping my relationships with both of them. Most times we'd go into the bush just the three of us, but this first time Mimi came too, along with a small army of relatives and friends. We hiked up to a series of mountain lakes northeast of Mt. Rainer. The skies stayed mercifully clear, there was a slight chill in the evening air, and the supply of hotdogs and flapjacks was enough to keep everybody fed and happy. I was delighted with how comfortable both my kids seemed to be in the wilderness, and how involved and curious they were to see a marmot's den or a glacier's snout.

My own experiencing would be challenged that summer. It had now been two and a half years since I'd first heard Francisco talk at the Holiday Inn in Arlington. Doubts about transcendental experience had turned into conviction and commitment. I'd become adept at exploring the realms opened though trance meditation and I appreciated the sense of confidence and direction these explorations had given me.

Suddenly, however, every time I went back to the place of light, instead of quiet joy, all I experienced was one very specific and insistent message: it was time to leave the nest and fly. I no longer needed IPM to get me to the place of light, or to show me how to talk to God. What I'd learned in trance states now provided the moral anchor I'd lacked in my first years in Washington, watching my ideals swept away by excitement and ambition. Now it was time to focus everything I'd become into service to the world. In New York I would be in a place of influence on issues that affected the lives of millions of people and that placement was no accident. I was to heal, but more than a boy's burned hand.

I accepted the guidance. I continued to meditate, and to return to the place of light, but I cut my links with IPM. I'd learned to meet God on my own and, through those encounters, I'd gained a moral context for my life, a compass that's guided me ever since. It's a compass I know I would never have found on my own.

It's been important for me to put down in this book the role mystical experiences played in shaping my life. In the 21st century, as fundamentalists gain more control over organized religion, fewer and fewer minds seem open to the possibility of alternative paths to God. Given my skepticism of my own experiences, I understand the difficulty. But if God is timeless and everywhere, why should we believe that direct communication with God is rare, or that it should be only the province of saints and mystics? Why shouldn't God speak and act through any of us in any place, at any time? Emerson, Thoreau and William James thought so. Quakers listen for the "still, small voice." Aboriginal cultures the world over trust in direct experience of God.

I describe my own experiences not because they are so dramatically different, but because I think experiences that transcend normal consciousness are far more common and accessible than most people are willing to talk about. Any of us is capable of deep reflection, and in that honest unvarnished space, to see the reality of who we are.

> *That is at the bottom the only courage that is demanded of us: to have courage for the most strange, the most singular and the most inexplicable that we may encounter. That mankind has in this sense been cowardly has done life endless harm; the experiences that are called "visions," the whole so-called "spirit-world," death, all those things that are so closely akin to us, have by daily parrying been so crowded out of life that the senses with which we could have grasped them are atrophied. To say nothing of God.*
>
> —Rainier Maria Rilke, *Letters to a Young Poet*

Chapter Eighteen
New York, 1977 – 1979

In New York, we moved into the bottom two floors of a renovated brownstone at 23rd Street and Tenth Avenue, a short subway ride from the center of the city. Our landlady was a local television star—the kids were in awe the first time they saw her face on the side of a bus. Our neighbor on one side was the actor Tony Perkins. The brownstone on the other side had been one of the city's best-known bordellos in the 1920s; there were reports that in peak times the house where we were living handled the overflow.

We enrolled the kids in the United Nations School—Jason in the first grade and Malory in the fifth. Mimi, far more than I did, helped them make the transition from lawns and Little League to subways and city parks. I would spend less time with my kids in New York than I had in Virginia. I felt bad about it, but in coming here I'd made my choice. What better excuse could there be for being an absent father than helping an idealistic American president change the world?

Mimi threw herself into the city's art world and spent more and more time with her own circle of friends. Both our lives became so full that it seemed to matter less, at least for a while, that none of that fullness came from being with each other. I talked very little to her about my work. The state of our marriage in New York was that our mail came to the same address.

The U.S. Mission to the UN was housed in a drab ten-story building just across First Avenue from the familiar UN complex. My job at the Mission was to help plan and present American positions on political issues in the Third World—the world outside North America, Europe, and the Communist bloc. In 1977, those issues included independence for the remaining colonies and peacekeeping and human rights challenges across the globe. Buoyed by my near miss in convincing Congress to limit arms sales, I was certain I could make a difference at the UN. When I crossed the street my first day on the job, it felt like heading across the tundra toward Mt. McKinley fourteen years before. Ahead of me was the adventure of my life.

It turned out my first challenge was more basic—getting Third World diplomats to talk to me. When I arrived at the UN, America's reputation throughout most of the Third World couldn't have been lower. American policies toward apartheid, foreign aid, Cuba, and Palestine were attacked by most of the Third World as unfair and insensitive at best, racist at worst. Nine months into the Carter Administration, most of the changes promised by the new president seemed nowhere in sight, blocked by conservatives both within the Executive Branch and in Congress. On courtesy calls that first day, diplomats from Niger and Somalia wouldn't even shake my hand. Others couldn't make it past the pleasantries without tearing into some perceived failure of American policy. Most of the rest greeted me politely, with cold eyes.

The UN's stuffiness didn't make things easier. In the first week of UN "debate" that fall, all I heard was one diplomat after another read canned, self-serving statements. The problems the UN grappled with were real, and affected billions of people, but the honest dialogues that might have helped solve them were not taking place.

Diplomats' kids at the UN School, ten blocks south, were doing a better job than their parents. The school enrolled kids from many of the national missions to the UN as well as from the UN's international staff. Malory and Jason came home every day with songs and games in multiple languages and their new friends had names like Ahmad and Jorge and Françoise. I wasn't the only parent who looked forward to parents' nights at the school, because of the feelings of acceptance and inclusiveness that surrounded them. Something at the UN was living up to the original dream.

Ten blocks north, Andy Young, my boss, understood the communications problems at the UN very well and did his best to break through formal UN procedures. His off-the-cuff, sometimes deliberately provocative style charmed the New York press and some ambassadors, but it infuriated others, who saw their status tied to protocol. I thought his style was brilliant, and it inspired me to challenge the UN's constipation at my level too.

The honest dialogues the UN needed required trust, and building trust meant taking the time, and caring enough, to put myself into other people's shoes and to let them into mine. I started asking other diplomats about their lives back home. I asked them about their kids, and told them about my own. Some Third World delegates remained suspicious that this tack from an American was a trick, but many more seemed genuinely eager to reduce the punishing formality of the place, and began to respond in kind.

My two deputies were as happy to humanize their work as I was. Henry Miller was a skinny, superbright young FSO whose preppie pedigree never got in the way of a fresh likeability and an unerring instinct to be human. Tony Jackson was about my age but a foot shorter, with receding salt-and-pepper hair that made him look like Haile Selassie. Everybody loved Tony—he was always first to say hello in the morning, to ask a waitress how her kids were doing, or to show up with flowers for overworked secretaries. Tony could keep any party rolling with his endless supply of jokes. He seemed almost permanently happy. He was also an agent for the CIA, using my office as cover for recruiting people to spy for the United States.

During the two-month General Assembly session each fall, three or four more FSOs came up from Washington to help Henry, Tony and me cover the hundreds of sessions that dealt with Third World issues. Every morning my small office was like the squad room on a cop show. We'd all crowd in to parcel out assignments, then fan out across the street to give a speech or listen to one and hopefully talk to people at a level that was real. At my urging that first fall, we learned what it was like to grow up in

Bhutan, explained how baseball worked, and shared complaints of New York City traffic.

Slowly we began to build some trust that allowed straight talk on issues that mattered. One of the people who'd refused to shake my hand when I arrived was Mahmadou Barré, an Oxford-educated Marxist from Somalia. I finally got him to agree to go to lunch. On the way to the restaurant we all but stumbled over a homeless man sprawled in a park across the street from the UN. "There are no homeless people in my country!" Mahmadou said triumphantly. "And no elections either," I answered. "What is so wonderful about democracy if it permits this kind of misery?" Mahmadou asked. "And so it's better to have everybody poor, and no right to change the policies that keep them poor?" I countered. "You do not understand the dialectic," said Mahmadou the Marxist, "and I am going to explain it to you over a wonderful capitalist lunch that you are paying for." The lunch went on so long we were both late for our afternoon meetings.

I'm sorry I lost contact with Mahmadou. Almost thirty years later, with every country except Cuba and North Korea abandoning the socialist model, I bet he manages a Coca-Cola subsidiary and has a Swiss bank account—provided he survived the chaos that overtook his country in the meantime.

At the U.S. Mission, my job exploded in size within weeks after I arrived. Some of that was inevitable, given that President Carter's campaign for human rights had expanded the workload of the entire Mission. And some of it was created by the intense focus of Andy Young on just one issue—the transition to independence of the white-dominated colony of Southern Rhodesia. Young's preoccupation sucked in most of the rest of the political staff, creating opportunities for me to play significant roles on other Third World issues, from Cuba to South Africa.

To my surprise, Andy Young's trust-building efforts didn't extend to his own staff. He'd brought with him to the UN a cadre of loyal lieutenants from the civil rights movement, and it became clear early on that unless you'd marched with him and Dr. King at Selma, you could never be a member of his inner circle. To him and his loyalists, any white Foreign Service officer—especially one that had gone to an Ivy League college—was incapable of understanding the colored peoples of the world, let alone treating them with fairness and dignity. Young never said anything like this directly to me or anybody else, of course, but he surrounded himself with gatekeepers who made the message clear.

These judgments rankled—especially as I began sticking my neck further and further out for the same Third World concerns that motivated Young and his inner circle. It wasn't much comfort to reflect that I was experiencing the kind of racist judgments that many black professionals experienced every day. Still, Young's attitude turned out to be a blessing. Consumed by the Rhodesia negotiations and blinded by his stereotypes, he rarely noticed what I was doing. Since my immediate boss was a hands-off type too, I ended up with far more freedom than I'd expected.

I needed it. As my contacts with Third World delegates became broader and deeper, my personal views on many of their issues shifted further and further away from the official policies I was supposed to carry out—policies still pretty much unchanged by Carter's promises.

Some of this shifting took place in the Delegates Lounge, a cavernous bar just outside the General Assembly hall. A few wall hangings and statues from around the world did nothing to dispel the feeling that you were drinking in an airport hanger. In its effort to be home to anybody, however, the Lounge boasted what must have been the longest beer list on the planet. Even the Mongolians could taste familiar suds. The written rule in the Lounge was that only official delegates could get in. The unwritten rule was that, no matter what posturing you'd just been forced to do for your country, this was a place where you could loosen your tie. The bad thing about the Lounge, at least for the traditionalists, was that everybody else could see whom you were talking to. Half the talk there was gossip on who was talking to whom and why.

I didn't care. I wanted to talk to the world, and I did. And I listened, trying to figure out on my own, absent propaganda from my nation or any other, what made sense and what didn't. I was convinced early on, for example, that there should be a Palestinian state on the West Bank. The arguments from my Arab colleagues echoed the passionate conversation I'd had with young Palestinians in that café in Jericho, a stop on the high road thirteen years before.

But the biggest catalyst for shifting my political views wasn't compelling arguments in the Delegate's Lounge. Important patterns of identity, ideals and responsibility were finally beginning to gel in my life, and to fit together in ways that were both shaping my political opinions, and hardening my commitment to act on them.

Since the *Golden Bear*, my life had been about adventure, driven for years by a selfish, misguided quest for manhood. I'd joined the Foreign Service as my path to power. At Wheelus and especially in Vietnam, however, I'd begun to see the dangerous shallowness of the motives that drove me, and to understand that playing on a larger stage demanded I be more responsible for my choices and actions.

In California, the men at Ben Lomond had helped me acknowledge that I was my father's son. Ideals long dormant had continued to rise in me, but, in Washington, that revival had faltered in the face of a surging career. By the time I arrived in John Glenn's office, however, my experiences with the Inner Peace Movement had finally begun to reveal a deeper sense of purpose for my life and to stiffen my resolve. Now, at the UN, challenges of injustice and poverty in the Third World presented huge new opportunities for acting on that purpose, and it all felt extraordinarily right.

What I sorely missed as these currents swirled together in my life, was someone with whom I could share my excitement. I said very little to Mimi. She did not think I was capable of these ideals and I saw no point in trying to defend or justify myself to her.

I did, however, find someone I could talk to, in the oddest possible place.

The United Nations was crawling with spies. You could usually tell who they were from their big expense accounts. The UN was ringed with great restaurants and most of the spy stuff went on, not in back alleys, but over three-martini lunches. The East European spy agencies had the biggest interest in me. Their agents, however, tended to be so completely humorless that sitting with them for two hours was almost not worth the meal. So I developed a special routine whenever an *apparatchik* from the Warsaw Pact was ordered to update my dossier over lunch. Even before the drinks had arrived, the earnest Bulgarian or East German or Ukrainian would start going through his biographical checklist, thinly disguised as small talk: "Zo, Mr. Graham—may I call you Dzohn—vat is it like the place ver you grew up?"

At which point I would take a résumé out of my jacket pocket, hand it to my host and say, "Mr. Zirinsky, here are the answers to all the personal questions you can expect me to answer. Now can we talk about something more interesting?"

I met a sad, square-faced Russian named Dmitri Probolof this way. He had a diplomatic title but was in fact a mid-level officer in the KGB, the Soviet intelligence service. When I handed him my résumé he seemed enormously relieved. He looked me in the eyes for what seemed a very long time. Then he said, "Please tell me who you really are" in such a way I knew he was not playing the usual game. So I told him—my youth, my adventures, my father, the Inner Peace Movement, my ideals—all of it. He responded in kind. Dmitri was a spy because the Communist Party had told him he would be a spy. He was also a mystic, whose struggles to come to grips with his ideals paralleled my own. It was an extraordinary conversation and it went on for almost four hours. It was the beginning of a friendship that could have got us both fired—or for him, worse. In the middle of the Cold War, it was treason for a Communist Bloc officer, let alone a KGB agent, to confide any tensions he felt with his job or with his life to anyone, and most certainly to an American diplomat. The risks for me were nowhere so grim, although it did occur to me that the FBI would never understand why I was talking about trance experiences to a Soviet intelligence officer.

When I got back from that lunch, Tony wanted to know what I'd learned that the CIA could use. I told him I'd learned nothing. But in fact I'd learned a lot. Dmitri and I had met at a place behind our eyes, not just as personalities but as souls, and that had changed the nature of our communication completely. We didn't blab official secrets that afternoon and we never did. But we did talk about politics not in terms of national priorities of power but of planetary priorities of peace. At the UN, we were each doing a delicate dance between what our ideals called us to do and what our masters demanded. That dance drew us together. For me the dance was exciting. For Dimitri, given his lack of freedoms, it turned out to be a matter of life and death.

I felt safer sharing my inner thoughts with a KGB agent than with my own wife. Mimi and I made all the routine decisions on raising the kids, on family finances—but there was nothing else between us except fifteen years of inertia. In New York we both tried to bring more respect and civility into our marriage. It's just that we didn't mean anything to each other, and we both knew it, and the pain of that thought sat in both of us like a toothache.

With the kids, the pressure was time. I'd often come home late, sometimes very late, and I'd work many weekends too. Given what I was doing at the UN and the opportunities I had in those years, I don't second-guess what I did. What saved my connections to Malory and Jason were the trips we took. Every summer there'd be at least one backpacking trip into the mountains of Washington State. That first winter in New York we went to New Hampshire to ski two or three times. Mimi wasn't much of a skier, so the kids and I spent days on the slopes where the three of us would have each other's total attention. As fathering, it wasn't much, but it was what I had to give. That I'm as close to my kids as I am now is a tribute to their resiliency far more than to mine.

By the spring of 1978, my new resolve as a healer—combined with a loose rein at work and my increasingly divergent political views—pushed me to operate less as an employee of the U.S. Mission and more as a "mission" of my own. I fulfilled my official job description well enough to keep the State Department happy—but what I did on my own became more and more the reason I was there.

The freelancing began with my role with the Nonaligned Movement.

For thirty years, the Cold War had shaped both American and Soviet policies toward the rest of the planet, as each superpower struggled to line up as many puppets as it could among the world's have-nots. From the point of view of Washington and Moscow, there was no integrity in staying neutral—the Cold War was the planet's end game, and any countries that failed to choose sides were flouting the rules.

Not surprisingly, most Third World states resented these pressures; they saw less to gain in becoming lackeys of West or East than in artfully playing one side off against the other: if the Soviets offered a steel mill, then the Americans should be good for at least a hydroelectric dam. Realizing that their strength lay in numbers, these same states had formed the Nonaligned Movement (NAM), a loose association that helped them pool their political power in a world where individually they were weak.

Until the Carter administration, the United States had paid little attention to the NAM. But when Jimmy Carter stepped up America's focus on the Third World, it became more important to know what those states were thinking and doing, not just individually, but collectively. Since all the NAM states were also members of the UN—where I already knew most of their delegates—in 1978 the Mission appointed me America's first formal link to the Movement.

The NAM met a couple of times a year, almost always in the capital city of one of its members. While as an American diplomat I couldn't be invited to these meetings, nothing stopped me from being in the right city at the right time and talking to my friends after their formal sessions ended. I hung out in restaurants and bars from Djakarta to Lagos, staying up until the early hours of the morning. While there was always some resentment of my presence on their turf, most NAM delegates—even those who weren't my friends—saw me as a fast, useful means of getting their views to Washington.

The Cubans, in particular, went out of their way to keep me informed— I was one of the few reliable channels they had to the State Department at a time of near complete breakdown in relations between Washington and Havana. For my part, I enjoyed hanging out with Castro's diplomats, not because I shared all their politics, but because they were fun, irreverent, and bold—especially Ricardo Santamaria, the deputy Cuban Ambassador. Ricardo was stocky and balding, with an accent that made him sound like a Latin ballplayer. He had anti-Castro cousins in New Jersey that he could never convert to the cause; he blamed the State Department, which would not let him travel outside New York City.

I told Ricardo once that his cousins reminded me of my parents—I might love them but I could never talk to them about things that mattered. Ricardo just laughed, and reminded me that at least I was free to fly out to Tacoma whenever I wanted.

Maybe so, but physical connection did not mean I could talk to my parents about my marriage, ideals, politics, spirituality... Every year it seemed another subject would go on the list. But these two people had raised me with love, they were getting old, and it was important to simply spend time with them in their world. In the summer of 1978, I returned from a NAM meeting in Ceylon through Tacoma, where Mimi and the kids had been since June.

My parents still lived in the same house where I'd grown up. The willow tree, spindly then, was now spreading into the neighbor's yard. The roof had been reshingled. A laurel hedge replaced the picket fence that had once separated our yard from the neighbor's.

This summer my older sister Wynne was in town as well, and the four of us spent good time talking around the blue formica table in the kitchen, outside the larger gatherings with spouses, in-laws and kids. "Remember the train trip we took around the United States in '53?" "Would Uncle Joe ever kick the bottle?" "Was it true Aunt Margaret had left the Church?" My father, now long retired from the newspaper, had taken up writing letters to the editor, and proudly showed me a book of clippings. For my mother, watching me down a second plate of her Croatian meatloaf helped her happily recreate the boy she knew.

With the kids, Jason was now seven and old enough to join me and his sister in serious trekking. This time we took an older cousin who was then studying to become a professional photographer. Christopher took some wonderful shots, including one I keep on my desk today. Jason is sprawled in front of me, with knobby knees and a mop of blond hair. Malory is nearing twelve, standing behind me, looking very thoughtful and beautiful. And I'm in the middle, looking like the father I wanted to be.

This trip we went to the north slopes of Mt. Rainier, just beneath the Willis Wall, a steep precipice of ice and rock. The first day we hiked to the edge of a cliff overlooking the Carbon glacier flowing from the mountain, and just sat there on sun-warmed rocks for most of the afternoon. We listened to marmots whistle and watched an occasional rock tumble down the mountain face in front of us.

Each day we scrambled up to a new high point and ran back to camp through meadows of wildflowers. The kids loved the exploring, and I loved sharing what I knew about the rocks and trees, the animals and the wind— stuff they would never learn in school. Every night we camped by a mountain lake. We had steaks the first night, and after that it was concoctions of rice and tinned meat and dried soups. None of us would have touched such stuff back in the city but it tasted wonderful as we pulled on jackets against the evening chill. After dinner each night we sat around a small campfire and talked and talked, about their lives and about mine. I told my kids what I was doing, and what I wanted to do at the United Nations, and why. After a year at the United Nations School, the questions they asked were better than most of those I heard at work.

Back in New York that fall, I kept pushing to expand the freedoms given me as the only American diplomat with access to the Nonaligned Movement. As my connections with the NAM and its members deepened, I wrung permission from the State Department to attach a page or two of my own views to my reports from NAM meetings. The reports went not only to Washington, but to every American Embassy in the world. In the beginning, I wrote cautiously, but as I gained confidence, I used the space to argue for changes in U.S. policies, or for speeding up the changes that Carter had promised. Conservatives in the State Department cried foul and tried to shut down this channel, but, to his credit, Andy Young stuck up for me, and it stayed open through a series of conferences all over the Third World.

The Havana Summit of NAM heads of state, in mid-1979, was the high point of this freedom. Because people like Qadhaafi and Arafat would be there, security in Havana was tight, and the sensitivity of NAM delegates that didn't want me there—including hard-liners in the Cuban government—was intense. It took three weeks of jawboning by the State Department before the Cuban government agreed to give me a visa. Even when they finally relented, teams of Cuban agents followed me wherever I went, making it difficult for me to talk to anyone. On my second night in Havana, a man took a swing at me in a hotel bar—almost certainly a deliberate attempt to provoke a melee that would have got me thrown out of the country. Luckily my friend Ricardo, who happened to be in the bar, pulled the man off.

I ended my final cable from Havana with a long analysis of why, having tracked the Nonaligned Movement, its issues, and its actors more closely than any other American for the last two years, I thought many American

policies on Third World issues were wrong. I argued for ending the embargo on Cuba, cracking down on apartheid in South Africa, talking to the
Palestinians, pushing harder for human rights, and adopting trade and aid
policies that would help close the gap between the world's rich and poor.

After the conference, I received a half-dozen very private letters and
calls from American ambassadors and other officials praising my analysis—and explaining why they couldn't afford to side with me openly. And,
of course, a lot of people called for my head on a platter. Even Andy Young
told me I'd gone too far.

The irony was that the biggest risks of my trip to Havana were posed by
the people I was trying to help. Back in New York, Ricardo told me over a
beer that my presence in Havana had caused a major row between the UN
Cubans, who wanted me to send my reports, and the hard-liners, who saw
my presence in Havana as a national affront. Ricardo added matter-of-fact-
ly that the dispute had exposed a plan by one of the Cuban security services to see that I had an "accident" in Havana. The plan had been blocked.
More he wouldn't say.

By this time it was late summer, and planning was already starting at
the Mission for the General Assembly session that fall. There was time only
for a short trip out to join my family in Tacoma, where they'd been for most
of the summer. I spent four days with Malory and Jason in the mountains—
another reconnecting but a poor substitute for the fathering I never had the
time for in New York.

Chapter Nineteen

New York, 1979 – 1980

Sending that gutsy cable from Havana—and watching the impact it had within the U.S. Government—obliterated any remaining cautions I had on risking my career. I was doing work that I believed in, that made me fully alive, and I wasn't about to be held back by bureaucrats.

I was careful not to involve my staff in my freelancing. Henry Miller was five years in the Foreign Service and while I was willing to put my own career on the line, I wasn't willing to risk his, too. I trusted Tony Jackson as a friend, but I knew he had other masters, and I had no wish for him to have to explain me to the CIA. But keeping Tony at a distance prompted one of the worst mistakes of my life.

It had always seemed to me that Tony's effervescence was skin deep. At cocktail parties, I'd watch him charm one group of people, but then, as he walked across the room, see his face sag just for an instant before he re-connected with somebody else. Unmarried, he seemed lonely, and in his business, it was hard for him to talk personally with anyone. In retrospect, I was probably his best friend at the Mission, but my talks with him never got anywhere near as deep as they did with Dimitri, his KGB counterpart. We'd reach a point, and then Tony would veer off. I thought then that he was just protecting his job. I think now that he just didn't know how to ask for help.

The last time I saw him was on a bitter winter night just before Christmas in 1979. I'd persuaded Mimi to help host a big-deal dinner party in our Chelsea home—an evening of witty jousting that I found exciting and Mimi found a bore. Midway through the salad, the doorbell sounded. It was Tony, shivering in a light coat.

"Was just passing by," he said. "Thought I'd drop in; see how you were."

He looked terrible, like he hadn't slept in a couple of days. His eyes were bloodshot, his voice a low mumble. He lived nowhere near Chelsea. Every instinct in me said he'd made a special trip to see me and that he was in terrible trouble. Behind me I could hear salad plates being cleared and the creak of the oven door as Mimi pulled out a tray of chicken breasts in cream sauce. I could feel the cold air pushing past me into the house.

"Tony," I said, "what if I meet you for breakfast first thing tomorrow morning. We've got a ton of guests for dinner, and now's a bad time to talk."

"Sure, sure," Tony said, backing down off the porch. "That'll be fine. I can see you've got guests. Tomorrow for breakfast. That's fine. Sorry I barged in. Tomorrow for breakfast. At the cafeteria?"

"That'll be good." I said. "At the cafeteria. About eight. And look, I'm really sorry I'm so tied up... Hey, you look freezing. Can I loan you a sweater?"

"No thanks," Tony said. "I got one in the car."

The Mission security officer woke me up at 2:00 A.M. Sometime around 11:00, Tony had picked up his girlfriend and taken her to a fancy midtown hotel. In the corridor outside a room he'd rented on the eighth floor, Tony had blown out his girlfriend's brains with a .38, then stuck the barrel in his own mouth and pulled the trigger.

I went to Tony's funeral, but I sat in the back so nobody could see my face. I saw myself as healer, but when a friend had come to me in need, I'd turned him away. It hadn't been any great challenge that had pulled me off course—just the chatter of a dinner party.

How could I match the insensitivity of that night with the ideals of healing that I thought were then driving my life? Flushed with my successes at serving the world, I couldn't understand this failure to help a friend.

What I didn't see then was that my spiritual growth would never be a straight-line path. It was—and still is—take one step forward, fall down, dust myself off, look sheepishly up at God and take another step. I live with a lot of falling downs, and my role in Tony's death is one of the worst. It was months before the pain eased, and it has never really gone away.

In January, 1980, I went to Belgrade for another meeting of the Nonaligned Movement. On the last night there, Ricardo and his boss invited me out for a "real workers' meal"—meaning beans and pork and cheap red wine. To this day, I'm convinced that what happened that night with the Cubans could have freed the American hostages in Iran a year before they were finally released.

The previous November, the entire staff of the American Embassy in Teheran had been taken prisoner by mobs controlled by the Ayatollah Khomeini, and for over two months, no amount of direct threats or diplomatic pressures had worked to get them freed. America needed somebody else's good offices and to me the Cubans, with their good links to Khomeini, seemed perfect.

The plan was hatched at a run-down restaurant in the industrial section of Belgrade. To the great discomfort of the Cubans, the Yugoslav government had insisted on supplying them with a huge black chauffeured limousine for their stay. Ricardo had directed the car to park a block away from the restaurant, and we'd walked the rest of the way. "We are socialists," he'd said. "No way we drive up to a workers' restaurant in a limo."

It took a half bottle of hot sauce before the Cubans pronounced the meal acceptable. That was also when they ordered the fourth bottle of wine. About two in the morning, after a rambling discussion that covered everything from the collapse of Red Sox pitching to changing U.S. policies toward Cuba, we sketched out a deal on a napkin that would have traded Cuba's help in freeing the hostages for a loosening of the American economic embargo on their island. We all thought it was a great idea.

I was afraid the notes might have disappeared with the hangovers, but two weeks later in New York, Ricardo took me aside in the General Assembly hall and whispered: "The man says we'll do it." When I looked puzzled, Ricardo sighed in frustration, wary of people watching us. "I mean," he said very deliberately, "that Fidel Castro wants to pursue our plan. He will help free your people in Teheran."

I all but ran across the street to my office with the news, but when the Mission sent Castro's offer down to the State Department, it was rejected outright. Under pressure from right-wing Cubans in Florida, the U.S. government was not willing to give Castro the kind of PR coup he'd score if he got our people out. Nor was it ready to loosen the embargo under any circumstances. I got my knuckles rapped for encouraging the enemy.

Considering Cuba's close ties to Iran at the time, it seems likely they could have pulled off their end of the plan. The hostages were finally freed in early 1981 when the Algerians played a role almost identical to the one the Cubans and I had sketched out on that napkin in Belgrade.

The lesson for me—repeated many times since—was that my enthusiasm for doing "the right thing" didn't necessarily make others more receptive. Boldness scared more people than it attracted, and ideals raised more suspicions than they dispelled. None of this discouraged me. But it made the challenges more interesting.

In addition to my work with the Nonaligned Movement, I represented the U.S. on the Security Council committee that policed the embargo on arms sales to South Africa. That embargo—set up to help put pressure on the apartheid regime—leaked like a sieve. Too many American and Western European arms merchants were making too much money selling guns to the South African police and military.

Through the 1970s, money from arms manufacturers bought the influence needed to keep national legislatures in the U.S. and Europe from tightening the ban—even as leaders in these same countries railed against the evils of apartheid. Most Third World countries saw failures to tighten the embargo as further proof that the West was long on rhetoric and short on principle. By the time I arrived at the UN, the issue had gridlocked: Americans and Europeans ignored Third World complaints, playing lip service to an embargo that was a farce. The angry rhetoric of many Third

World states, on the other hand, was so shrill it stood no chance of being heard.

In February 1980, I flew to South Africa to see apartheid for myself. I went first to visit Robert Sobukwe, Nelson Mandela's partner in the early fights for freedom in South Africa. Sobukwe and Mandela had both been jailed for life. In 1978, dying of the tuberculosis he'd contracted in prison, Sobukwe had been released into house arrest in Kimberly, a diamond mining center in the Transvaal.

He lived in a small, one-story house on the end of a narrow treeless street on the edge of town. A police car was parked across the street, and two plain-clothes cops lounged in beach chairs beside it. Sobukwe could not leave his house, and could receive only one visitor at a time. In talking to anyone, Sobukwe had to sit in the front window where both he and his visitor could be seen by the police.

He met me at the door, walking slowly with a cane. His body was emaciated, shiny skin stretched tight across his cheekbones. Death was on his shoulder, but his eyes danced and his handshake was full of life. He motioned for me to sit down near the window, then poured two cups of tea from a metal pot.

I'd come with a list of political questions, but Sobukwe waved them away. Apartheid would end, he said impatiently, leaning across the small table that separated us, staring into my eyes. That was not the issue. The problem was how to bind the country together when it *did* end, when the fears of whites and the anger of blacks might be even greater than they were then. "As South Africans, black and white," he said, "we need to find reconciliation. We need to forgive each other."

He turned away to cough, then wiped his mouth with a handkerchief. Not once, in the course of an hour's conversation, did Sobukwe—a man who'd endured every suffering at the hands of a ruthless police state— show the slightest flicker of anger or blame. Knowing his death was near, all he wanted to talk about was forgiveness for the people who'd killed him. Reconciliation was the goal, he kept saying; anger and blame were the obstacles.

Immediately I understood why the South Africans were keeping this frail, dying man under house arrest. His personal charisma was overwhelming. It flowed not just from his fierce pursuit of justice, but from his commitment to serve, to forgive, to reconcile—and his total ability to keep his eyes on the great issues that transcended his own pain.

These qualities were what gave Sobukwe (and Nelson Mandela, it would soon be clear to the world) the power to convince others that a stable peace in South Africa demanded more than the transfer of political power. The goal had to be building a new country and that could only happen by building peace in the hearts of all South Africans, white and black. That meant forgiveness, each of the other.

What a huge, bold, impossible vision—and to hear it from a man dying under guard in a country controlled by the people who had killed him! But it happened. Against all odds, apartheid would end, Nelson Mandela would become President of South Africa and the organization he and Robert Sobukwe had created would present a breathtakingly powerful model of healing to the world. The higher purpose that guided these two men gave them the insight, compassion and courage to challenge the odds and inspire the world.

I left Sobukwe's house feeling both uplifted and incomplete. Then struggling to implement a higher purpose for my own life, I saw in Sobukwe the model I needed, and I measure myself against it still.

But, for me, Robert Sobukwe was not just a model of morality. He was a model of manhood, one completely different from those of my youth. Men like Roy on the *Golden Bear*, the foreign Legionnaires in Algeria and the other swashbucklers I'd admired, all had a physical toughness and bravado that was seductive to me when I was young. Then Ben Lomond had suggested a new model, one that combined toughness with compassion. Now here was its avatar. Hacking out his tubercular lungs, Robert Sobukwe never doubted the outcome of his work. As I drove away from his house, past the huge open pit mine that gave the town its name, all I could think about was that this delicate, dying man was much tougher than all the heroes of my youth put together, and tougher than I had ever been.

From Kimberly I went to Johannesburg and, the next morning, to the segregated black township of Soweto just outside the city. I watched blacks lining up for buses that would take them to serve drinks and clean swimming pools in areas of the city where they could not live. I saw miles of tin-roofed shacks, piles of uncollected garbage and bands of teenagers, looking for trouble. I felt angry eyes boring into my back. A few hours later, I was at a diplomatic cocktail party in Johannesburg's fanciest white suburb, in a mansion surrounded by iron fences and guard dogs.

Apartheid stank.

And Western refusals to tighten the embargo on arms to the masters of apartheid stank even more. Returning from the trip to South Africa, I finally saw something I could do: I would use my position on the Security Council to make the arms embargo work.

"What if," I said one afternoon to Thuelo Mbeki, a Zambian friend on the arms embargo committee, "you and the others had an insider—me—in the American government willing to help you strengthen the embargo? I'm willing to tell you what I think will put real pressure on my own government. Then you turn the screws. Then I follow up with my own arguments to the State Department. Once we've got the U.S. on board, the British, the French and the Germans will have no choice but to go along. Why not? All we do now on this committee is posture. You guys scream at us, and we play innocent, and the arms are still getting through. It's crap, Thuelo. This is a chance to bust things loose."

At six feet two and at least 250 pounds, Thuelo looked like he belonged in an NFL backfield. He shifted in his chair. "Sure," he said, eyeing me carefully. "I'll do it. But first I want to know why *you're* doing this. I know how you feel about apartheid, but this could get you sacked. And there are people in my government who'll say I'm being duped."

"Look," I answered, "I'm not stupid. I'm not going to give you anything with my fingerprints on it. And why *not* take a bit of a risk?"

Two days later I sat down with Mbeki and outlined the strategies I thought would work to force the U.S. and others to tighten the embargo. Over the next few weeks, I convinced the Filipinos that a tough position on tightening the embargo would play well back home as a low-cost way to show some independence from the United States. I suggested to the Bolivians and the Bangladeshis ways they could forcefully remind the U.S. of Carter's election promises.

It worked. Messages began to come in from American ambassadors in the Third World, describing an "upsurge in pressure" to strengthen the arms embargo against South Africa. Once, Secretary of State Vance received a strong message from an African Foreign Minister that I myself had helped draft two weeks before.

When the wires from abroad were humming, I started writing my own memos, suggesting to my bosses that it was now time to take on the conservatives in Congress, and the arms lobbies. To keep ignoring such determined pressure from the Third World, I argued, would make it doubly hard for President Carter to convince anyone that his crusade for human rights was real.

That worked too. The State Department caved. Unwilling to stay out on a limb, the British, French and Germans went along, grumbling all the way. A tougher embargo was adopted in April of 1980, and, in time, it helped end apartheid.

The caper didn't stop there, although it would have been better if it had. When the arms embargo committee gathered to celebrate, the chairman, Ambassador Mahmoud from Bangladesh, ordered the tape recorders turned off. After he'd congratulated everyone on the victory, he turned in my direction. "We all know the role Mr. Graham played," he said, "and we are very grateful."

The European delegates glared at me, now hearing proof of a role they'd suspected but never been able to prove. I'd started to respond to the ambassador, when a big hand gently pushed me back in my seat and Mbeki added his personal thanks, describing his friendship with me in ways I never knew he felt. Three more Third World delegates followed him, each speaking with a candor and emotion that I never heard in any UN session, before or since.

All three European missions made official complaints to the U.S. Mission the next day. With no taped record of the meeting, however, they still couldn't prove I'd done anything out of school. Nor could my own government. I would have been fired if the State Department had discovered my plan—even though all I'd done was force my own government to honor its own policies against apartheid.

My role in strengthening the arms embargo against South Africa was perhaps the bravest thing I'd ever done. In part, I took those risks because I was inspired by Robert Sobukwe and angered by the contrast between the squalor and oppression in Soweto and the defended wealth of white suburbs in Johannesburg.

But at a deeper level, I stuck my neck out to help end apartheid for the same reason I'd risked my career to openly criticize my own country's policies in the Third World, to open dialogues with America's opponents, and to involve Castro in freeing U.S. hostages in Iran. I took these risks because fighting for justice in the Third World was part of the higher purpose that by then was guiding my life and giving it meaning. In the end, the motivation was so strong, I couldn't *not* do what I did.

The experience was like learning to swim. I couldn't forget what I'd done or how to do it. I couldn't forget the joy and fulfillment I felt in making a difference like that.

There were other lessons that last heady year at the UN. One of them was about handling the roar of the crowd.

I felt very good about what I'd done to pursue my own foreign policy at the UN. Others were noticing—not just those who wanted to squash me, but many who praised me for what I was doing and how I was doing it. I fed on the praise, and part of me was starting to see myself as a knight on a white horse. What I failed to see, as my actions attracted more and more attention, was that the praise was becoming *too* important, and that my mission as healer was only distracted by the sound of applause.

But I was coming to love that sound.

In May 1980, I agreed to speak at a symposium on Cuba at Riverside Church, a center of liberal politics in Manhattan. It was clear that the far-left organizers of the event had invited a government officer only to provide token "balance" to a panel of prominent pro-Castro speakers who would then tee off on my remarks.

That's not the speech they got. I delivered a blistering condemnation of my own government's policy on Cuba that brought the two thousand people to their feet. The lefties on the panel could only mumble their agreement.

I thought it was a great speech. In many ways it was. But it was also an irresponsible speech, raising hopes about shifts in American policies toward Cuba which were totally unjustified. In retrospect, I'd gotten swept up by my fifteen minutes of fame. Andy Young called me into his office the next morning, mad at having to repair the mess I'd made. "Look," he said, pointing to a press account of my speech, "there's room for only one preacher at this Mission—and it's me, not you."

Stung by my mistake, I stayed close to my desk for a week. Selflessness had never been one of my virtues. But it didn't take a lot of introspection to see that ego could undermine a mission far more meaningful to me than seeing my name in lights.

At home, Mimi seemed more distant after my successes at the UN, even though I knew she shared my political views. I guessed then that there were two possibilities. Either she thought I was grandstanding at the UN—and was the same glib phony she'd long thought I was. Or she accepted that the feelings and ideals I was putting into my work were real—and she resented my not bringing them to our marriage.

I don't know what the truth was for her then, and I still don't know. A year or so after we'd finally split, she came to my apartment in the West Village to pick up something that belonged to her. She knew that I was by then very much involved in the peace movement, speaking and writing. I can still see her hesitating on the landing, outside the heavy black door. "I'm sorry I wasn't married to this person," she'd said softly, and left.

In 1980, however, we were still married. New insights and commitments were about to shatter old patterns and our marriage would be one of them. My career in the Foreign Service, however, would end first.

By mid-1980, I'd spent nearly three years at the United Nations, focused not on serving America's interests as defined for me by the State Department but on finding real answers to problems of war, injustice and poverty in the Third World. I'd tried to build trust inside an untrusting system, to create honest dialogues that reached the core of the issues, and to move people to take risks to implement solutions that would work. My freelancing had succeeded more than I had any right to expect, and everything I'd done had made my life meaningful, responsible and happy in ways I'd struggled to find ever since Vietnam.

The State Department should have fired me. Given the discipline it demanded, I was a growing threat, not just for what I'd done, but for how I'd done it and for the example I'd set for others. The cable I'd sent from Havana, the South African arms embargo caper, my friendships with Cubans and with a KGB agent…all were way past the limit where my elders might pat me on the back for courageous dissents and colorful idiosyncrasies. Graham was now nearing the senior ranks and it was time for him to be a team player.

But a team player was not who I was, not by that point in my life. My path was the path of a healer, and I needed to go wherever that path led. My assignments both in Vietnam and at the UN had given me huge amounts of autonomy that I couldn't expect to enjoy anywhere else—a fact that became very clear when Andy Young was fired and I found myself under the heavy thumb of his replacement, a dull academic.

Ever since getting slapped down for dealing with the Cubans over the Iran hostages, it had been clear to me that the State Department was too top-down, bureaucratic and unimaginative for me to survive for the long term. I'd become too good at operating on my own, and accustomed to that freedom. It was also clear that, once in the senior ranks, my moves would be watched more closely and the pressures on me to conform would increase.

Another factor was politics. When the Ayatollah's minions had taken the American hostages in Teheran, a kinder, gentler American policy toward the Third World was no longer politically supportable in Washington—if it ever really was. Most of Jimmy Carter's promises went unfulfilled, and what he and Andrew Young did manage to accomplish would not soon be repeated. Asked to write yet another speech defending timid American policies, I sat at my desk, aiming paper clips into a wastebasket and smoking so many pipefuls of strong tobacco that my mouth tasted like an ashtray. My political views were already to the left of a Democratic president. If Ronald Reagan won the election that November, how could I possibly carry out the policies of a Republican Administration?

The State Department made the choice easier. They refused to extend my tour at the U.S. Mission and ordered me into a temporary exile where I would be neither seen nor heard from for years. I was given a choice—either I could go to the Congo as Chief Political Officer or I could quit.

If I went to the Congo and stayed in the Service—and somehow kept from rocking more boats—in five or six years I'd be Ambassador to a small African country, at the mercy of a bureaucratic world in Washington that would force one crippling compromise after another. And if I somehow managed to hang on to my ideals through all of that, in ten more years I'd be part of the power structure myself. But the highest a Foreign Service Officer could rise in the State Department was the Number Three job. Real power was held by elected officials and their appointees, no matter how incompetent or ideological they might be. Even if I survived in the Foreign Service, I would always be taking orders from *somebody* who probably wouldn't share my views. I couldn't see myself doing that.

I had a higher purpose that gave meaning to my life. I was a healer. By June of 1980 it seemed clear that to serve that purpose I needed more independence than the Foreign Service would ever allow. If I was going to make a difference, I knew then I couldn't do it following somebody else's plan, not even Jimmy Carter's. It had to come from what was burning in my own core.

I never presented quitting the Foreign Service to Mimi as an option, because I knew that nothing she could say or do would change my mind. I told her that I intended to quit, and why. She was strangely passive, other than saying that, if I *did* stay in the Service, she would not go with me to any more jungles or deserts. If I went to the Congo, I would go alone. She did not complain about the financial risks of my quitting; we both knew that she could go with the kids back to Tacoma any time she wanted, where her wealthy parents would always be a safety net.

I mailed my resignation on June 15. When I put the envelope in my outbox, I had no clear idea of next steps. All I had was a conviction that I could figure it out.

The next day I called my parents. My father had never stopped living through my achievements and he was stunned when I told him I was leaving a successful diplomatic career to follow my heart into a very uncertain future. And that I was leaving five years short of the 20 years needed to vest a government pension was madness to him. He urged me to stick it out for those five years no matter how I felt about the job.

I felt angry listening to him suggesting I should sidetrack my life just to collect a pension. In retrospect he was simply being who he was—the man who'd turned down the job at the *Honolulu Herald* when his dreams were still intact, who'd crippled whatever ambition remained with drink, and then let the Great Depression trap him into a dead-end career that paid the bills.

My mother said very little, other than to agree with my father about the pension. Neither of them seemed to have heard anything I'd said about my reasons for quitting. That was no surprise, given how little I'd shared with them about my life over the previous fifteen years. To both of them, I think, I was still the kid in the Harvard cap and gown, out to make a name in the world they understood.

In late June, the State Department set September 1 as my final day.

Chapter Twenty

The *Prinsendam*, 1980

For fifteen years, the Foreign Service had been my life. It had given me adventures and status beyond even the wildest dreams I'd conjured in Tennant Creek, sitting by my campfire, blundering into the future. What I'd wanted then was a way I could keep adventuring, but in ways that would make me powerful, that would boost me above the bullies of my youth. The Foreign Service had delivered on this—and now I was quitting because the dreams I'd had fifteen years before had been replaced by other dreams, ones that gave my life meaning beyond my youthful images of what it meant to be a man.

I was committed to go where my heart was leading, and I knew I couldn't do that working for the government. But the more I thought about what I was leaving, the more naked and alone I felt. I looked out the window of my office toward the UN buildings across the street and wondered: shorn of all the Foreign Service meant to me—who was I? What would my life be like?

As the summer lengthened, money worries pushed into my mind like a fat man into a crowded elevator. I'd decided to quit solely on the basis of where I felt my life was headed. I'd done no financial planning—I'd simply trusted that, if I went where my heart was leading, the money would follow.

When, over lunch, I told my KGB friend Dmitri about my plans to quit, his soft oval face broke into a rare smile. On opposite sides in the Cold War, we each kept up a delicate dance at the UN between what our ideals called us to do and what our masters demanded. It was still that dance that drew us together, in the quiet space behind our eyes. Now I was leaving the dance, and Dmitri wished me all the best.

The day of our lunch, he seemed sadder and more tired than usual. I knew he opposed his country's recent invasion of Afghanistan even as he read speeches defending it. Unlike me, however, Dmitri couldn't leave his dance. He could only stop dancing, and that is what he did. On July 12th, A few weeks after I'd last seen him, I got a midnight call from the same Mission security officer who'd notified me of Tony's death seven months before. This time, when I got to the Mission, I was taken into a small room and grilled by three men from the FBI. Dmitri had left the UN early that afternoon, locked himself in his bedroom and chug-a-lugged vodka until his heart stopped. The FBI said it was suicide.

Tony, now Dmitri, both victims of a sadness that destroyed them from inside. I never knew what made Tony sad, but perhaps he, like Dmitri, simply couldn't keep up the dance between what was in his spirit and what he was paid to do. It was no coincidence both men were intelligence agents— two good people paid to prey on the weaknesses of others.

It was Dmitri's death that finally pushed me to start planning for my own future. I had choices that he didn't, and I needed to start making them. Mimi and I had saved very little of my modest government pay. My severance check would amount to less than $20,000, which wouldn't last long, especially if we stayed in New York. I needed to find a new source of income, even if the search delayed my efforts to save the world. I had the whole rest of my life ahead, I told myself. Wouldn't it be better to start my mission without having to worry about money?

Making money shouldn't be hard, I thought. Over the long term, I could make money from speaking fees and book advances, but it might be years before those sources could pay the bills. In the short term, I knew there was good money to be made advising international banks and corporations on the political risks of investing in the Third World. With my contacts and experience in the Third World, I could make as much in an hour as a consultant than I'd made in a day in the Foreign Service. I knew two or three foreign ministers personally, and scores of lesser officials. I knew how to maneuver through bureaucracies from Dakar to Karachi. I had friends all over Washington D.C.

I printed up a slick brochure, complete with glowing recommendations from VIPs. The State Department gave me time off to start talking to prospective clients. I stayed behind in New York that August to launch my new business, while Mimi and the kids went back to Tacoma without me.

A consulting business could have worked for me. The trouble was, I couldn't take making money for corporations as a serious goal. I didn't give a damn if those companies sold more bonds or cars or if they pumped more oil. What I cared about was how they could use their power and influence to help bring more peace and justice to the countries in which they operated. I looked at engines of greed and saw engines for social change. The results of this mismatch were predictable. I was shown in plenty of doors— and shown out as soon as I opened my mouth.

Some of my failures that summer were embarrassing. Given a great chance to showcase my new business before a hotel ballroom full of top executives, I lectured them on the evils of apartheid. Ten people clapped. My first real client agreed to pay me $500 to talk to him about investing in Angola over breakfast at the Plaza Hotel. He didn't show and I ended up paying $43 for the ham and eggs. My consulting career ended before it ever began. Desperate, I interviewed for jobs at Citibank and Bankers' Trust— bureaucracies far more deadening than the Foreign Service. Both banks turned me down.

Then a friend tipped me to the possibility of lecturing on cruise ships. He'd heard that cruise lines were looking for professional people with interesting stories, and that they paid well.

How bad could that be? I could do a couple of cruises now, make a little money, collect my thoughts—*then* pursue my ideals. And if it worked, what would be wrong with living on cruise ships for part of every year and saving the world in the off-season?

I saw what I was doing. I heard my prattle. And I wondered what had happened to the courage that had propelled me through all the risks I'd just taken at the United Nations. I was just being practical now, I told myself, ignoring the fact that if I'd "just been practical," I would have taken none of those risks. By late summer my job search reflected more panic than prudence. I felt ashamed about it, but saw no other course.

On my first try, I landed a job with Holland American Lines. My first ship, the *Prinsendam*, would be leaving from Vancouver for Alaska and Tokyo on October 3. I'd be a member of the ship's entertainment staff and be paid $2,000 for two half-hour talks. I could take my spouse. I took my daughter Malory instead, who was then thirteen.

With a contract for my speeches signed, I was breathing a little easier when my career in the Foreign Service formally ended, after fifteen years, two months, and ten days. On October 1, Malory and I flew out to Vancouver to join the ship.

Small by today's standards, the *Prinsendam* carried 320 passengers and 204 crew, including me and a dozen singers from a touring company of *Oklahoma!* She was then the newest ship in the Holland American fleet. With the latest in navigation and safety gear, she was, said the company's brochure, unsinkable.

For the first three days, the ship picked her way slowly north through the Inland Passage into Alaskan waters, stopping in Glacier Bay and Sitka before heading out across the North Pacific. Malory had my total attention, and the two of us explored the ship from bilges to bridge. Of course it all rekindled memories of another sea adventure, now more than two decades behind me. My daughter listened to all the stories she'd heard before about her father, "just a little older than you are now," shipping out, wide-eyed and expectant, aboard the *Golden Bear*. That trip had launched the first part of my life and the *Prinsendam*, I thought, would launch the second. I had no idea how right I would be.

On the fourth night, as the ship picked up speed in the open sea, the wait staff distributed Dramamine at dinner. The tail end of Typhoon Vernon would hit us at dawn, they said, and the seas would be rough for at least the day.

The day came early.

The ship's firebell jerked me awake like a telephone call in the night.

"Attention passengers," said a calm, insistent voice over the public address system. "Attention passengers."

I rolled over and opened my eyes. The clock said 1:30. I'd been in my bunk for an hour.

"We have a small fire in the engine room," the voice said. "It is under control, and there is no danger. I repeat—there is no danger. However, we ask all passengers to come up to the promenade deck while the smoke is being cleared. We are very sorry for this inconvenience."

I was tired. I could smell no smoke in Cabin 416. I ignored the message and lay back on the bunk, listening to the throb of the engines.

"Passengers are requested to proceed at once to the promenade deck," repeated the voice, this time with an edge. I sat up and flicked the light switch at the head of the bunk. Nothing happened. I opened the door to let in some light from the emergency bulbs in the passageway, and in the dimness saw my tuxedo jacket where I'd left it, thrown across a chair. The pants were on the floor, on top of a crumpled shirt. Two hours before I'd been in the ship's nightclub, making small talk on the dance floor. It was, I'd been told the first day out, part of my job. If I'd left the Foreign Service to save the world, for the moment I was doing it one blue-haired widow at a time.

"Attention passengers," the voice over the PA system began again.

"Malory, wake up," I said, reaching across the narrow cabin and giving the familiar lump under the blanket a gentle shake. "Wake up."

Malory sat up, rubbing her eyes, and we both listened as the message was repeated: no instruction to dress warmly or to bring life vests—just come to the promenade deck.

"What's it mean, Dad?" she asked.

"I don't know, Mal," I answered. "But I think we better get dressed and do what they say." We pulled on jeans and shirts, then thin windbreakers. On the way out the door I noticed that the sound of the engines had stopped. The *Prinsendam* was dead in the water.

"Dad, we can't get through," yelled Malory from down the passageway, pointing to an automatic firedoor which had slammed shut across our path to the main stairs. I stopped pulling on my jacket zipper. How could a "small fire" short out the cabin lights, stop the engines and trigger the firedoors? The first curls of acrid, brown smoke began drifting in front of the light bulbs.

We headed in the opposite direction, slowly making our way to a forward stairwell now clogged with jittery, coughing people, a few of them still in pajamas and robes. The smoke coming up from below was thicker than it had been in the passageway, and smelled of burning paint and insulation. I thought of going back for our life vests but crewmen in oxygen masks hurried us onward.

On the promenade deck, passengers huddled in deck chairs or stood in small groups. Some of them had pulled cloths off the tables in the ship's lounge, now filled with smoke, and were using them as blankets. Malory and I sat in a corner of the darkened deck, and I hugged her.

The air, on this October night in the Gulf of Alaska, was cold but clear. A few people seemed to be crying softly. There were a few nervous wisecracks. Other than that, the ship was eerily silent. There was no moon. A dancing green belt of Northern Lights lit the sky, so bright it hid the stars. Beneath, a dark, still ocean spread in all directions.

Every ten minutes the loudspeaker voice assured us that the danger had passed. But any fool could see that the smoke billowing up from the stairwells had gotten blacker and thicker since we'd climbed through it. This was no small fire and it was not under control.

"May I have your attention, please," said a new loudspeaker voice with a throaty Dutch accent. "This is the captain. We have succeeded in sealing the engine room and have flooded it with carbon dioxide foam. The fire should now choke itself out. It will take more time to clear the smoke. In the meantime, please move to the stern of the ship. Thank you for your patience."

A murmur of relief, then of anger, washed across the crowded deck. In the morning, I thought, they would tell us how serious it had really been.

In fact, the ship was already doomed. The first distress signal had been sent out at 1:15, and even as we huddled on a cold deck, an armada of rescue ships, planes and helicopters had been organized and was heading in our direction. Five hundred people, most of them elderly, were trapped on a burning ship 140 miles from land, in the most dangerous part of the North Pacific, with a typhoon bearing down on them. To the Coast Guard and Air Force officers then planning the rescue, it was a disaster in the making.

Malory and I moved with the passengers to the outdoor cafe at the ship's stern, and helped set up tables and chairs. Strings of colored lights from the evening's cocktail party broke the darkness. Booze flowed. The ship's orchestra had formed up on the shuffleboard court, but whatever good feelings its music raised were overwhelmed by dread for anybody who knew the story of the *Titanic*. At least *this* orchestra played show tunes, not *Nearer My God to Thee*. Malory and I sat back, munching peanuts.

Any optimism created by the captain's message was short-lived—the smoke spilling up from the stairwells kept getting blacker and thicker. Worse, heavy dark smoke was now coming up the outside of the ship's hull and curling over onto the deck. There was no way that the fire had been contained. Somewhere, below, it was eating away at the ship. A man in silk pajamas and a camel's hair blazer demanded to know what was going on. Nobody answered him.

Just before 4:30, the ship's purser pulled me aside. "Don't tell your daughter and don't tell the passengers," he said, "but the dining room is burning. Help us move the passengers to the sides of the ship. A helicopter is going to drop more firefighting gear and we need a clear deck."

The dining room was only one deck down. If it was burning, then the firewalls around the engine room had been breached.

Fifteen minutes later the center of the stern deck was clear, with the passengers huddled along the rails on either side. A helicopter hovered over the deck, sweeping the ship with its searchlights. Slowly, a pallet of CO_2 canisters swung down at the end of a cable. When the canisters had been stowed, crewmen began passing out life vests.

There were a few wails, but by and large, no panic. The man in the camel's hair blazer sat silently, a glass of whiskey in his hand, his eyes un-focused. Several of the *Oklahoma!* singers started belting out songs from the show and urged people to sing along. Not many did. Suddenly, in mid-verse, one of the strings of colored lights broke loose from the deck above and came crashing down, just missing an old couple trying to cinch their life vests. Bulbs shattered in showers of sparks. This time people screamed. The music stopped.

"Please do not panic," the captain's voice said over the loudspeakers. "Proceed directly to your lifeboat stations. I repeat, there is no cause for panic."

Malory and I were assigned to Boat #2, far up on the port bow.

We edged forward through a crowd of frightened people. Looking through dark windows into the lounge, we saw flames for the first time. On the deck above us, crewmen were knocking away the restraining pins on the lifeboats with sledgehammers. Winches clanked, ropes flew. One by one along the port side, three lifeboats swung out over the water, then were lowered from their davits until they were level with the deck where we stood.

A young Dutch officer, apparently in command of Lifeboat #2, ordered his Indonesian crew to strip back the canvas cover. The boat was thirty feet long by ten wide. It was entirely open except for a tiny radio shack in the bow. A narrow wooden bench curved down each side. A dozen more benches straddled the boat. There was no motor. A sign in the bow said in red block letters that the boat's capacity was sixty. I asked Malory to count how many people were waiting at Lifeboat Station #2. "Ninety-two," she said.

No sooner had the seamen peeled back the canvas cover than a dull explosion rocked the ship, followed by the shattering of glass. The heat had blown out the windows in the dining room and lounge. The fire gulped the rush of oxygen, and within seconds flames were leaping twenty feet into the night sky.

Malory didn't move a muscle and didn't say a word, staring into the flames. Tongues of fire reflected in her dark eyes. "When the going gets tough, Mal..." I began, dredging up a chestnut I'd taught her in the mountains years before.

"I know, Dad," she answered with a weak smile. "The tough get going."

Malory was cool, but others weren't. Now panic was in the air, like coal dust before a mine explosion. Jammed back against the railings by the flames, a few people screamed. Others moaned quietly. A panic would have pushed people into the water, but to be in the Gulf of Alaska, at night, in October, meant death in minutes. Even if you could swim, you'd die from hypothermia. "Oh my good Jesus," a woman said softly just behind us.

Now the captain appeared on the bridge, in full-dress uniform, with a bullhorn in his hand. "I regret to inform you," he said slowly, his Dutch accent somehow adding authority to his words, "that the fire is now completely out of control. We must now abandon the ship. Please follow the instructions of the crew."

The ship's six lifeboats and four life rafts began to load. There were goats, and there were heroes. At our station, many of the Indonesian crewmen pushed passengers out of the way to jump into the lifeboat first, and their Dutch officers did nothing to stop them. But other people gently lifted infirm or very old passengers into the boat, and wrapped them in blankets. Malory and I got into the boat almost last, wedging ourselves onto a bench near the starboard bow.

The crewmen on the deck above paid out the ropes unevenly, so the lifeboat began to careen from side to side as it went down, banging hard against the side of the ship on each swing. Several of us on the starboard side tried to fend off the ship with our hands and shoulders, trying to keep the impacts from tossing someone out of the overcrowded boat, or cracking its sides.

We hit the water with a dull thud. It was 5:30 A.M. and very dark. The sea was calm so the little boat floated low but well, even overloaded, and being packed together helped keep us warm. Within minutes, the other boats and rafts were in the water too. The *Prinsendam* also had two motorized tenders, whose job in an evacuation was to string the lifeboats together, once in the water, and tow them to the ships that would answer the SOS. One of the tenders got hung up in the lines that were lowering it to the promenade deck, and dangled helplessly at a 45-degree angle. The second tender managed to load passengers and make it to the water, but its tow ropes were rotten and broke at the first pull. So the *Prinsendam*'s six lifeboats and four rafts, none of them with power, began to drift away from the burning ship, and from each other. In these tiny craft, and the tender, were 475 passengers and crew, huddled, wondering, waiting for the dawn. The captain and fifty of the crew had stayed on board in what would be a hopeless effort to put out the fire and save the ship.

We'd been in the water no more than half an hour, when a stiff breeze began to blow from the west and dark clouds erased the Northern Lights. The lifeboat began to roll gently in a light chop. Typhoon Vernon was on schedule. It didn't take a seaman to know that a storm of any size would be fatal to a small boat as crowded as ours. Any rescue would have to beat the storm.

The darkness, clouds and wind fanned the fears in that little boat. We were in the middle of the Gulf of Alaska, 140 miles from the nearest land. Nobody was dressed for the cold, let alone for an oncoming storm that could swamp us. There was no cover. Rain was already beginning to fall, sharp pellets so cold they stung the skin. Wind and currents continued to push us further away from the other boats and from the *Prinsendam*.

Crammed against each other, Malory and I tried to doze. Unfortunately, the guy in the camel's hair blazer was in our lifeboat; he was outraged again and he wouldn't stop mouthing off about how he was going to send a letter to the president of the shipping line. Someone near him started a singalong and drowned him out with a chorus of *Old Man River*.

There were twenty members of the crew in the boat, mostly Indonesian cooks and stewards who whined and complained louder than anybody else. None of the Dutch officers aboard took charge. Suddenly, one of the stewards stood up in that overloaded boat—a very bad idea. Panicked out of his wits, he screamed in broken English that we were all going to die. A wave of fear washed over the boat, drenching us like seawater.

A woman in her seventies immediately stood up next to the panicked crewman, slapped him hard across the face, and ordered him to sit. The man stopped yelling and stared at her, stunned, while she lectured him on his behavior. He sat down, shamefaced. The moment of panic passed. The singing resumed.

It was a lesson in leadership I never forgot. That woman was fully aware of the dangers. And I don't think she was without fear—anyone who *wasn't* afraid in that lifeboat, feeling the cold deaden their limbs, watching the storm coming on, wasn't human.

But I'd waltzed that woman around the dance floor eight hours before, and I had a sense of what moved her. She was from one of New Jersey's oldest families. With three hundred years of family pride in her veins, to her any crisis was a call to action; panic was unthinkable. Where the crewman saw only saving his own skin, this woman saw service.

She also sensed, I'm sure, that when that steward had panicked, some of the passengers had started to panic too, since they figured he was a member of the crew and therefore must know what the real dangers were. So this woman quickly became a more powerful model of how to deal with fear.

Storm clouds masked the rising sun, but at 7:00 A.M. the tanker *Williamsburgh* appeared on the horizon, answering the SOS. The *Prinsendam's* motorized tender maneuvered alongside the huge ship, her passengers clambering up a forty-foot rope ladder swaying in the wind.

But the *Prinsendam's* lifeboats and rafts had no engines. We couldn't reach the *Williamsburgh* and the behemoth was too big to maneuver to us. Worse, we were now widely scattered, just as the storm was moving in. As the swells grew, we could see each other only from the crests.

But there was no mistaking the sight and sound of the three helicopters that also appeared at first light. Each hovered over a lifeboat, lowering a metal chair at the end of a cable, like the ones that whirl screaming kids around at county fairs.

In Lifeboat #2 we waited forever for our turn. When a helicopter finally hovered fifty feet above our stern, we just looked at each other, uncertain who should go first. The only guidance any of us had came from the movies: "Women and children first."

And so it went. Two men grabbed the chair as it came down, helped the first woman belt herself in, then signaled to the chopper to hoist her up, spinning and swaying in the wind. Seven more women were taken up the same way, before the helicopter flew off to the deck of the *Williamsburgh*.

The rest of us cheered. An old man in a dark overcoat threw his flashlight into the ocean—as it turned out, the only one we had. "We'll not be needing that now," he said, watching the helicopter. I wasn't so sure. The choppers went as fast as they could, but there were still hundreds of people in the boats and steadily rising winds and seas slowed the rescues, making each trip more difficult and dangerous.

More and more waves were now breaking over the sides of the boat, soaking clothes and blankets and numbing us with cold. A yachtsman named Dick showed us how to rig a sea anchor by lashing together the few oars in the boat and every other loose thing we could find and dragging it behind us at the end of a rope. That pulled the stern around so we hit the waves more head on. For a time it helped.

Malory and the woman from New Jersey were the last women to be lifted off Lifeboat #2, about 3:00 that afternoon.

That left thirty-two men. Four helicopter loads. Our sea anchor had by now been ripped away, and we were now drifting broadside into the waves. Every ten seconds buckets of icewater broke over us. We kept bailing, but as the little boat pitched more strongly in the storm, letting go our holds became more and more dangerous.

When the helicopter returned, the Indonesian crewmen went first. We were sick of their whining. So eight crewmen went, then a second eight.

That left sixteen—twelve passengers, three Dutch officers—and me. Two helicopter loads. It was now 5:00 P.M. Rain lashed the little boat, driving through our clothes. Visibility was less than a hundred yards. Winds were gusting fifty knots or more. The waves were mountainous. How the helicopter found us for the next trip I'll never know. The pilot fought to keep his machine stable over the lifeboat, but he had to hover low, risking downdrafts, to have any chance of getting the rescue chair on target.

The situation in the lifeboat was desperate. Waves slammed into the little boat and the half-inch planks bent inward with an awful creaking sound. Spray lashed our faces and the bitter salt tasted like our fear. Each time the chopper got close, we had to grab with frozen fingers at a twenty-pound metal chair swinging wildly in the wind, without getting smashed in the head or flung out of the pitching boat. Eight times the pilot brought that metal basket down. Eight times we got it. Eight times another body went swinging up into the helicopter, with the rotors pounding over the roar of the storm. On the final pass, the pilot sent down a note that he would radio our position to the two Coast Guard cutters steaming in our direction—but that he could not come back. It would be suicidal to challenge the storm again from the air. We watched the helicopter disappear into the storm, and waited for the cutters, now the only chance we had.

I struggled hand-over-hand to the radio shack and tried to power up the radio. The battery was dead. The SOS I was tapping on the telegraph key was going nowhere. The lifeboat had a light, but it was powered by the same battery as the radio. There were no flares.

It was now 5:30. We'd been in the lifeboat twelve hours. The choppers had gone for good. The critical factor now was not Typhoon Vernon but the fading light. There was a small enough chance that the cutters would find us in the storm in daylight. But the chances of finding us at night—with no flares, no lights and no radio—were nonexistent, and the cold would kill us before the dawn. Our fates would be sealed by the darkness, now an hour off.

By 6:00 P.M. visibility was down to fifty yards. In the bow, facing the oncoming seas, I watched thirty-foot waves tower above us in every trough, then braced myself as they flung the boat skyward and rammed it down again. The wind ripped off the tops of the waves, sending seawater into the lifeboat so cold it sucked the breath out of us.

We bailed furiously, but how much longer could we last? The eight of us were all deathly seasick. There was no cover. My windbreaker was the heaviest jacket anyone had. All of us were hypothermic. It was taking every bit of energy we had just to stay in the boat. If we weren't rescued before the cold drained that energy, one of three things would happen: we would die of hypothermia where we sat, we would be thrown out of the boat, or the boat would swamp.

None of us talked, or even tried to. There was nothing more we could do. We clung to the benches, dry-heaved our guts out, bailed—and waited.

The winds blew stronger; the waves rose higher; the rain hit harder. An old man who'd refused rescue earlier—the same one who'd thrown away the flashlight—told me he had emphysema and put his head on my lap to die. I recognized the progression of hypothermia in me, and in the others. The cold had now become less painful. A certain calm was setting in; it would be followed by an enormous temptation to sleep, a sleep from which none of us would wake.

It was time to take stock.

Up until that moment, I'd assumed that this crisis, like all the others in my life, would take me to the brink of death but not beyond. It was another adrenaline rush, another adventure that I would walk away from with another story. The stories always ended the same way—I survived. Even when that last helicopter had left, I'd figured there'd be another way out. There always was. That was the lesson from the McKinley River.

But sometime after 6:00 P.M., as gray seas merged with gray sky, it occurred to me that this time I was actually going to die.

Before when I'd come close to death, I'd never had time to think about it. All the other near misses—bullets, avalanches, falls—had been swift and swiftly over. This time I had half an hour before my fate was sealed by darkness—then maybe three or four more hours before I was dead. It was all the time in the world.

I tried to talk to God, to the universal presence. My intent was not to beg for my life, but to put myself back in that place of light I'd first reached in Sara Bassett's living room. I just wanted to check in, to find out what was going on, to make sure there was no mistake.

I never got to that place of light. Every time I closed my eyes and tried to drift there, I was pulled back by anger. The more I thought about it, my dying now *must* be a mistake. In the years since Vietnam, I'd slowly crawled out of an unconscious, self-centered hole. Now I was about to put everything I'd learned to work to make a better world—I'd even left the Foreign Service so I could devote myself to this new life. So how was it that now, on the brink of this beginning, I was being wiped out? I'd always assumed there was an order and logic to the universe. But my death now didn't make any sense. It didn't make one damn bit of sense. I had a right to know what was going on. I glared into the teeth of the storm and hurled one word into the slashing rain: "Why?"

The answer came at once, not as a physical sound that others could hear but as a voice that enveloped me as if I was standing inside a circle of loudspeakers.

"There will be no mystery in your death," the voice said, in so many words. "You know your purpose is to heal but now you are fleeing it. You tried a consulting business, then a job at a bank, now a cruise ship. If you get out of this alive you'll find something else to pull you away from what you know your life is about.

"You have a choice. You can choose not to live your ideals, and you'll die out here, and that will be better than a lifetime of excuses and regrets.

Or you can get serious about your life's purpose and do what you know you need to do."

I looked at the other seven shapes in that lifeboat. None of them seemed to have heard anything. Then I looked back into the storm. I was so seasick I couldn't even dry heave. I could hardly feel my feet and hands. I was exhausted, dying of the cold. I had nothing left.

"OK," I mumbled, looking straight into the storm, rain lashing my face. "OK."

What happened next sounds straight out of a grade-B movie, but it's the truth. At that instant of surrender, a dark shape burst out of the storm off the port bow. It was the Coast Guard cutter *Boutwell*, heading right at us. The searchlight picked us up before the cutter sliced us in two.

The ship used sideways-pushing engines to edge as near to the lifeboat as possible without capsizing us. A seaman threw us a rope. Somehow with wooden fingers I caught it and tied it to a cleat on the bow, but an instant later a huge wave ripped off both the cleat and the entire board it was fastened to. Water rushed in over the shattered wood. The lifeboat began to founder. I stared, unable to react. Just as the storm began to toss us away from the cutter, two frogmen rappelled into the boat and fixed lines that held.

Four Coast Guardsmen on the deck of the cutter manned a heavy ten-foot pole, at the end of which was a strong rope noose. The old man with emphysema went first. The frogmen in the lifeboat fitted the noose around his chest, then drew it tight. Timing the waves perfectly, the seamen on the cutter's deck heaved up on the pole just as the lifeboat was cresting. The man took off like a shot, flying through the air onto the cutter's deck. When my turn came, I landed heavily on the deck and was immediately wrapped in a blanket and hustled below.

I gave my name to an officer with a clipboard, then was helped into a hot shower. When the hot water had thawed me out, I was handed a mug of hot soup, then tucked into a dry, warm bunk.

One other lifeboat with 20 men was still out in the storm, but it had a cover, lights, a radio, and two Air Force survival experts aboard. That boat was found just after midnight, the final action in the greatest peacetime air/sea rescue ever. Only one life was lost, and that was a guy whose heart stopped. The man with emphysema survived. The *Prinsendam's* captain and the other crewmen who'd stayed aboard were rescued by helicopter. The burnt-out hulk of the *Prinsendam* sank in 9,000 feet of water, six days later.

Twenty-four hours after our rescue, the *Boutwell* landed us in Sitka. A day later I was in Seattle. Malory had been taken to Valdez on the *Williamsburgh* and arrived at SeaTac airport a few hours after I did. The picture of her jumping into my arms made the front pages of newspapers all over the country.

"Hey, Dad," she said to me when I put her down, "When the going gets tough…"

"Yeah," I answered with a smile, "the tough get going." She was thinking about the adventure. I was thinking of my promise to that voice in the storm, and where it might take me next.

My parents and Mimi's parents met us at the airport, looking relieved but tired. Mimi picked us up at JFK three days later, and her welcome was more complicated. The cutter *Boutwell* had shortstopped a resolution of our awful marriage and I can't believe that all of her was delighted with that.

Chapter Twenty One

A Promise Kept, 1980 – 1981

How did I know the voice I'd heard in that lifeboat was God? Seasick, dying of the cold, I could have been hallucinating.

But I *knew*. I'd been screaming at God and immediately there was this answer, not from me, not from a hypothermic brain.

I've also long since realized that it doesn't make any difference whether that voice had been from God or not. *Something* communicated that specific message to me in a way so powerful it changed my life. If it was the wind, or my own imagination, then so be it. What moved me was not just the messenger, but the message.

That voice hadn't told me what to do. It had posed a choice, or rather re-posed one that had been framed long before Malory and I had ever gotten on the *Prinsendam*. Piss or get off the pot. In the lifeboat, that choice had been put in the starkest possible terms: either start living my life's higher purpose, or don't live at all. When I'd said "OK"—hanging on to that bench in the lifeboat, puking my guts out—I had no idea that cutter would show up. When it did, however, I knew I had to deliver on my promise, not just because I'd made a bargain to do so, but because I'd finally accepted that the success of my life depended on it. The voice was right: my life's purpose was to heal and to serve. If I kept running away from that purpose, I could look forward to nothing but excuses and regrets.

When the movie *Titanic* came out, twenty years after the *Prinsendam* went down, Malory and I went together to see it. Afterwards, we just looked at each other, remembering without words the fire and the lifeboat and the storm and the thought that we could die.

But back in New York that fall of 1980, Malory refused to talk about the ordeal at all. She insisted it was "no big deal" and even wrote an article for *Seventeen* magazine that made it sound as if surviving burning cruise ships in the North Pacific was summer camp with helicopters. If she was burying her feelings, I knew where she'd learned to do that. So I kept bringing the subject up.

One night in early November, I heard quiet crying from her room. When I went in, she blurted out that being on a sinking ship had taught her that she could die at any time—and she was crying because she hadn't yet figured out what to do with her one, fragile life. She said she was afraid she could die before she started.

I held her for a long time. Then I told her that there weren't many people thirteen years old who'd settled on a life direction, and she had a lot of exploring to do. Her father was thirty-eight and only then getting a grasp.

What I told her reassured me more than it did her. The promise I'd made in the middle of that storm had focused my path. Now, in New York, I set about to walk it.

I abandoned any more thoughts of making money as a consultant and threw myself into giving workshops on political action in a dingy basement room of the Lexington Hotel that I rented for $35 a day. One high, barred window opened onto the sidewalk from that room. A row of steam pipes hung from the ceiling, burping and banging to keep pace with the autumn chill.

I called my workshops "Change the World." Actually, I called them "Change the World!" with an exclamation point, which pretty much reflected both the vision I'd taken from that lifeboat and my ignorance of how hard it would be to get that vision across to anybody else. I thought that if I could only train enough people in what I knew, the nuclear threat would ebb, global violence would lessen, and hunger and poverty would end.

At first, I didn't even cover my expenses, but after the deal I'd made in the lifeboat, there was no way that lack of money was going to hold me back. Money wasn't all I lost with those workshops. Many of my old contacts in the government, even people I considered my friends, thought I was nuts or a traitor or both. They refused to come to hear me, or even to take my calls.

In the beginning, I based the workshops on lessons from my own life. I told the stories of my failures at Wheelus and in Vietnam as a way of talking about the importance of personal responsibility, and I urged people to see how their individual actions all shaped the larger systems of which they were a part. I used my experiences at the United Nations to show how trust could work as the key to resolving conflicts, and I taught that caring was the key to trust. I talked about the importance of taking risks for one's ideals.

It was a hodgepodge, clumsily delivered, and I made a fool of myself just about every time. I was too intense. I scared people. I made them feel guilty, or confused the hell out of them.

Not many people came, and some of those were friends who owed me favors. I asked each one to fill in a four-page questionnaire telling me how I could improve. There were a lot of brickbats in those questionnaires—and that's not counting the people who walked out after the first half-hour. But the criticisms showed me where I needed to get better. A few people said they were intrigued, and urged me to keep at it.

In the middle of this, in November 1980, my father, Al Graham, died. Officially he'd died of old age—a half-dozen parts of his system just shut down at the same time. I will always think it was my leaving the Foreign Service that killed him, however, or at least hurried his end. He'd been in and out of the hospital for a good part of 1980, but worsened when I'd told him of my decision to quit.

My mother called when it looked as if he might be going down for the last time. Two days after I got to Tacoma from New York, she and I took him back to the hospital to die.

It wasn't pretty. The more death closed in on him, the more frightened he became. He began to hallucinate that he was being run over by a truck, again and again and again. The hospital finally sedated him because people could hear his screams all over the floor. My mother and I sat, holding his hands, urging him to let go. And then he did, finally. The pulse in his throat just rippled lower and lower until it disappeared.

Leaving the hospital that night, I'd hated myself for what I felt—that even in dying, my father was a failure. That he couldn't even end his life with dignity. But those thoughts didn't make it into the eulogy I gave at his funeral. I said that my father was a kind, gentle and thoughtful man, which he had been. I said that I loved him, which I had. I didn't talk about the disappointments and distances I'd felt. I didn't mention the afternoon I'd spent with him at his favorite fishing hole, trying to apologize for my judgments. When the first shovelful of dirt thudded onto the surface of his coffin, I felt only minimally complete with him—thankful for that afternoon at the fishing hole, but not finished.

The end of my Foreign Service career, the *Prinsendam*, the workshops, and now my father's death—all happening within a few months—pushed me into the future like an avalanche.

In January I started giving speeches to anyone who would listen. At first, the peace movement was the only audience I could attract, and, even there, I was often accused of being a government mole. At one gathering in Manhattan a thin, dark-haired woman all but flew at me with her fists. "Now why do you think this slick guy, this John Graham here," she screamed to a ballroom full of people, "wants to help us get rid of nuclear weapons—out of the goodness of his heart? Yeah sure. Isn't putting someone like him up here to give us advice *exactly* what the FBI would do?"

Peace activists had a hard time accepting converts. And a convert was who I was, several times over. Gentle child—then eagerly into war. Catholic faith, then no faith, then faith only in myself. In Vietnam, I'd faced-off with the dark side of my soul then, years later, started the strangest possible journey to God.

But there was no way I could explain all this to the woman screaming at me from across the stage. And in any case, doubts of my conversion weren't the biggest problem I faced in being heard.

The real challenge was my message. What I was teaching wasn't just politics—but a way of doing politics that brought people together instead of pushing them further apart. Political work, I told my audiences, had to be healing, or it just fed a downward spiral of attack and defend in which nobody came out ahead. I spoke with commitment, but telling activists they should be healers was, for many of them, like telling a Muslim that Mecca didn't matter. They saw jabbing a sharp stick in an opponent's eye as the only way to win.

I made it harder by insisting that the most powerful way to change the world was through changing people, including ourselves. I told audiences that individual courage and compassion were the keys to positive political change. I told hard-core activists, for example, that the anger they felt toward "the system" could be a reason why they kept failing to change it, and that the smartest way to resolve conflicts was to build trust with their opponents.

This was not what many wanted to hear. They'd come to learn new ways to bash their opponents, and Gandhian messages from a guy still wearing Foreign Service suits disappointed them. Many left shaking their heads.

But I was stubborn, and I was convinced that my message would change the world. After all, it had changed *me*. I'd finally found that what made my life meaningful wasn't chasing adventures or status or power. My purpose was to heal, to bring people together to solve public problems. That discovery made my heart sing, and I preached with the fervor of the converted. I passed out leaflets for my workshops and speeches on the street in Greenwich Village and tacked them on telephone poles next to flyers about Alanon meetings and lost cats. I spoke in dimly lit church basements to earnest audiences of three or four. I sat in a director's chair next to a music stand that held my notes in neat little plastic sleeves.

Three months after my father died, in February 1981, I went to India to spend a week on a Gandhi pilgrimage with two men from a group called Moral Rearmament. For over forty years MRA had done quiet, behind-the-scenes work to resolve conflicts all over the world. It had played an important role in bringing France and Germany together after World War II, in a process that led to the European Union and the Common Market.

The year before, when I'd still been at the United Nations, I'd seen how a few dozen very brave people from MRA had quietly helped create a peaceful transition to majority rule in Southern Rhodesia—something British and American diplomacy had failed to do.

MRA worked by bringing people in conflict together in small groups, to tell their stories and to listen to the stories of the others. By putting a human face on conflict, MRA created small centers of peace that radiated outwards. MRA believed what I believed—that personal change was the key to political change. When the group invited me to India, I saw it as a chance to deepen my connections with people whose passion and strategies for change matched my own.

My two companions on that trip had also left traditional careers for lives of service. Dick Ruffin had walked away from a job as a Pentagon planner five years before. Larry Hoover had left a law practice to teach mediation skills in small communities in the Blue Ridge Mountains. Both men were affable Southerners with infectious drawls that soon crept into my own speech.

The three of us walked where Gandhi had walked, and talked for hours with his disciples about how strategies of nonviolence could be applied to current conflicts, as in the Middle East. And I had plenty of time alone, to walk and think about the workshops and speeches I'd begun, about my marriage and my family, and about the role as healer I wanted to play.

I came back from that trip clear that if I could spend a week in India talking about changing the world, I could sure as hell try harder to change my life at home.

In one way, Mimi had made it easier. The year before, she'd started pouring her life into volunteer work at women's prisons in New York City. Somewhere in the course of that, she'd started an affair with a Presbyterian minister. In February 1981, just after I'd returned from India, she and the minister had gone to Toronto for a conference on prisons—where the minister had broken off their relationship.

Mimi came back from Canada more distraught than she could hide. She told me about the affair, then, to my surprise, assumed my support in helping her deal with being dumped by someone she obviously loved very much.

If Gandhi could feel compassion for the British in India, I told myself, then I could manage some for an unwanted wife. I gave Mimi the shoulder she asked for. In a curious way, for a week or so we actually seemed to come closer together. Mimi wanted my help and, even after fifteen years, I was still grasping at any form of emotional life with her. There was something desperate for both of us in those embraces, but I was too close to see the picture—it was like looking at a Monet from six inches.

It took a friend named Michael Wyman to help me make sense of what was going on. Michael was about my age, short and balding, scratching out a living delivering his own personal-growth seminars in the City. We'd met at some event in Soho, and hit it off immediately. When I'd decided to move my workshops out of the Lexington Hotel basement, he and I had rented a joint seminar space above a used-book store on University Avenue in the Village.

Two weeks after Mimi had returned from Canada, I shared my confusion with Michael, over breakfast at a little Greek coffee shop around the corner from our space.

After I'd told him the story, he stared at me for a long time. Then he asked me if I thought Mimi had any positive feelings for me. I said no.

"So let me get this straight," he said. "She asks you to hold her, not because she loves or even likes you, but because she expects you to help her deal with the pain she feels because she's been dumped by a lover. And you've got no assurance that when she recovers from this she won't take up with somebody else. Have I got this about right?"

He did.

So Michael called me a fucking idiot. He started yelling at me, right in the middle of the coffee shop, over plates of greasy eggs and ham. I can still see the veins in his neck, still hear what he said.

"John, this is sick. This is not compassion. It's self-destruction. It's like those Buddhists barbecuing themselves in Vietnam. Christ, now you've had a week running around playing Gandhi or whatever the fuck you were doing in India, and you come back with the same pathetic bullshit you left with. How can you stay in a marriage that hasn't worked for fifteen years, that's never going to work?

Then Michael took my head in both his hands and stared at me. "What are you waiting for?" he said softly. "What are you waiting for?"

This being New York, the dozen or so other people in the coffee shop were ignoring this. They weren't interested. But I was. Michael had gotten through to me.

I walked around the Village for half an hour after that breakfast, then called a lawyer and started looking for an apartment. That evening I told Mimi I was moving out. She said nothing. I think she was relieved that one of us had finally made the move.

Then I told my children. Malory, then fourteen, didn't seem surprised. Jason, at nine, was too young to fully understand what I was saying.

By mid-March 1981 I was gone, living by myself in the West Village. Mimi and I signed the papers for a divorce as soon as a lawyer could draw them up.

Once the move was made, all the old reasons for not making it seemed ridiculous. Surely we couldn't have stayed together for fifteen years because of what our parents thought, or the Catholic Church, or own dogged refusal to admit failure. But we had.

There'd been another reason, one I didn't see until I'd left. What had kept me in that marriage, at least for its final months, wasn't fear of failure, but fear of actually fulfilling my dreams, of keeping the promise I'd made in the teeth of that storm.

In New York, so much in my life had begun to come together. I'd tested my ideals at the United Nations, with some success. I'd left the Foreign Service to play on a bigger field. The *Prinsendam* had focused my resolve. Even my workshops and speeches had started to improve. Every sign but one was pointing up.

And that one sign was at home. After every workshop, I'd get on my bicycle and the excitement and passion I'd just generated seemed to push me without pedaling back to the brownstone on 23rd Street. But I'd no sooner enter that door than I'd be pulled down from my vision and the excitement and passion would vanish in one glance from the woman I'd married in a snowstorm in Tacoma fifteen years before.

There was a weird comfort in that, in checking my dreams at the door and descending back into being that poor poignant son of a bitch who lived with someone who despised him. Descending not only tempted me to break the promise I'd made in that lifeboat—it gave me a rationale for doing so, for not trying to fulfill the potential of my life. How could I change the world—what right did I have to even try— if I couldn't change my own marriage?

Five minutes in that house and I'd forget every vision I had. My marriage was my anchor in a safely miserable harbor and, until Michael Wyman got through to me, I hung onto that weight for all it was worth. I hung on because I was scared, not of failing, not of giving a clumsy workshop or a bad speech, but of living full-time the passion and meaning and power that pursuing my dreams was beginning to unlock. I called my workshops Change the World! How could *I* do that—me the skinny kid, the adrenaline junkie, the failed husband? I knew that if I kept the promise I'd made on the lifeboat, there'd be no turning back. What I was afraid of was living my life on that level. It was the possibility of success, not of failure, that was terrifying. And my rotten marriage offered me a way out.

When I finally moved away, that fear just disappeared. It was as if I'd broken a spell.

Now, Mimi and I saw each other only to deal with the children. We'd been strangers for fifteen years. Now that a marriage no longer held us together, it was a relief to act like a stranger without feeling guilt or failure.

We managed to divide our assets without killing each other, and she agreed to child support payments that I could handle. The toughest part of the divorce was Jason. Malory adjusted, but the divorce turned Jason into the saddest little guy in the world. He wore torn jeans and wouldn't comb his hair and kept looking down at the ground. I used to pick him up after school a couple of times a week and take him to Ray's for pizza or to Blimpies for a hamburger, and he'd hardly ever talk. When he did say something, it was usually not more than a word or two.

Jason didn't understand all of what was happening, but he also blocked out a lot he did. I was convinced he wanted to talk about how he felt, but I couldn't find the words to make that conversation safe for him even though, in workshops, I could get other people to talk about the deepest parts of their lives. I'd take Jason back to the brownstone on 23rd street and hug him and watch him trudge up the steps to the door, and know that I was failing.

When I telephoned my very Catholic mother to tell her about the split, she understood it even less than did my son. To her, divorce was unthinkable, impermissible—a sin. Following so soon after my quitting the Foreign Service, the *Prinsendam* and the death of her husband, the news was almost more than this very tough woman could bear. In that first call to her after I'd moved out, she'd said very little. When she did start to talk to me again, it was to find a place to lay the blame. To her, statements like "We were both at fault" were incomprehensible. Indictments had to have a home.

As March turned to April in 1981, I poured myself into improving my workshops and booking speeches. Given the intensity of mission I felt, I happily created a monkish life. I would live by myself, partnered only with my ideals, and that, I thought, would last forever.

It lasted two months. By June, to my surprise, and I think a little to my disappointment, I was beginning to feel distinctly lonely. I went to a few singles bars but the music was too loud and the talk too shallow, and I never went back.

The one social event I allowed myself was a writers' group I'd joined two years before, following a weekend conference on creative writing in the West Village. The conference promoters had organized dozens of small follow-up groups where people could read their writings, hear critiques, and improve their skills. By chance I'd been assigned to a group that met every Tuesday night in Ann Medlock's apartment on Central Park West.

Ann was a single mother, making a living as a writer and publicist. Nine years before, she'd ended a marriage to a guy who'd literally left her in the hospital where she'd just given birth to their son David. She was older than I was, but I never knew that until she told me. She'd been an ac-tress and model in college, with head-turning good looks. She had fair skin, blond hair to her shoulders and deep blue eyes that let you know she called her own plays. The novel she was working on in our group was witty and sharp; if there was any consensus in the group, it was that Ann's work would see the inside of a bookstore before anyone else's.

Until the last Tuesday of June 1981, there'd been not a hint of romance between Ann and me. I thought she was terribly aloof. She says she'd thought of me then as this nice, married State Department dork. Married men, she said, were invisible to her. So, I suspect, were dorks. I remember inviting her to a Halloween party that Mimi and I had given just after the *Prinsendam*. Ann and I were friends—nothing more.

Everything changed that Tuesday night. Three months separated from Mimi, I came into Ann's living room for the writers' group and something was very different about her, about me—about everything. I didn't hear a word of anybody's writings and neither, I think, did Ann. As the meeting was breaking up she asked if anyone wanted to go see *Superman,* and I answered "Yes" so loudly and quickly that anybody else would have been a fool to come along. As the Man of Steel and Lois Lane were falling in love in the crystal cave, either my hand crept over Ann's or hers over mine—we still differ on that—but however it happened, the other hand did not pull away.

After the movie we went to an Irish bar and fell in love, instantly and completely, then went back to her apartment and made love until dawn.

In Australia, afraid of losing control, I'd fled the fires I'd ignited with Jean, then committed to a marriage where I should have known—where I *did* know—those flames would never burn. For fifteen years that decision had stored passion in me like stresses on the San Andreas Fault.

That Tuesday night the earth moved, and making love to Ann was explosive and driven. In the morning we just looked at each other and held each other and then went out for breakfast at a little café down the block. I can't remember anything we said. For me at least, I was still overcome by wonder. Two days later I moved into her apartment for good.

Ann was in 1981 bailing out of her own career to start the Giraffe Project, a nonprofit whose purpose was to move people to stick their necks out for the common good. Frustrated by what she saw as a culture that had lost its nerve, she'd started the Project as an antidote to ordinary media fare—to the mind-numbing mayhem and sappy trivia that were eroding civic energy and hope. People needed to know about heroes and the good things heroes did, as models for their own courageous, compassionate citizenship. The idea was hardly new. People had been telling the stories of heroes for thousands of years as a way to communicate core values. A writer and publicist, Ann had invented the Giraffe Project to do the same thing for our times.

Her strategy with the Project was simple: she found people acting with courage and compassion to solve public problems, then started interviewing these "Giraffes." When she recorded a good story, she'd write a radio public service announcement around it, convince a movie or Broadway star to record it, then send the story to hundreds of radio stations. Other people, she hoped, would hear Giraffes' stories and be inspired to stick their necks out too, on problems of concern to *them*. Giraffes were people like Gene Gitelson, a Vietnam vet who'd left the security of his banking career to help down-and-out vets, and Elsa Hart, a gems expert who'd faced down crooked middlemen to get an Apache tribe in Arizona a fair deal for the gemstones from their mine. Other Giraffes took on issues like environmental pollution or blew the whistle on corporate or government crime.

In many ways, Ann's Giraffe Project and my speeches and workshops were trying to do the same thing—to spark people into acting for the common good. When I first learned about what she was doing, however, I admit I thought it was too lightweight to succeed. I couldn't see how just telling stories would change anything. I thought it was political trainings like mine that would *really* make the difference.

But I couldn't ignore that Ann's work was attracting support much faster than mine. Convinced that changing the world was *serious* business, my workshops and speeches were still too preachy. I thought that if I made my case well enough, people would see its merits and begin to act on my advice.

 Eight years before, the men at Ben Lomond had freed me to open my heart, and I'd done so, to a degree that had lit up my life. But the boards I'd hammered over my heart as a young man were heavy and some of them were still in place. In 1981, I still needed to learn that motivating people to do difficult things was much more an emotional and spiritual challenge than an intellectual one.

Ann became my teacher. Gradually I began to see that the Giraffe image was a far more powerful way to get people's attention than anything I was doing. I began to feel the archetypal power of the stories Ann was telling and to see her genius in using the giraffe metaphor to get them into people's heads and hearts. I could see that people were listening to Giraffe stories, and that the Giraffe Project was already changing lives. It was anything but lightweight.

Ann also knew that nobody felt comfortable around a paragon or trusted a know-it-all. Even the title of my seminar, Change the World!, put many people off, by implying I had "the answer" when I'd only pulled up a corner of the rug.

Other lessons were even more personal. When Ann and I came together, being madly in love had not really altered twenty years of my living as a loner. Even living with her, I kept my own schedule as I always had, knowing where I was and what I was doing. When I'd leave the apartment for an appointment, I never thought to tell Ann where I was going—or sometimes even to say goodbye. I meant no harm, so when Ann protested, at first I saw it as an issue of control. It was months before I could see that the kind of partnership Ann offered and expected was not about controlling possibilities but about expanding them. Coming together with Ann was for me a whole new way of being, and I needed training wheels.

It turned out something less would do. A month after I moved in, Ann gave me a beautiful, polished chip of bark, about the size of a silver dollar, to carry in my pocket. When I'd reach for change, I'd feel the warm, smooth wood among the metal coins and remember that I was part of something new, something that made me incredibly happy, something I didn't want to lose. I began to get it.

Another connection wasn't so easy.

David, Ann's son, was nine years old when I moved into the small apartment on Central Park West he'd shared just with his mother for most of his life (Ann's older son, Courtney, was already out of the nest, a college student in Oregon). David's father had abandoned him before his birth, so I was the first father figure in his life. Neither of us was comfortable in our role. Suddenly, for David, his mother's attention had a competing focus, and, worse, there was now another adult telling him what to do. For my part, my own sad son, only a year older than David, was living two miles away, wondering why I'd abandoned him for another boy. Jason couldn't or wouldn't talk about what he felt. David was only too happy to talk to me, and it was usually to express his wish that I would go a long way away as soon possible. Not much that Ann or I could do or say eased his feelings.

The more David wished me gone, the more I'd missed Malory and Jason. I saw them often, but now only as a visitor in their lives. I spent more time with Jason than his sister because he was the one most damaged by the divorce, and the one I feared most could slip away from me. Malory would never slip away. It wasn't because she was older, and better able to understand what was going on. It was because of the *Prinsendam*. What we'd faced together had forged bonds that would never loosen. We felt that then, and we still do.

Chapter Twenty Two
New Paths, 1981 — 1984

I dreaded coming to Tacoma that first summer after Mimi and I had separated. Mimi had already taken the kids there in July, and I followed late that August. I stayed with my mother, in the apartment on Yakima Avenue where she'd moved after my father's death. I talked with her for hours in her little kitchen, but none of my explanations for why I'd ended my marriage penetrated her tough Croatian head. She'd learned about my moving in with Ann, so the issue of the separation was now compounded by the fact that I was living in sin with somebody else—presumably the Jezebel. My mother did not, could not understand. She rattled pans on the stove, eyes down, and muttered. Hugging her was like holding a redwood.

Trekking in the mountains with Malory and Jason, I did better. Malory, then almost fifteen, was old enough to understand what I told her about her parents' failures, and to ask questions. Jason, nearing ten, could at least see that his mother and father were not friends. I talked to both kids about how sometimes old paths simply closed off and new ones appeared. Ann was my new path, and I intended to move forward with her without in any way leaving them behind.

I'd said that to them just after the three of us had finished lunch, on a part of the trail around Mr. Rainer that wove through a grove of ancient trees, some of them ten feet across. As we adjusted our packs and started on, we passed a huge tree that had been dead for decades. It was full of holes made by insects and birds, and the whole top third had been blown off by some long-ago storm. There's a reason why loggers call old dead trees like this one, "widow-makers;" they can stand for decades, then come crashing down with no notice.

Malory passed the tree, then Jason, then me. Seconds later we heard a grinding, crushing sound and turned to see this huge tree fall across the path we'd just traveled, leaving behind us a wall of wood six feet high. Frankly, given all the near misses in my life, I didn't even count this one as close—the tree missed me by twenty feet, although, had it hit me, it would have pounded me into the ground like a tent stake. The kids looked at me. "Is that what you meant, Dad?" asked Jason, I think in all seriousness. "Old paths closing and you're moving on?"

The State of New York officially ended my marriage to Mimi on December 18, 1981. Now marriage became an issue between Ann and me. She made it very plain that, no matter how much we were in love, she wanted me in her life not just as lover but as husband. At the same time, she was nervous that anyone as newly separated as I was, was in no shape to make good decisions about another relationship. For my part, I just wanted the whole marriage issue to go away, given the last fifteen years stuck in one that didn't work.

That impasse sparked our first big argument. Afterwards I went for a long walk in Central Park. I thought about that tree on Mt. Rainer, and Jason's innocent question. I couldn't move backward. I had to move forward. I hadn't looked for Ann to enter my life but it had happened; she was the perfect partner and everything in me knew it. And now she was saying—commit to me formally, or move forward someplace else.

I proposed to her in the apartment a few days later. Ann, always with more a sense of drama, proposed to me a week after that, in the restaurant atop the World Trade Center, with all of New York City at our feet.

On June 13, 1982, my fortieth birthday, Ann and I married in a friend's country house near the Delaware Water Gap, two hours west of New York City. Our guests brought food instead of gifts. Malory was a bridesmaid. David, Jason and Ann's older son Courtney were ushers. It rained all day, and we were married in front of a roaring fire. I walked in to the soundtrack of *Superman* and Ann, to John Denver's *Annie's Song*. In Quaker fashion, the sixty friends we'd invited all signed beneath our vows, and that framed promise, in fading ink, hangs in our house today.

By the fall of 1982, I was speaking to larger audiences, including a panel on "life-changing experiences" at a major conference center in upstate New York. The other panelists were Robert Muller, a top official in the UN who'd been in the French Resistance during the Second World War, and Edgar Mitchell, the astronaut. Muller talked about a narrow escape from the SS, Mitchell described his first views of earth from the moon, and I told the lifeboat story. For all of us, these experiences had dramatically revealed or reinforced paths to deeper meanings for our lives.

When we'd finished, a young man in the back of the room asked a question that, judging from the murmurs, seemed to be on everybody's mind: "How is it you guys get these clear, bold signs that change your lives," he asked, "when stuff like that doesn't happen to most people? Do I have to fight the SS, fly into space, or be in a lifeboat lost in a typhoon to finally get the direction for a meaningful life?'

At first the five hundred people in the room laughed and applauded, as if that question had been on all their minds. Then there was silence. I didn't have a ready answer, and neither did Muller. But Mitchell leaned into his microphone and started to speak. There are signs to help guide us to meaningful lives all around us, Mitchell said. Mostly it's little stuff, subtle stuff. Maybe it's something in a book, an ad or a movie, or something you hear on the street that leads to a deeper reflection. Most of us ignore these signs, Mitchell went on, especially if they don't match the agendas we've already set for ourselves. And some of us are so stubborn (and here Mitchell waved a hand at the three of us on the panel), that there's no way any of these subtle signs are going to get through. We're the slow learners, he said. We have to get hit over the head with a two-by-four before we notice something is trying to get our attention.

In the more than two decades since that evening, I've been asked that young man's question many times by people who've read my books or heard my speeches: "How do I find the path to a meaningful life?"

I still start my answer with what Edgar Mitchell said. What I add, however, is that, from my experience, the signs pointing toward a higher purpose and a more meaningful life may not be small and subtle at all, but large doors that suddenly open or close in our faces. Here the challenge is not in seeing the path, but in finding the courage to walk it. The opportunities I had to freelance at the United Nations were large open doors and, still supported by a government paycheck, I boldly walked through them. But when those UN experiences led to an even bigger open door—a life of service outside the Foreign Service—I balked because of money fears. Even when other doors were slamming shut all around me, including my hopeless attempts at consulting and banking, I would not move through the one door that gaped open. It took the "two-by-four" of the *Prinsendam* experience to finally push me past my fears.

To find a meaningful life, I also add, it's often not enough to be open to individual events as signs, no matter how subtle or obvious they might be. It's also important to see the *patterns* that events form in our lives—the way they're woven together in time and space to point the way. I can see guiding patterns in my own life now that I couldn't see when I was younger, patterns going back to my childhood, woven from schoolyard bullies, disappointments in my father, adventures on the high road and in the Foreign Service, revelations from Ben Lomond and the Inner Peace Movement, challenges at the United Nations, and much more.

What feels almost unfair, I tell people, is that it's hardest to see the patterns that are forming in one's life at the time when the forming is going on—when the guidance would be most useful. But the patterns of a life are like crop circles that some people think are mystical signs carved in farmers' fields. You can't see the patterns unless you fly over them—from the ground it all looks like trampled hay. Just because it's hard to see the patterns doesn't mean they aren't there, no matter how chaotic and confusing life may seem.

The guiding patterns in our lives are not set just by the events and experiences that seem positive at the time. In crop circles, it takes both the grain that's standing and the grain that's flattened to form the design. It's clear now that a lot of the patterns that formed my own life were the result of bad choices—or good choices made for shallow reasons. I'd joined the Foreign Service in part to get back at the bullies—but the skills and experiences I'd gained in the Foreign Service are important to what I teach now.

I'd run out on my Australian girlfriend—but if I'd had the courage to stay with her, my life now would be completely different. My consulting business in New York, started in a panic over money, had been a bust—but if it hadn't, there'd have been no *Prinsendam*, and I'd be a rich, corporate consultant. For years I'd sought manhood through adrenaline highs because I'd lost sight of who I really was. But that rough history now made me credible to a lot of audiences who might otherwise dismiss what I was saying as too "soft;" when they understand that I'm no untested do-gooder, it's easier for them to hear what I'm saying about meaning and compassion in their lives.

In short, all those patterns that have formed my life, all those connections of events, have been pointing from the beginning to—and now support—the life I'm leading now.

I tell audiences now what I wish I'd been told when I was young: that the path of a meaningful life is out there for each one of us. The signs and patterns that point to it may be obscure, and there will be obstacles and risks along the way. The only real mistakes we can make are to back away from that path when we find it—or not to seek it at all.

———————————————

As my new life with Ann Medlock and the Giraffe Project hurtled into the 1980's, I needed less and less the polished piece of bark to remind me I was not alone. I understood now that I didn't have to be Atlas nor Sisyphus. I had a loving partner as smart and tough as I was. We were ping-ponging ideas, plans and options, and what was coming out of our collaboration was better than what either one of us could do alone. By 1983 the Giraffe Project had become the umbrella for all of it—the media work, and the speeches and workshops.

We were now together twenty-four hours a day, and that hardly seemed enough. We interviewed Giraffes in delis and read radio scripts and workshop notes on benches in Central Park. We'd call on magazines and media companies to urge them to use Giraffe stories. We'd bounce ideas for speeches back and forth. We'd walk to meetings to save bus fare and every month was a challenge to pay the rent. We held hands walking down Fifth

Avenue, and we laughed a lot. We were consumed by each other and by the work, which steadily grew. The Project began attracting major press coverage, from *Parade* to the *New York Times*. When we got our first foundation grant we celebrated over roast pig at a Cuban restaurant called Victor's.

There were still sour notes from Tacoma. My mother refused to accept or forgive my ending a Catholic marriage. Finally convinced that Ann was not the homewrecker, she blamed me for everything, including being a terrible model for my children. My older sister Wynne, then raising a very Catholic family of her own near Philadelphia, shared my mother's judgments. I felt sold out by both of them, and couldn't understand how, for them, ideology could be thicker than blood. For years, their judgments became a wedge and a sadness for all three of us.

In the fall of 1983, Mimi moved with Malory and Jason to Seattle. I didn't see my children until the following May, when I flew out to Seattle to keynote the 1984 King County Democratic Convention. I gave a huge hall of delegates a red meat barnburner, tearing into Republican policies and shouting and waving my arms in the air. I finished to a thunderous standing ovation. Hooked by the moment, I stayed at the podium waving my fists. In the hall afterwards, a couple of the state's major politicos heartily shook my hand. I felt the same breathless seduction I'd felt after my errant speech on Cuba in New York four years before. There was no doubt after that speech to the Democrats that, if I came back to Seattle to pursue a career in politics, I wouldn't be starting from scratch.

I stayed in Seattle for two days after the speech to see my mother and my kids. Jason was almost thirteen. In the eight months since I'd seen him, puberty had thinned his face and dropped his voice. Out of New York, he was emerging from the shell that had hardened around him after the divorce. Malory, now seventeen, had become a high school revolutionary, taken a lover, and generally was driving her mother and her grandparents nuts. To me she seemed just fine, an opinion that only widened the gulf between my mother and me. Unable to comprehend Malory, Mother doted on Jason, in an effort to keep at least one of my kids in line.

Back in New York, I talked with Ann about the opportunity my speech had opened of launching a political career in Washington State. I remembered the evening in front of my campfire in Tennant Creek almost twenty years before, when I'd made the right decision to join the Foreign Service for all the wrong reasons. Power now was not the seducer it had been then, nor did I need to prove my manhood to schoolyard bullies. As the ovations from the Seattle convention faded, I remembered my life already had a higher purpose, a mission. I was a healer, and I needed to be free to go wherever that healing mission led. The Giraffe Project was the perfect vehicle for me and Ann, the perfect partner.

A career in politics, as in the Foreign Service, would box me in with obligations and responsibilities I did not want. And one great speech did not change the fact that getting into position to run for Congress would mean years of retail politicking that I had no stomach for. Politics was not my path and I chose not to walk it.

I returned to the Northwest that June of 1984, ten days ahead of Ann and David, to take Malory and Jason back into the mountains. I'd seen them for barely a day after the speech to the Democrats in May so this would be the first real time I spent with them in almost a year.

The sun had melted the last bits of snow off the high country trails, and the three of us hiked high up into the Goat Rocks Wilderness, just south of Mt. Rainier. On a soft evening, just past the solstice, we were cooking our steaks on a ridge so close to the mountain it seemed we could put out our hands and touch the snowfields. A sap bubble exploded with a loud pop, scattering embers from our campfire into the evening sky, lighting our faces against the fading light.

The soft boom of an avalanche on Mt. Rainier pulled our eyes north. Jason pointed to a white plume of snow, barely visible in the evening light, sliding down from a high glacier two miles away. A few seconds later, we heard the sound of boulders falling, clicking and thumping as they tore into the mountain's side. Then it was silent, and the dark outline of the huge peak filled the night. The three of us just stared. There were good reasons the tribes living at its base called Rainer "Tahoma'— the Mountain That is God.

Mt. Rainier, and a few other places like it in the Cascades, had been where I'd finally found a way to talk to my kids about God. It was important to me to open both of them to a spirituality they would never learn from priests, nuns, or grandmothers. My counsel to them had always been what I'd learned from the Inner Peace Movement: develop a spiritual life, but don't look to intermediaries to tell you how to do it. Find God through your own direct experience. In the beginning, I'd tried to talk to them about what I'd seen from out-of-body trances, but they were very little and all I'd done was frighten them and undermine my own credibility.

In the mountains it was different, especially as the kids grew older. Our trips to places like Mt. Rainer, away from man-made things, made it easier for the kids to use their own experiences to probe for answers to spiritual questions, just as Native Americans had. I told them that I thought God was everyplace and in them, but I also told them they must find the truth for themselves. I suggested they'd have more luck finding truth from listening to the mountain wind or watching the mists rise on a lake than from kneeling in a wooden pew. I took them into the woods in the dead of night, without a flashlight, and we would sit quietly as moonlight lit distant cliffs and feel the presence of God.

Mimi's Catholic mother and my own, of course, managed to wheedle descriptions of these trips out of the kids. Especially after the divorce, my filling my own children with heresy only darkened the coat of an already black sheep.

I was tired of being that sheep and my mother's blame had worn me down more than I realized. It all came apart when Ann and David arrived in Tacoma that summer.

The two of them had driven across the country in Ann's old Pontiac, with Ann doing Giraffe radio interviews in stations along the way. They reached Tacoma three days after Malory, Jason and I had returned from the mountains.

Introducing them to my mother was a disaster, not because anything they did, or even anything my mother did, but because my own nerves failed to meet the challenge. Twenty-three years later, Ann still wrinkles up her nose in thinking of that first evening. "We'd driven across the country, calling you every day," she will say, "and when we finally made it to Tacoma, it seemed to David and me that you didn't want us there."

I understand how she would think that. For three years I'd gotten nothing but blame about my divorce from my mother and my sister. I'd defended Ann until the blame had turned on me, then I'd defended me, then more or less given up. I really thought I'd done pretty well with a very difficult situation, avoiding the kind of brawls with my mother and sister that might have separated us forever.

But when Ann and David had walked in the front door of my mother's apartment on Yakima Avenue, all I could feel was my mother's wrath. She was civil and polite that evening, but I could feel her judgments about Ann and me churning below the surface. Where I should have ignored those judgments, where I should have defused the meeting with some humor, I instead just stood there, doing little to help the woman I loved and her son deal with the awkwardness. The evening was wooden, but far worse, I'd given Ann reason to doubt my commitment to her and to our marriage.

We all managed to get through the rest of the visit. My mother more or less kept her thoughts to herself in front of Ann, which was a miracle. Ann, of course, let me know of her disappointment in me.

The easiest part for me was the apology to Ann. The hardest part was acknowledging that, at age forty-two, I could still be controlled by my mother's judgments.

Chapter Twenty Three

Whidbey Island, 1985 – 1989

By 1985 Ann and I needed help in running an expanding Giraffe Project, and we needed more office space than the dinner table in Ann's apartment. The price for both people and space in New York City was very high. It was time to move. I could book speeches from anywhere. We were finding Giraffes everywhere. Media operations in some ways were easier in New York, but even before the Internet, we could promote Giraffe stories with an 800 number and a fax machine.

Another factor was me. Ann would have been happy to stay in New York forever, but I was getting increasingly restless on the East Coast. My roots were out west. My kids were in Seattle. Except for a trip to Peru in 1979, I'd done very little real climbing since my college days and I missed it. The gentle slopes of the Appalachians were no substitute for the crags and glaciers of "real" mountains. With New York in the middle of a real estate boom, we decided to cash out and move.

Focusing on the northwest, we began looking for a place that was both rural and close to a major city. In 1983 I'd spoken at a conference center on Whidbey Island, reachable by ferry about an hour north of Seattle. The island was rural, it was beautiful, it sat midway between two major mountain ranges—and land was cheap. When I brought Ann to the island in early 1985, it told us in one afternoon that it would be our home.

Two months before, in Santa Fe, I'd bought a pair of Rudy Rios cowboy boots. They were way out of my price range but I'd bought them at a strange sale that knocked everything off 50% at 3 o'clock in the morning. I'd hung in with my cup of coffee and come away with the boots. But fine boots like these demanded Levi button-fly 501 jeans—wearing zippered jeans with those boots would be like wearing tennis shoes with a tuxedo. The problem was, I couldn't find a pair of 501s anywhere in New York that would fit my long thin frame. Walking with Ann down the main street of Langley, a village of 800 people on South Whidbey Island, I saw a stack of 501s in the local general store. My size was on top.

Across the street, I found the same blend of pipe tobacco I thought existed only at the Wilke Pipe Shop at Lexington Avenue and 48th Street in Manhattan. Down the block, Ann found a print shop doing exactly the quality of work she needed for Giraffe Project publications. Another storefront, just the size the Giraffe Project might need for an office, was for rent a block away—and above it was a space that could be converted into living quarters. All this discovered within thirty minutes.

Ann and I just looked at each other. How many more signs did we need? We rented the office space on the spot, and within a week convinced the owner of the building to convert the upstairs space into an apartment.

We moved to Langley in September 1985, put David in seventh grade at the Langley Middle School, and hired an assistant for the Giraffe Project. When Ann's rental building in New York was converted into co-op apartments that November, we bought her tiny apartment on credit, then resold it for enough money to launch the construction of a dream house on an isolated ridge, looking across Puget Sound to the mountains on the Olympic peninsula.

Meanwhile, Malory and I had switched coasts. Just as I'd moved west, she'd headed east to Hampshire College in central Massachusetts. Her brother, however, was now only an hour away in Seattle. I'd come into town for school events or a movie and Jason would come out to the island for weekends when he could.

Jason was more willing to talk to me than he had been in New York, but a large part of him still lived in a private world. To me (and Ann) he was always a polite and respectful teen—the exact opposite of David. Jason's dark side was a penchant for binge drinking that I then had no clue about, or rather whose clues I refused to accept. I ignored warnings from Malory and David about Jason's drinking, so I never acknowledged let alone talked to my son about whatever personal demons were driving him to anaesthetize himself. Something pulled him out of the hole before any real damage was done—but it wasn't me.

My mother was ninety minutes away, in Tacoma. I saw her every month or so, but she hadn't stopped blaming me for my divorce. The only world she was comfortable in was her own, with all its rules and judgments, so my visits were still hard. I would drive her to her doctor's appointments, handle whatever insurance and banking business had to be done, and take her out to dinner at Johnny's Dock, an undistinguished eatery she'd enjoyed with her husband for thirty years. She would order her usual baked salmon or meatloaf, and reiterate her complaint that the baked potatoes were too large. I steered the talk away from my own life, because there seemed so little about it that did not frustrate and disappoint her. Of course she appreciated the practical help I gave her, and came to depend on it, but forgiveness was still foreign to her, like a language from the far side of the world.

It was ironic that, just as I was shaping my life as a professional communicator, I could not talk to my own mother about anything that mattered to me, and I was willingly incompetent to see past the closed doors in my own son's heart.

But the hardest thing in my life those years was David. He hated being uprooted from New York against his will—especially to a place he regarded as nothing but rain and country bumpkins. That, combined with the onset of adolescence, created a perfect storm in his relationship with me.

I'd always thought that I was the target for the anger David felt toward the real father who'd abandoned him. He was very smart, and relentlessly found ways to insult the things he knew were important to me. He sneered at the Boy Scouts, 4-H, athletes, studying, hard work, and at the beautiful rural place we now called home. He began dressing in black and acted just like the creeps who'd made my life miserable in high school.

Ann was in the middle. She could not get David to change the way he felt and acted. And she was frustrated with how often I lost my temper over the provocations. David was, after all, a kid, an angry kid, and I was the adult. There were awful arguments over David that scared us both.

In workshops, I could advise other people on how to solve their conflicts, but I struggled to follow my own advice at home. None of the training from the Inner Peace Movement kept me calm enough, or supplied the compassion that might have let me deal with David better than I did. All I can say for the years he lived with us was that I tried, and to this day, am ashamed that I couldn't be the father he never had. After two years of simmering conflict on Whidbey Island, David went to live with his older brother Courtney, then living in Olympia, fifty miles south. Courtney was about to be married and was struggling to establish himself as a musician, but he loved David and was generous enough to take him in.

My own relationship with David improved dramatically once he was out of the house, but I take no credit. David liked his brother and never focused his anger on Courtney the way he had on me. Thirteen years his senior, Courtney was also old enough to be the adult male that David so desperately needed in his life. David's life began to stabilize.

From the beginning, Malory and Jason had swept David up in their world. The more they treated him as a brother, the easier it became for him to accept me as a father, and for me to treat him as a son. But by far the biggest reason for the healing was that David simply grew out of his rage, or at least the part of it directed at me.

I'd see Malory on an occasional visit to her campus in Massachusetts, or she'd visit Seattle during the summers, but she was building an independent life and soon a career. Hampshire College had kindled in her a passion for film and video production, and I assumed—wrongly as it turned out—that after graduation she'd head for New York or Los Angeles. In fact, she would return to Seattle to start and run a series of video-based nonprofits helping at-risk kids, and, in the 1990's, start an *aikido* center.

Back in the northwest, I started climbing mountains again, and within a year was teaching courses in advanced ice and rock climbing for the Seattle Mountaineers. David wasn't interested, but I began taking Jason on trips more ambitious than our usual backpacks. Guiding him up steep cliffs in the Cascades, taking small risks together, gave us more than literal common ground. Jason remained a private person, but at least we had something to share.

In the summer of 1987, he and I headed north to climb a series of peaks on Vancouver Island. Jason was nearly sixteen that summer and running high school track. Trim and athletic, he was beginning to look like that buff picture of my father taken at the beach in the 1920s, when Dad was starting out with the *Tacoma News Tribune*.

We climbed a minor peak one afternoon and were descending un-roped. Suddenly Jason lost his footing and couldn't stop his slide down a steep snow slope. He bounced over several rock outcrops, then landed face down on a snow-covered ledge, a hundred feet below me. His body was still. I stopped breathing. I'd survived plenty of falls worse than that. Surely he was OK. He had to be OK.

It took me a few minutes to climb down to him. Just before I reached him, he stirred, then got up, unhurt. I hugged him for a long time.

We talked in the tent that night about what had happened.

Jason had survived a fall that easily could have killed him. He'd walked away with only a few bruises. He knew how often I'd done the same thing, surviving close calls and bad choices. He also knew that I thought my deliverances were not luck but signs, and that signs and patterns had, in my interpretation, finally pointed me toward finding and living a meaningful life.

If miraculous escapes were signs for my life, he wanted to know that night, was the same true for him? Had God just saved him too, and for some reason? Or had his survival that afternoon been dumb luck? What if life was nothing but random events? What if there were no such things as "signs" or "God" or "higher purposes?" What if that was all a crock?

Both of us were already in our sleeping bags. I looked at him, remembering all those Tuesday afternoons at Ray's Pizza or Blimpies in New York when I couldn't get him to talk, and so grateful now that he wouldn't stop.

Jason knew my stories. He knew most of the twists and turns my life had taken. I think, deep down, he also knew that he'd have to eventually answer all his questions for himself, to face his own demons, and to live out his own stories.

I remember telling him, in candlelight so dim I could barely see his face, that ever since the incident on the McKinley River, I'd seen my deliverances as a pattern, one of several that had shaped my life. Years later, my mystical experiences had convinced me that my life and the patterns that formed it were part of an infinite design, an unknowable tapestry which I called God.

Patterns and designs, to me, implied purpose. I couldn't accept that life was some well-crafted but random game. There had to be a point to all this complexity, and that meant there had to be a point, a meaning, to my life and to his. Life without meaning would be like a fancy Swiss watch with no hands on it. Who would make such a thing? I had things to do in this life, and so, I believed, did he.

As Jason knew, I'd found the meaning of my life in service, in healing. At 45, I didn't expect that to change; the patterns had coalesced. For me, the choices now were not so much about the path I was on as about finding ways to walk it better.

But why, Jason pressed, why did it all seem to be working out so well for me? Even when I'd messed up I'd come out ahead. And my explanations made it all sound too tidy.

I told Jason that I wasn't sure, but that, as a veteran bullshitter and backslider, I knew I would never have found a meaningful life if it hadn't been for an extra bit of courage or guidance, or an unexpected opportunity, just when I needed it. That help had to come from something bigger than I was, and for me that could only be God, the universal presence I'd first met in trance experiences. That help, I thought, was what Christians called "grace." Grace was like drawing an Advance-to-Go card just when you're about to land on another player's hotels.

But "grace" was not "luck," as far as I could see. There was a purpose behind it. It came from God, but with strings: "Here's grace —now use it to find and carry out the meaning of your life."

Why did I get grace? All I could say for myself was that, after the McKinley River, I'd never lost faith, at least not completely, that there must be some higher purpose to my life, even if I had no clue as to what it was. So I'd kept trying to figure it out, no matter how many wrong alleys I'd gone down. And for all my mistakes, I'd eventually started finding some answers and then making tough decisions to carry them out. I'd hung in there and then grace happened.

So the lesson for me was that grace was attracted by faith—faith that our lives mattered, that each of us had a meaningful role to play on the planet, that we weren't just marking time. Faith that each of us could find that personal role and fulfill it even if we felt unprepared and unworthy.

Faith gave us the courage and persistence to stay on the quest long before any results were clear. And sometimes, maybe when we least expected it, the reward for faith was grace. Amazing grace. Advance to Go.

Jason looked at me, saying nothing. Then he nodded slightly, bunched up his sweater as a pillow, and put his head down. I blew out the candle. The sound of wind in high hemlocks stirred the night.

Ann and I often said that the place where we'd built our house was the best campsite we'd ever seen. The hemlocks on our land framed a spectacular view of Puget Sound and the Olympic mountains. The Giraffe Project office was six miles away, down a country road where the only traffic delays were caused by deer that had a hard time sharing the island with the rest of us. Listening to Seattle traffic reports on the car radio in the morning produced quiet smiles.

At least once a week now, I'd take the ferry and drive through that congestion down the interstate to Tacoma, where my mother was getting frail. In 1988 she was 86, still living by herself in the apartment on Yakima Avenue, although things like cooking and getting to church were becoming bigger challenges for her every year.

She had finally begun to mellow. She may not have forgiven me for my divorce, but at least she stopped talking about it and began to welcome Ann and David into her family and her heart. She took an interest again in what I was doing with my life.

I think part of what moved her to soften was practical: she sensed the risk of pushing me away, just as she was growing very old and needing my support. But I also think that the blaming just got too pointless and bitter, even for her, and that her natural instinct to be loving finally won out over her allegiance to rules and standards that had controlled her since she was a child.

Ann and I finally convinced her to come out to the island. It turned out, to our surprise, that she had a history there, one she'd never mentioned. Fresh out of teachers' college, she'd taught the 1923-24 school year in a tiny two-room schoolhouse on South Whidbey Island, near the present ferry landing and only a few miles from where Ann and I had built our house. A city girl, she'd hated the outdoor privies and kerosene lanterns of rural life at that time and fled for more civilized postings once her one-year contract had expired.

Still, she was remembered. An enterprising writer for the *South Whidbey Record* brought four of her former students to meet her that first time she came out to the island—after an absence of 65 years. Those students, all men in their seventies, came with their hats in gnarled country hands. They called my mother "Miss Xitco" or "Ma'am" and generally looked as if they had all missed a homework assignment and feared the worst. I couldn't help the thought that eighteen years before I was even born, my mother had been instilling fear.

The Giraffe Project continued to grow. In August 1988, Ann and I were invited to speak at a conference in Aspen hosted by John Denver. A group of Soviet officials and media types were also there. The week of the conference, there was a whole page on the Giraffe Project in *Time* magazine, so when we started to speak, in a large white tent under a blue Rocky Mountain sky, there wasn't an empty seat.

As Ann and I talked about Giraffes and about our work that afternoon, a Soviet broadcaster named Vladimir Pozner sat in the audience, listening intently. Afterwards he asked us to dinner, where the three of us connected as if we'd known each other all our lives.

Vladimir was stocky, balding, with penetrating eyes and a grin that gave them warmth. Born in Paris of a Russian father and a French mother, brought up in Greenwich Village, he'd gone with his parents to Moscow in the 1950's. For the Pozners that move was a mistake—any Russians who'd lived abroad as long as they had were suspect, and the Iron Curtain slammed down around the family just as surely as the Berlin Wall. More at home at Ebbetts Field than in Red Square, Vladimir was forbidden to leave the Soviet Union for the next 33 years—until Gorbachev, and *glasnost*, began to open the USSR to the outside world. Suddenly Vladimir, with his perfect American English and his knowledge of the West, found himself a key interpreter of the USSR for American television audiences, and an important champion of Gorbachev's reforms in his own country.

In Aspen that evening Vladimir asked dozens of questions about the Giraffe Project. By dessert, we'd become allies, and Vladimir asked Ann and me to come to Moscow that winter, to start a Giraffe Project there. Under Communism and under the czars, he said, anybody in the Soviet Union who'd stuck their necks out got sent to Siberia or shot. Now Gorbachev was trying to get people to become active citizens overnight. It wasn't happening. People were scared and puzzled by the whole concept. They needed examples. They needed to hear about Giraffes. Soviet Giraffes. Would we come?

Ann and I agreed instantly. It was a chance to help shape the future of an entire country, and, for all we knew, the world. And for me, taking on a challenge that big was the kind of high-stakes, long-shot adventure that had fueled my life for decades. It was also a huge chance to carry out the mission of service that had finally brought meaning to my life after fruitless struggles to find it in status and power, or in the risk-taking that had so many times almost got me killed.

Chapter Twenty Four

Moscow, February 1989

They said it was the mildest Moscow winter in twenty years. All I know is that standing in Red Square, waiting for the photographer from *Argumenti I Facti* to set up his shot, drained the warmth of a late afternoon sun out of us. The man wanted Ann and me *just so* with the cathedral in the background, the Kremlin to our left. A gaggle of Japanese tourists passed, several giving us quick, quizzical stares. Ann's breath rose in little bursts from the smile she held. The camera finally clicked.

As it did, policemen in long gray coats began blowing whistles and waving their arms to clear a path for a convoy of black limousines, coming straight at us from an opening in the Kremlin wall. The tourists scattered. Our photographer hesitated, needing one more shot and not wanting to reset his tripod on the uneven stones. The cop closest to us blew his whistle louder, then ran toward us, yelling in Russian. Ten feet away he stopped, studying our faces. He grinned. "Giraffe!" he said, touching his heart with his left hand and pointing at us with his right. "Giraffe!" Then he spun about and waved at the VIPs to drive around us.

Three days earlier, the man would have chased us off. Ann and I were invited guests of the Gorbachev government, but we'd quickly learned the limits of our welcome. The Ministry of Information had given us a paper bag full of rubles to cover our expenses for two weeks. The trouble was, our clothes and speech tagged us as foreigners, so waiters asked us for dollars and refused to seat us when we said we'd be paying in rubles—whose value was falling by the day. One of the waiters, in a restaurant in our hotel, began pushing a chair against the glass door when he saw us coming. When we weren't guests at some official meal, we survived on little ham sandwiches bought from a street vendor near Red Square. We'd come to Moscow to support a new era in the Soviet Union, but missing meals wasn't a hopeful way to start.

That all changed when we went on Vladimir Pozner's show, one of the first live, uncensored television programs in the country. After decades of canned propaganda and party-line news, the press freedoms introduced by Gorbachev had shocked people across eleven time zones. *Sunday Evening with Vladimir Pozner*, loosely patterned on *Donahue* in the United States, was watched by tens of millions of Soviets every week, and its host had become an instant celebrity.

The show that night started with video clips of American Giraffes and of some Giraffe candidates in the USSR, followed by questions from the studio audience. There were about 200 people there that night, in two banks of seats on either side of a long red carpet. Ann and I sat in the front row on one side and Vladimir roamed up and down the carpet and into the seats, bringing his microphone to people who raised their hands.

A woman with very red hair asked Ann how she'd found the courage to start the Project and Ann responded with the story of her struggle to become self-confident after a young life of reversals and putdowns in pre-feminist America. As for the Giraffe Project—the challenge was pressing and the opportunity to do something was right in front of her. Nobody else was acting—she couldn't look away.

An old man thundered from the next to last row, chopping the air with his right hand: "Why do Americans want war?" The man looked like Leonid Brezhnev and wore three rows of World War II service medals on a worn gray suit. Vladimir said nothing as he came back to the carpet and shoved the microphone under my chin.

I answered that Ann and I had been to meetings all over Moscow that day, and that, though I'd never been in the city, I had a fair knowledge of where the major buildings were. "Do you know why?" I asked. "It isn't because of hotel maps. As part of a job I had in the U.S. Foreign Service I helped plan nuclear war and I saw all the targeting maps for Moscow, and all the important places where American warheads were aimed and probably still are aimed. And do you know that somewhere in the USSR a Soviet planner is targeting missiles at Washington D.C., and he or she knows exactly where the Pentagon and the CIA and the White House are for the very same reason?"

I said I thought that neither the American nor the Soviet people wanted war, but that my experience was that war is often made by good people who lack the courage to make peace. It takes courage to acknowledge that planning for nuclear war is lunacy. When people take the risks to call for change, then change can happen. My own life had taken a 180-degree shift, from planning nuclear war to Giraffes, and I was no saint. If I could do it, others could.

Feet crossed and uncrossed in the television audience. Somebody coughed. Then the audience applauded. Our part of the show ended. It seemed all of Moscow must have watched; instantly, Ann and I went from counting out kopecks for ham sandwiches to rerouting traffic in Red Square.

Over the next ten days Vladmir helped us find the people who could help us set up a Giraffe subsidiary in Moscow. We met with government people, journalists and private citizens. We'd even met with Andrei Zhukov, a Communist Party boss. With my history in the Foreign Service, going into Party headquarters was going into the belly of the beast. But the first thing we saw inside the building, a drab six-story cube hidden down a narrow avenue, was a cart of manual typewriters and stacks of file folders bound with cloth ribbons. Some beast.

Inside a conference room with nearly bare walls, Zhukov told us he was worried that his countrymen lacked the attitudes and skills to take advantage of the Gorbachev reforms. He thought that finding Soviet Giraffes and telling their stories could help get things moving. Before we left, he gave us helpful suggestions and contacts.

Everywhere we went, the Giraffe vision went straight to the Russian soul; our audiences understood that what we were talking about wasn't just politics and social change—it was a spiritual journey, it was about finding what was important in each human heart and using it to heal the world. We talked about the importance of courage and compassion, and about the power of one or a few to make a difference. And we told stories of Giraffes.

Within a month, "Giraffes USSR" was in business, finding Soviet Giraffes and broadcasting their stories.

Its finest moment came two and a half years later, on August 21, 1991. Boris Yeltsin had barricaded himself inside Parliament and called for the general strike that would pull the country back from civil war. Listening to the news broadcasts in Langley, Ann and I had talked to our people in Moscow, getting a sense of what was happening and what was needed. Then we'd collaborated on a Giraffe response that Radio Moscow had broadcast across the entire country that same day. That message was everything we believed. It said:

> "Giraffes USSR salutes all the brave citizens who stood tall and refused to give up their right to be free. They have stuck their necks out to preserve freedom for all of us. And they have won.
>
> "Now it's up to all of us, each and every citizen, to accept responsibility for the success of reforms in our country. It is not enough to hope that others will fix everything that is wrong. The bravest among us have refused to accept tyranny and repression—they have shown us the way. Now we must all stand tall, living new lives as active participants in a new society that was almost lost to us. The time for passivity is over. We can no longer just wait and watch and hope, doing nothing.
>
> "It is up to us. We can, each of us, declare ourselves responsible for making sure that our country succeeds in building democracy and in its even harder challenge of building a healthy economy. Leaders cannot do it all for us. A few brave citizens cannot do it all for us.
>
> "Giraffe USSR salutes the citizens who will stand tall and meet the challenges that face us now."

Our staff in Moscow faxed us the text of the message as it had gone out. Ann and I were at home, sitting down to dinner on the front porch of the house, overlooking the sea and the mountains. On the table was barbecued salmon, chard from the garden, and a Semillon from a vineyard down the road. In the near distance, a container ship moved slowly up the channel, heading for Asia. Behind the ship, five ridgelines climbed one behind the other into the sky, each fading a different shade of purple. Above them, narrow bands of cloud were reflecting red and orange off a sun that still had a diameter to fall. The cedar boards of the house glowed gold.

Did our message make a difference, going across the Soviet Union, at that cusp in history? Did broadcasting stories of Giraffes, did my giving speeches, change anything? Was all this worth it?

Ann and I just looked at each other and grinned. What had happened that day was another step on a path that we'd come to expect was full of miracles.

I thought how often people looked at me and Ann, and the work we did and how we lived, and told us how "lucky' we were. We always answered—respectfully—that our success had nothing to do with luck. We'd each given up safer options and taken many risks to go where our hearts led. God may have given us grace, but grace, as I'd tried to tell Jason on Vancouver Island, was not the same as luck. Grace had come to us because we'd never given up a faith in a positive purpose for our lives, and now had found it with the Giraffe Project and with each other. Most of the people who called us "lucky" were ones who'd chosen safer paths—and who were now wondering why something seemed to be missing.

I let my breath out slowly. Ann had waited patiently for my reverie to stop. A squirrel chattered from a half circle of large trees to our left, a place we called the Sacred Grove. Evening birds began to tune up. A swallow, then a swift bat, darted into a cloud of gnats above the small pond I'd built. The last of the sun lit Ann's blonde hair and framed a face as beautiful as it had ever been. She put her hand out across the table, palm up, as she often did and I put my hand in hers.

I could count nothing missing from my life. I looked again at the fax from Moscow and thought of everything that had come before. And I heard again a song, a song I hadn't heard for years:

They say you've been out wandrin'; they say you traveled far.
Sit down young stranger, and tell us who you are.
The room has all gone misty; my thoughts are all in spin
Sit down, young stranger, and tell us where you been.

About the Author

John Graham shipped out on a freighter when he was sixteen and took part in the first direct ascent of Mt. McKinley's North Wall at twenty, a climb so dangerous that no one's done it since. He hitchhiked around the world at twenty-two, covering every war he found along the way as a stringer for the *Boston Globe*. A Foreign Service Officer for fifteen years, he was in the middle of the revolution in Libya and the war in Vietnam.

To the young Graham, adventure was everything, and each brush with death only pushed him to up the ante—and to bury ever deeper the emotional life needed to make him whole.

Then it changed, sometimes slowly, sometimes dramatically. Over the last quarter century, Graham has been actively involved in peace-building initiatives all over the world. He's helped end apartheid in South Africa, avert a major strike in Canada, save what's left of the Everglades, settle a war in the Sudan and find long-term environmental solutions in the Pacific Northwest. Today he's a mentor and coach to the Young Leaders Integrity Alliance, a group of young activists working to promote ethical, accountable and effective leadership worldwide. He also works with a variety of international nonprofits to help resolve conflicts in the Middle East and elsewhere, with a focus on building bridges between the Muslim world and the West.

John Graham is President of the Giraffe Heroes Project, an international nonprofit moving people to stick their necks out for the common good (www.giraffe.org). The Project finds real heroes and tells their stories, inspiring others to take action on the problems important to *them*. The Project's other work has included everything from supporting the transformation of the Soviet Union in the early 1990's to developing programs that (to date) have helped over a quarter-million young people lead lives as courageous and compassionate citizens.

Graham brings his lessons-learned to speeches that bring people to their feet and into action, inspiring them to solve the public problems that concern them most. His workshops are street-smart trainings in the nuts and bolts of getting the job done. For more information or to book a presentation, see www.johngrahamspeaker.org.

There's also a website, www.sitdownyoungstranger.com, you can use to quickly tell your friends and contacts about this book.

Graham lives with the love of his life down a dirt road on Whidbey Island, Washington, on the end of a ridge overlooking the Olympic Mountains and the shipping channel into Seattle.

Made in the USA
Lexington, KY
19 January 2015